From the Pages of
The Prince and Other Writings

There is nothing more difficult to manage, or more doubtful of success, or more dangerous to handle than to take the lead in introducing a new order of things.   (from *The Prince*, page 25)

A prince, therefore, must have no other object or thought, or take up anything as his profession, except war and its rules and discipline, for that is the only art that befits one who commands.
(from *The Prince*, page 63)

The distance is so great between how we live and how we ought to live that he who abandons what is done for what ought to be done learns his ruin rather than his preservation; because a man who wants to make a profession of goodness in everything is bound to come to ruin among so many who are not good.
(from *The Prince*, page 66)

Men have less hesitation about offending one who makes himself loved than one who makes himself feared, for love is held together by a chain of obligation which, because men are sadly wicked, is broken at every opportunity to serve their self-interest, but fear is maintained by a dread of punishment which never abandons you.
(from *The Prince*, page 72)

There are two methods of fighting, one with laws, the other with force: the first one is proper to man, the second to beasts; but because the first one often does not suffice, one has to have recourse to the second.   (from *The Prince*, page 75)

Whenever the majority of men are not deprived of their property or honor, they live contentedly.   (from *The Prince*, page 79)

It is better to be impetuous than cautious, for Fortune is a woman, and it is necessary, if you wish to keep her down, to beat her and knock her about. And one sees that she lets herself be conquered by men of this sort more than by those who proceed coldly. And therefore, like a woman, she is always the friend of the young, because they are less cautious, fiercer, and command her with more audacity. (from *The Prince*, page 107)

"Fortune, who wants to be the arbiter of all things human, did not give me enough judgment to have understood her early on, nor enough time to overcome her."
(from *The Life of Castruccio*, page 135)

When evening arrives, I return home and go into my study, and at the threshold, I take off my everyday clothes, full of mud and filth, and put on regal and courtly garments; and decorously dressed anew, I enter the ancient courts of ancient men where, lovingly received by them, I feed myself on the food that is mine alone and for which I was born, where I am not ashamed to speak with them and to ask them about the reasons for their actions, and they, in their humanity, respond to me. And for four hours at a time, I do not feel any boredom, I forget every difficulty, I do not fear poverty, I am not terrified at death: I transfer myself into them completely. (from *Letter to Francesco Vettori*, page 151)

He who creates a tyranny and does not kill Brutus, and he who establishes a free state and does not kill the sons of Brutus, will not last long. (from *Discourses on Livy*, page 196)

The Prince
and Other Writings

Niccolò Machiavelli

Translation, Introduction, and Notes
by Wayne A. Rebhorn

George Stade
Consulting Editorial Director

BARNES & NOBLE CLASSICS
NEW YORK

ℬ

BARNES & NOBLE CLASSICS

NEW YORK

Published by Barnes & Noble Books
122 Fifth Avenue
New York, NY 10011

www.barnesandnoble.com/classics

Niccolò Machiavelli wrote *Il principe* (*The Prince*) and *Discorsi sopra la prima deca di Tito Livio* (*Discourses on the First Ten Books of Livy*) in 1513 while he was incarcerated. Machiavelli wrote *Vita di Castruccio Castracani* (*The Life of Castruccio Castracani*) in 1520.

Published in 2003 by Barnes & Noble Classics with new Translation, Introduction, Notes, Biography, Chronology, Comments & Questions, and For Further Reading.

Maps "The Papal States" and "The Italian States of the Late 15th Century" are reprinted by permission of Waveland Press, Inc., from Niccolò Machiavelli, *The Prince* (translated by Leo Paul S. de Alvarez). (Long Grove, IL; Waveland Press, Inc., 1980 [reissued 1989].) All rights reserved.

Introduction, Notes, and For Further Reading
Copyright © 2003 by Wayne Rebhorn.

Translation, Note on Niccolò Machiavelli, The World of Niccolò Machiavelli and *The Prince*, and Comments & Questions
Copyright © 2003 by Barnes & Noble, Inc.

The Prince and Other Writings
ISBN-13: 978-1-59308-060-0
ISBN-10: 1-59308-060-3
LC Control Number 2003106736

Produced and published in conjunction with:
Fine Creative Media, Inc.
322 Eighth Avenue
New York, NY 10001

Michael J. Fine, President and Publisher

Printed in the United States of America

QM

24 25 23

Niccolò Machiavelli

Statesman, political theorist, republican, essayist, historian, biographer, poet, and dramatist, Niccolò di Bernardo de' Machiavelli was born May 3, 1469, in the city of Florence, during an era of political upheaval on the Italian peninsula. The Machiavelli family had held numerous positions in the Florentine government, but Niccolò's father was not wealthy and could not give his son access to Florence's most powerful families. Little is known of Niccolò's youth, save that he studied Latin and the classics, including Livy's *History of the Roman Republic.*

In 1494 the Medici family, which had controlled the politics of Florence for a century, was driven out of the city, and the Florentine Republic was established, heavily influenced by the monk Girolamo Savonarola, who preached against tyranny and corruption. When the Savonarola regime collapsed in 1498, Machiavelli was installed in the newly elected city government; he was appointed Head of the Second Chancery, was secretary to the governing council that directed foreign affairs and defense, and exercised influence in his unofficial role as counselor to the head of the government, Piero Soderini. Machiavelli served for fourteen years in these powerful political and diplomatic positions, which allowed him to experience the behind-the-scenes world of European politics—including missions to the Holy Roman Emperor Maximilian, King Louis XII of France, Cesare Borgia, who was the son of Pope Alexander VI, and Julius II, who followed Alexander as pope—and his observations profoundly influenced his political philosophy. Machiavelli's work for the Florentine republic awakened him to the challenges facing the Italian city-states, and his later writings reflect his keen desire to rescue Italy from its subjection to foreign powers because of its fractionalism.

Machiavelli's fortunes changed in 1512, when Spain invaded Italy and dismantled the republic of Florence. The Medici family reclaimed power and promptly dismissed Machiavelli. In early 1513 Machiavelli was imprisoned and tortured on charges of conspiracy against the Medici. He maintained his innocence and was pardoned on the condition that he withdraw to his villa in Percussina, seven miles outside the city. It was there, cut off from Florence's political milieu, that he wrote *The Prince*, as well as his other enduring political works, *The Art of War* and *Discourses on the First Ten Books of Titus Livy*.

Composed in a matter of months following Machiavelli's release from prison, *The Prince* was an effort to secure the future stability of Italy, and especially Florence, through unsentimental, pragmatic, and strategic statecraft, and to gain the trust of the Medici, which would allow Machiavelli to return to public life. But this was not to be: Although he was eventually given a relatively small political office by the Medici, he never regained the important political position he had held in the Republic. Moreover, the two successive Medici princes to whom *The Prince* was dedicated died before Machiavelli's hopes could be realized, and of his political works, only *The Art of War* was published in his lifetime. Machiavelli was an active member of the Orti Oricellari intellectual circle, and he continued to write on a wide range of subjects during the remaining fourteen years of his life. He wrote the popular comedy *The Mandrake Root* in 1518, and a biography, *The Life of Castruccio Castracani*, in 1520. In that same year, Machiavelli succeeded in regaining the favor of the Medici; he was given a commission to write the *History of Florence*, which he completed in 1525. Before his death, the lifelong republican saw the fall of the Medici and the return of the Florentine Republic in 1527, although officials refused to restore him to his old political position because of his association with the Medici. Niccolò Machiavelli died in Florence on June 21, 1527.

Table of Contents

The Italian States of the Late 15th Century

C. Brandon Schmitt 1979

The World of Niccolò Machiavelli and The Prince

1453   Constantinople falls to the Turks, who begin their relentless spread, which will last some 300 years, into the Balkans and central Europe. Greek scholars flee to Italy with important manuscripts, enhancing the study of Greek and the printing of Greek texts.

1469   Niccolò Machiavelli is born on May 3, the third of four children of Bernardo Machiavelli, an impecunious lawyer, and Bartolomea Nelli, an educated woman who writes poetry.

1492   Christopher Columbus, sailing under the banner of Ferdinand of Aragon and Isabella of Castile, travels to the New World. Ferdinand succeeds in expelling the Moors from their last stronghold in Granada in southern Spain. In Florence, Lorenzo de' Medici (Lorenzo the Magnificent) dies. His family had controlled Florentine politics for the past century. Well educated and himself a poet, Lorenzo patronized artists such as Botticelli, Filippino Lippi, and Michelangelo, and scholars and writers such as Angelo Poliziano and Marsilio Ficino.

1494   The French king, Charles VIII, invited into Italy by the Venetians, who wish to extend their territory in Lombardy, invades the peninsula in order to claim the Kingdom of Naples. Lorenzo de' Medici's son Piero and the rest of the Medici family are driven out of Florence, and the Republic is established. The charismatic Dominican preacher Girolamo Savonarola, the head of the Convent of San Marco, becomes the spiritual leader of the city.

1495   Charles VIII captures Naples and partitions it with the Spanish king, Ferdinand of Aragon, but is soon thereafter driven out of Italy.

1498   Excommunicated by Pope Alexander VI, in March Savonarola is brought to trial by the Signoria, the governing body of Florence, and after being tortured, is condemned to death and is burned at the stake together with two of his disciples. On June 19 Machiavelli is made Head of the Second Chancery, which is primarily concerned with foreign affairs.

1499   The French king, Louis XII, invades Italy and occupies Milan and Genoa.

1501   Machiavelli marries Marietta Corsini. He will have four sons and a daughter with her.

1502   Piero Soderini is made the *gonfaloniere a vita* (chief magistrate for life) of the Florentine Republic. Machiavelli is sent on several diplomatic missions to Cesare Borgia, the son of Pope Alexander VI.

1503   Pope Alexander VI dies and is succeeded for a short time by Pius III and then by Giuliano della Rovere, an enemy of the Borgias, who takes the name Julius II.

1504   Machiavelli writes his *Decennale Primo (The First Decade)*, a history in verse of the first ten years of the Florentine Republic.

1504– Louis XII signs the Treaty of Blois, by which he retains
1505   Milan and Genoa, while the Spanish get Naples.

1507   Machiavelli goes on a diplomatic mission to the Holy Roman Emperor Maximilian I, passing through the German-speaking areas of Switzerland on his way to Austria.

1508   Pope Julius II forms the League of Cambrai against Venice with France, Spain, and the Holy Roman Empire. Machiavelli writes his *Rapporto delle cose della Magna (Report on German Affairs)* based on what he had observed in Switzerland and Austria.

1509   The League of Cambrai defeats the Venetians at the battle of Agnadello (Vailà). The Florentine citizen militia, which Machiavelli argued for, retakes the rebellious city of Pisa. Machiavelli writes the *Decennale secondo (The Second Decade)*, but work on it is interrupted, and it is never completed.

1510   Pope Julius II forms the Holy League against France with Spain, the Holy Roman Empire, Venice, and England.

Machiavelli is sent on a diplomatic mission to France in a futile attempt to persuade the French to allow Florence to remain neutral in its struggle with the papacy and Spain.

1512   The French win the battle of Ravenna but lose their best captain, Gaston de Foix, and are later driven from Milan by the Swiss. A Spanish army marches on Florence, where partisans of the Medici take the Palazzo della Signoria on September 16 and restore the Medici to power. Machiavelli loses his position as Head of the Second Chancery on November 7; three days later he is exiled from Florence but refused permission to leave Florentine territory. He begins an eight-year exile from the city on his farm at Sant'Andrea in Percussina near the town of San Casciano.

1513   The French are routed by the Swiss at the battle of Novara and withdraw from the peninsula. Machiavelli's name is found on a list of conspirators against the Medici; he is arrested on February 12 and tortured but is released on March 11, when a general amnesty is proclaimed to celebrate the election of Giovanni de' Medici as Pope Leo X. Machiavelli begins the writing of the *Discorsi* (*Discourses*) and begins and possibly completes that of *Il principe* (*The Prince*).

1515   The French king, Francis I, invades Italy and with his Venetian allies defeats the Swiss at the battle of Marignano. Thomas More begins writing *Utopia*, which he will finish the following year. Machiavelli begins taking part in conversations in the important philosophical, political, and literary center called the Orti Oricellari, in the gardens of the palace of Cosimo Rucellai.

1516   Desiderius Erasmus publishes *The Education of a Christian Prince*. When Giuliano de' Medici dies, Machiavelli dedicates *The Prince* to Lorenzo de' Medici instead.

1517   Martin Luther posts his ninety-five theses on the door of the castle church in Wittenberg, an event that marks the beginning of the Protestant Reformation.

1518   Machiavelli completes the *Discourses* and, most likely, writes his original play, the comedy *La mandragola* (*The Mandrake Root*).

1519   *La mandragola* is published in Florence; it will be published in Venice in 1522, and in Rome in 1524. The Spanish king Charles I is elected Holy Roman Emperor as Charles V.

1520   In March a meeting is arranged between Machiavelli and Giulio de' Medici. After a trip to Lucca in July, Machiavelli writes *La vita di Castruccio Castracani da Lucca* (*The Life of Castruccio Castracani of Lucca*). On November 8 Giulio has the Studio fiorentino (the University of Florence) appoint Machiavelli the official historiographer of the city. Machiavelli probably writes his one story, "Belfagor, arcidiavolo" ("The Arch-Devil Belfagor").

1521   Machiavelli publishes his *Arte della guerra* (*The Art of War*), a dialogue that is set in the Orti Oricellari. He is sent to the town of Carpi to negotiate the separation of the Minorite convents from the other convents in Tuscany.

1523   Giulio de' Medici is elected pope as Clement VII.

1524   Machiavelli writes the comedy *Clizia*, a play that is a free reworking of Plautus's *Casina*; it is produced the following January.

1525   Francis I once again invades Italy and is decisively beaten at Pavia, where he is captured, taken to Spain, and the next year forced to sign the Treaty of Madrid, by which he renounces his claims to Italy and cedes Burgundy to Charles V. Machiavelli completes the *Istorie fiorentine* (*History of Florence*) and presents it to the pope. He writes the *Discorso o dialogo intorno alla nostra lingua* (*Discourse or Dialogue on Our Language*).

1526   Francis I repudiates the Treaty of Madrid and forms the League of Cognac with Clement VII, Henry VIII of England, Florence, and Venice against Charles V. Machiavelli is made secretary to the commission in charge of the fortification of the walls of Florence.

1527   Charles V sends an army under Charles de Bourbon to attack Rome, which is brutally sacked for a week in May.

Florence throws out the Medici and reestablishes the Republic. Machiavelli is refused an office in the new government. He dies on June 21.

1529   The French are defeated by the forces of Charles V and sign the Treaty of Cambrai, renouncing their claims in Italy; however, they will return to Italy several more times in the next two decades.

1531   *The Prince* and *The Life of Castruccio Castracani* are published together by Blado in Rome. The *Discourses* is also published there by Blado.

1559   The Treaty of Cateau-Cambrésis, by which France yields Milan and the Kingdom of the Two Sicilies to Spain, marks the definitive expulsion of France from Italy and completes Spain's domination of the peninsula.

The Papal States

C. Brandon Schmitt 1979

Introduction

In the late summer and autumn of 1512, Niccolò Machiavelli's world came to an end. Until then, his life had been a Renaissance success story. Although he was born into a prominent Florentine family in 1469, his particular branch of it did not have much social standing in the city, a situation only made worse by the fact that his father, who was a doctor of laws, had been declared an insolvent debtor, which prevented him from holding any sort of public office and deeply depressed his law practice. As a result, the young Machiavelli did not receive the usual humanist training in the classics that his more affluent contemporaries enjoyed. Nevertheless, even though he never learned Greek, he did learn to read, write, and speak classical Latin, an essential prerequisite for any sort of public employment in late-fifteenth-century Italy, and on his own he read widely in the works of Latin authors, including Virgil and the love poets and historians such as Livy and Tacitus. It is not certain exactly how deeply he immersed himself in Florentine politics during the 1490s, a tempestuous decade that saw the fall from power in 1494 of the Medici family, which had controlled the city for much of the previous century; the brief rule of Girolamo Savonarola, the ascetic Dominican who initially moved the masses to renounce their worldly ways but soon lost their support, angered the papacy, and was tried and executed in 1498; and the re-creation that same year of the Florentine republic. If we do not know exactly how Machiavelli had been displaying his intellectual and other talents up to this point, we do know that on June 19, 1498, this relatively obscure twenty-nine-year-old was made the Head of the Second Chancery, which may have been slightly less important than the First Chancery, but which nevertheless did have the function of managing the foreign affairs of the city and consequently thrust Machiavelli squarely into the center of Florentine politics.

For the next fourteen years, Machiavelli employed his considerable talents in the service of the republic and the city that, he remarked in a letter dated April 16, 1527, was dearer to him "than my own soul." On a number of occasions, he was sent on diplomatic missions to other city-states within Italy, to Germany, and to France, with which Florence was joined in an alliance that would cost it dearly. On most of these trips, Machiavelli was not the head of the delegation, since his family did not have a sufficiently high social rank to gain him appropriate recognition in states where kings and princes and dukes held the reins of power, a situation that must have rankled because he was always the keenest observer and shrewdest diplomat in the Florentine delegation. Nevertheless, he did go on these missions and sent back to his superiors detailed reports that had a significant impact on policy. Machiavelli's star was at its zenith from 1502 on, for in that year the republic, unable to find stability in the midst of its feuding factions, named Piero Soderini the *gonfaloniere a vita*, "chief magistrate for life." The amiable Soderini, who sought—foolishly, in Machiavelli's opinion—to achieve political concord in the city by mollifying its factions, generally recognized the political brilliance of the Head of the Second Chancery, and Machiavelli gradually became his chief confidant and adviser, his *manerino*, or "little hand," as his enemies in the city called him with derision. Machiavelli managed to persuade Soderini to create a citizen militia in 1505, a project dear to Machiavelli's heart since he saw such a militia as a re-creation of the Roman military model and the one best hope for Florence—and Italy—to fend off the powerful invading armies of France and Spain that had been fighting in the peninsula since the mid-1490s. And that militia, which Machiavelli helped train and lead, acquitted itself well in June 1509 when a rebellious Pisa was once again brought under the control of Florence. Clearly, if Machiavelli was not the head of state himself, he was practically the next best thing.

In 1512 all that came to an end. Machiavelli had been worried about the survival of the Florentine republic because its long-standing alliance with France made it the enemy of the pope, Julius II, and his powerful allies, Spain and the Holy Roman Empire. Julius II was obsessed with making the papacy a major political power in the Italian peninsula. Having allied himself with France, the Holy Roman Empire, and Spain in 1508 in order to check the growing power of Venice, the pope defeated the Venetians at the battle of

Agnadello in 1509, but then turned on the French and sought to drive them out of Italy. Aware that the traditional alliance Florence had with France had become a liability for the city, Machiavelli went there in September and October 1510 in a desperate, and ultimately futile, attempt to persuade the French to allow Florence to remain neutral. By May of the following year, the armies of France had been driven out of Milan, beginning what would become a complete withdrawal from the peninsula in 1513. Meanwhile, in April 1512, Spanish troops moved toward Tuscany and in August attacked the town of Prato only a few miles away from Florence. The militia that had been created to defend the town was defeated, most of its members choosing to flee rather than fight, and the town was brutally sacked. Seeing the handwriting on the wall, Soderini fled the city on August 31, and on September 16 partisans of the Medici stormed the Palazzo della Signoria, the seat of the government, and restored them to power. Julius II favored this change, as did his successor Leo X, the former Giovanni de' Medici, and for the next ten years his cousin, Cardinal Giulio de' Medici, ruled Florence.

The fall of the republic could not have been more devastating for Machiavelli. On November 7, 1512, he was removed from office as Head of the Second Chancery, and three days later he was forbidden to enter the Palazzo della Signoria and was exiled from the city, though confined to Florentine territory, for the next year. This exile would continue until 1520. Essentially, Machiavelli was rusticated to a small farm he had inherited from his father at Sant' Andrea in Percussina, a tiny hamlet near the town of San Casciano. Not only was he now stripped of his former place in Florentine politics, but he was thoroughly impoverished, having to support himself and his family on the meager income afforded by his small estate. Even worse, a few months later his name was found on a list of potential conspirators against the Medici, and although he was not actually involved in the plot, he was arrested on February 12, 1513, imprisoned, and tortured; he was finally freed on March 11 only because a general amnesty was proclaimed to honor the election of Giovanni de' Medici as the new pope. Deprived of any active life in politics and largely confined to his farm—although he did get back to Florence from time to time—Machiavelli turned to writing, putting his thoughts on politics, among other things, down on paper. He did this partly in order to have an outlet for his frustrations and to satisfy vicariously his desire to walk the halls of power, and partly, at least as far as *The Prince* is concerned, as an attempt to curry favor with the Medici and get them to allow him to reenter the city and its government. He dedicated the book to Lorenzo de' Medici, the duke of Urbino, after the original dedicatee, Giuliano de' Medici, died in 1516, but Lorenzo remained hostile to Machiavelli, seeing him as a republican opponent of Medici rule. The result was that Machiavelli spent the eight years between 1512 and 1520 in exile, eight years that must have felt devoid of meaning for him. Ironically, of course, we are the richer for it, since in those years he composed not only *The Prince*, but the *Discourses*, his great republican commentary on Livy's *History of Rome*; his comedy *The Mandrake Root*, which many feel is the most original dramatic work of the Italian Renaissance; and his brief *Life of Castruccio Castracani*.

Machiavelli did, finally, return to Florence in 1520, although he never regained the politically important position he had held under Soderini. During his exile, his undeniable intellectual abilities were clearly in evidence not only in his writings, but also during the discussions he participated in with other Florentine intellectuals in the gardens of the house of Cosimo Rucellai, the so-called Orti Oricellari, an important philosophical, political, and literary center, where he was often the center of attention. Medici supporters attended those gatherings, and they and other powerful intermediaries interceded on his behalf with Giulio de' Medici. However, it was only in March 1520, several months after Lorenzo's death in 1519, that Giulio finally was persuaded to receive him. Later that year, on November 8, he had Machiavelli appointed official historiographer of the city, a position that paid him a substantial annual salary in exchange for which, over the next four years, he produced his *History of Florence*. He dedicated the *History* to Clement VII, the former Giulio de' Medici, who had been elected pope in 1523, and in response he received 120 gold ducats and some vague promises about reviving the idea of a citizen militia, promises that never really bore fruit. Machiavelli had been entrusted with several small missions by the Medici just before his return to the city, but he only truly entered political life again, albeit in a small way, in April 1526, when he was made the secretary to the five-man council that was charged with managing the fortifications of the city.

Once again, however, events conspired against Machiavelli. The Medici had not learned the lessons of the Soderini regime and had continued the city's traditional alliance with France. The French had returned to Italy in 1515 under the leadership of their new king, Francis I, but after some initial successes, they and their allies, including the papacy and Florence, were defeated by the forces of the Holy Roman Emperor Charles V, first at the battle of Pavia in 1525, and then, more decisively, at Civitavecchia, a coastal town not far from Rome, on May 6, 1527. This last defeat led to the infamous Sack of Rome, in which Charles's army, many of whose mercenary troops were Swiss and German Protestants, took the city and spent a full week in it, pillaging, looting, raping, and killing. In Florence, republican sympathizers took this opportunity to throw out the Medici once again. Machiavelli expected to be awarded his old position as Head of the Second Chancery and was bitterly disappointed when he was passed over, mostly because his service to the Medici had made him seem untrustworthy. Disillusioned, he died just a few weeks later.

The personal crisis Machiavelli lived through during the second decade of the sixteenth century was also a crisis for Italy, as well as being a time of transition for Europe in general. In the late fifteenth century, western Europe witnessed the formation of the nation-states of England, France, and Spain while Italy remained a welter of tiny city-states in the northern and central portions of the peninsula and the large Kingdom of Naples in the south. Five states dominated the political life of the peninsula—Venice, Milan, Florence, the papacy, and Naples—and for several centuries a rough balance of power had obtained among them. However, this balance was destroyed in 1494 when the French king Charles VIII invaded Italy. Invited in by the Venetians to assist them in their expansion onto the mainland, France's real aim was to seize the Kingdom of Naples. When Charles I, who had come to the Spanish throne in 1516, was elected Holy Roman Emperor as Charles V in 1519, Spain became the principal competitor with France in the Italian peninsula for the next half-century. In his works, Machiavelli comments on the wars that pitted shifting coalitions of Italian states, allied with

France or Spain, against one another, and he laments the profound weakness of Italy in relationship to the nation-states around it. Machiavelli recognized that the French and Spanish invaders threatened the autonomy of the Italian city-states, and by and large, he was right. For although the French continued to fight the Spanish, they finally gave up completely and signed a treaty in 1559, giving Milan and the Kingdom of the Two Sicilies, which included the Kingdom of Naples, to Philip II of Spain. This meant that most of the city-states in the peninsula were either directly or indirectly under Spanish control. These Italian wars did bring the culture of the Renaissance from Italy to the rest of Europe, but they also left Italy with only a marginal role to play in the politics of the continent. What Machiavelli was witnessing, then, was the end of the feudal order in Italy, as its tiny cities and duchies and principalities proved themselves no match politically and militarily for the much larger nation-states around them. Machiavelli may not have been cognizant of these broad developments, but his works consistently register their effects.

As Europe developed strong nation-states in the late fifteenth and early sixteenth centuries, it also experienced a revolution in political theory. To put it simply, states and governments were beginning to be seen, at least by a few thinkers, not as something God-given or inscribed in the nature of the universe, and thus as something ahistorical and unchangeable, but rather as human constructs, the results of people's needs and desires and fears, and thus as things that were historical, contingent, and capable of transformation. Although some political theorists proclaimed the divine rights of kings and defended absolute monarchy, others now saw the state as a fabrication and its ruler as something like an actor. To take just one example, consider Thomas More's revolutionary work *Utopia*. This text is based squarely on two assumptions: first, that human beings can be made better if they are raised in a better environment—that is, in a better state; and second, that a state is a man-made entity that can be changed in quite radical ways if necessary—such as by the elimination of private property—in order to create that better environment. By the second half of the seventeenth century, Hobbes and Locke would develop a contract theory of government in which those who ruled did so only because the people in general ceded to them the right to do so. The notion that the ruler was something like an actor, rather than God's deputy on earth, is strikingly evident in the drama of the period: kings and princes, like Shakespeare's Richard III and Henry V, are players who may, in some cases, have some sort of inherited right to rule and may even claim to be supported by divine authority, but their ability to govern rests on their ability to manipulate their subjects by the skillful use of rhetoric and the occasional application of force. To say that rulers are cunning rhetoricians adept at power politics is to say exactly what Machiavelli was saying in *The Prince*. It is not surprising that although many thinkers understood the real complexity and subtlety of his thought, in the popular mind he came to stand for a kind of political ruthlessness summed up in the caricature of him that one finds on the Elizabethan stage, the "Machiavel," or that one sees in the fact that his first name was confused with "Old Nick," a synonym for the devil. By identifying ruthless politicians and rulers as Machiavels, people in the period were using Machiavelli as a scapegoat, making him represent what they feared but did not wish to acknowledge about their supposedly legitimate rulers—namely that they, too, could be seen as Machiavels.

All of Machiavelli's works, and especially *The Prince*, can be read as a series of responses to the crises he was living through, to the personal crisis he experienced when the Florentine republic fell in 1512, and to the larger crises involving Italian and international politics, the theoretical conception of the state, and the vision of the ruler. Or perhaps it would be better to say that his texts are not just passive responses to those crises, but active attempts to define, to give voice to, what was happening in the world around him, and indeed to promote action in that world as well. In them Machiavelli is asking over and over the same questions: why are we Italians so weak, so much unlike our Roman ancestors? Why have we become the prey of the larger states around us? And how can we remedy this situation? What sort of state and what sort of ruler will allow us not just to maintain our independence, but perhaps to regain some of the glory of ancient Rome? Bound up with these questions was Machiavelli's more personal one: why did I fail, and how can I get back the political role I once played in the republic? As he tries to answer these questions in *The Prince*, the *Discourses*, and his other works, he also grapples with the problem of how to make sense out of history, how to extract useful lessons from it so that we can avoid the mistakes of the past.

Although Machiavelli theorizes about politics throughout his works, he takes pains to separate what he is doing from the work of pure theorists. Thus, at the start of chapter 15 in *The Prince*, he distinguishes himself from those who "have imagined republics and principalities for themselves which have never been seen or known to exist in reality." Instead, he tells us, he writes about *la verità effetuale della cosa*, "the effectual truth of the matter." By "effectual truth" he means a truth—about politics as well as about human nature—that has an *effect* in the real world, rather than something more purely speculative or contemplative. Although More's *Utopia* might seem to be the sort of work about an imaginary republic that Machiavelli is objecting to here, it was written in 1515 and 1516, some two years or so after Machiavelli started working on *The Prince*. Nevertheless, More's thought-experiment about the best of all possible states grows out of a long tradition, which Machiavelli surely knew, of imagining ideal states and rulers, a tradition that stretches back into antiquity and that has Plato's *Republic* as one of its clear progenitors. Moreover, there was a genre of political writing to which both authors are responding in their books, a genre called the *speculum principis*, the "mirror for princes," in which authors composed idealized portraits of princes and their duties in order to offer instruction to rulers and rulers in training. The great Dutch Humanist Desiderius Erasmus had written just such a volume, the *Institutio principis christiani* (*The Education of a Christian Prince*), for Charles V, and published it in 1516. Like many works in this genre that stretch back well into the Middle Ages, Erasmus's book offers sober advice stressing the importance of Judeo-Christian morality as the basis for governing. While More's *Utopia* fits quite comfortably into this genre in many ways, Machiavelli's *Prince* can almost be read as a parody of its idealistic moralizing, for his book repeatedly underscores the gap between morality and politics, insisting that a prince who tries to do good in a world full of bad people will inevitably come to grief. Machiavelli takes the name of the genre seriously: he tries to reflect in the "mirror" of his book what real princes really do—and must do—in the real world if they are to obtain and maintain political power.

In keeping with his preference for an effectual truth that bears fruit in the real world, Machiavelli stresses the importance of judging human beings and their deeds in terms of how things turn out in the end. This is not the same thing as saying that the end justifies the means, although sometimes Machiavelli is interpreted that way. Revealingly, in chapter 18 of *The Prince*, "How Princes Must Keep Their Word," he uses a phrase that shows just how different his thought is on this subject. The phrase occurs just after Machiavelli has declared that a prince must appear to be "all mercy, all loyalty, all sincerity, all humanity, all religion," although he need not actually have any of these qualities. The reason is that men in general judge things by appearances and that the few who may perceive the truth will be overwhelmed by the many who do not. Moreover, he continues, "in the actions of all men, and especially of princes, where there is no court of appeal, one looks at the outcome." "One looks at the outcome": *si guarda al fine*. Machiavelli's statement here may seem to suggest he is saying that the end or outcome justifies whatever means the prince might use to achieve it—in other words, that a good end makes even the most wicked means morally acceptable. But what he is really saying is that people will judge a prince's means to be good as long as he succeeds and the outcome is beneficial to them. Machiavelli admits, both here and in his works generally, that morality may be a good thing, but it is not what drives people's behavior in the real world. What he is *not* saying, however, is also important, for by not declaring that the end justifies the means for the prince, he is not offering the prince a convenient way out of the moral dilemma he faces, which results from the fact that if he wants to gain and keep political power, he has to do despicable things that cannot really be justified *morally* by the end he pursues. If one could argue that a prince who does evil does it simply in order to bring about some greater moral good—defined as, say, political stability or economic welfare—then this problem would vanish. Such a move was precisely the one made by political theorists in Machiavelli's wake who came up with the idea of *ragione di stato* or *raison d'état*—namely, that some serious and morally unimpeachable "reason of state" could justify the most criminally culpable acts. By contrast, what Machiavelli is saying is harder, more uncomfortable, more thought-provoking, and more cynical: sometimes the prince must do evil simply because he cannot gain or preserve power otherwise, but as long as he succeeds and people benefit from it, they will not be upset.

Actually, Machiavelli never advocates the pointless or wanton commission of crimes or suggests that the prince should get some sort of sadistic thrill out of inflicting harm on others. Rather, such things as assassinating one's enemies or severely punishing one's followers when they err are presented as necessities—duties, almost—that are imposed upon the prince, for if he did not act in that way, he would run the risk of losing power. Thus, in chapter 15, just after Machiavelli tells us that he is not interested in imaginary republics, but in the "effectual truth of the matter," he goes on to say that a man "who abandons what is done for what ought to be done learns his ruin rather than his preservation; because a man who wants to make a profession of goodness in everything is bound to come to ruin among so many who are not good." He then concludes that a prince must "learn how not to be good, and to use this knowledge and not use it as necessity dictates." What he says here acknowledges the importance of morality and goodness, even as it also acknowledges, perhaps with a rueful sigh, that such things must be set aside if political necessity dictates otherwise. Indeed, considering that Machiavelli often says directly that human beings are a wicked lot and that he has been caricatured as a gleeful advocate of evil, the fact that he goes out of his way to say that a prince must "learn how not to be good" almost comes as a shock. For it suggests that he sees some fundamental tendency toward decency in human beings, who must overcome an enormous inner resistance in order to do evil.

The full complexity of Machiavelli's response to the problem of squaring morality with political effectiveness can be seen in his assessment of Ferdinand of Aragon's accomplishments. In chapter 21 of *The Prince*, which is concerned with how princes must do striking and unusual things—he calls them "rare"—in order to acquire the esteem or prestige necessary to rule, the first example is that of Ferdinand, who started out merely as king of Aragon but became the king of Spain and extended his dominion to Naples and even to part of France. Declaring that "if you consider his actions, you will find them all very great and some even extraordinary," Machiavelli mentions how Ferdinand manipulated the barons of Castile to keep them from rebelling against him, how he obtained money from the Church to fund his army, and how he used religion as a pretext to extend his empire. He then concludes on the positive note that Ferdinand "has always done great deeds which he contrived and which have always kept his subjects' minds in suspense and amazed and occupied with their outcome." Ferdinand thus seems an ideal prince according to Machiavelli's standards: ruthless, cunning, energetic, larger than life. And yet, in the middle of this celebration, when he notes how Ferdinand used religion to further his aims, the first example given is one whose morally problematic status Machiavelli himself underscores: "in order to be able to undertake greater enterprises, always making use of religion, [Ferdinand] devoted himself to the pious cruelty of driving the Marranos out of his kingdom and despoiling them—this example could not be more pitiful or rare." Machiavelli's sentence starts out as praise: Ferdinand is one of those admirably cunning princes who know how important it is to appear religious. But then, the reader is surprised to read that Ferdinand's treatment of the Marranos—his expulsion of converted Jews and Moors from Spain in 1502—was a "pious cruelty." If Machiavelli had spoken of it as a pious *act*, there would be no problem: Ferdinand would simply be a clever trickster who knows how to use religion, and Machiavelli's adjective could be read as either straightforward praise or delicious irony. However, since "pious" qualifies "cruelty," the reader suddenly sees things not from Ferdinand's perspective, but from that of his victims. And lest one should think this a slip of the pen on Machiavelli's part, he repeats the procedure at the end of the sentence. This time he does not merely praise Ferdinand's "example," that is, his exemplary action, as something "rare," but also calls it "pitiful," thus, again, preventing the reader from feeling an uncomplicated admiration for the Spanish king's political astuteness untouched by any sort of moral qualm. Although the passage is generally filled with praise, "cruelty" and "pitiful" introduce jarring notes into the presentation of Ferdinand, and if they do not undermine his status as an ideal prince, at the very least they make the reader feel some sort of moral hesitation in responding to him.

There is one other way in which Machiavelli complicates the relationship between morality and politics. In chapter 8 of *The Prince* he considers those who became princes through crimes and offers an extremely complicated assessment of the two figures he uses as examples, the first of whom, Agathocles of Syracuse, will be looked at closely here. Machiavelli starts off the chapter by declaring that "I will give two examples, one ancient, the other modern, without otherwise entering into the merits of this method, because I judge them to be sufficient for anyone forced to imitate them." Essentially, he seems to be shying away from making a straightforward moral pronouncement here about the use of crimes to acquire a principality. He will not debate the "merits"—the "demerits"?—of such actions because, considering such things as the prince's situation, human nature, and the goal of achieving and maintaining political power, it is sometimes simply what he has to do. Clearly, Machiavelli dislikes making such recommendations, but he seems about to do so, albeit, perhaps, while holding his nose. And yet, although he then goes on to say many positive things about Agathocles, it turns out that he is really not recommending that would-be princes imitate Agathocles.

While admitting right from the start that Agathocles employed "wickedness" in order to get ahead, Machiavelli emphasizes, instead, his political success, describing how, for instance, after tricking the people of Syracuse and having many of its citizens murdered, he "seized the city and ruled over it as a prince without any civil dissension." Indeed, Agathocles's brutal acts ensured his control and allowed him not just to defend Syracuse from the Carthaginians, but eventually to force them to make peace and to leave Sicily in his hands. Thus far, it seems as though Machiavelli wants his readers to overlook, or at least tolerate, Agathocles's wickedness, just as they were to accept Cesare Borgia's betrayal and killing of his lieutenant Remirro de Orco in the preceding chapter. Indeed, the next paragraph begins with praise for Agathocles for having faced "a thousand hardships and dangers" in order to rise through the ranks of the army and for having maintained his rule over Syracuse "by many courageous and perilous efforts." Nevertheless, Machiavelli insists that Agathocles is not to be imitated or admired, declaring simply that it is wrong "to betray one's friends, to be without loyalty, without mercy, without religion." "By such methods," he concludes, "one can acquire power, but not glory." If one judged Agathocles simply on the basis of his courage and energy and daring, Machiavelli admits that he would be praiseworthy, but "his ferocious cruelty and inhumanity, together with his countless crimes, do not permit him to be celebrated as being among the most excellent men." What has complicated Machiavelli's view here? It would be difficult to claim that he is repelled by the idea of betrayal and murder, for he seems to accept such things elsewhere as political necessities. In part, his revulsion seems to be inspired by the sheer scale of Agathocles's wicked deeds. In part, Machiavelli condemns Agathocles because, although he acquired power, he did not achieve *glory*. Thus, complicating the act of judging princes for Machiavelli is not just his moral reservation about such deeds as Ferdinand's expulsion of the Marranos, but also a concern for the glory that constitutes the judgment history confers on the deeds of princes.

No matter how the prince is judged in Machiavelli's works, he is always distinguished from the vast majority of human beings who are referred to as "the people" or "the masses" or "the multitude." Machiavelli scorns them because they are blinded by their appetites, their carnal lusts, and, especially, their material desires. Thus, in chapter 17 of *The Prince*, he warns the prince not to arouse hatred in the people, something he can avoid "if he does not touch the goods and the women of his citizens and subjects." He goes on to warn the prince also not to take someone's life without providing public justifications for it, although he then returns to the preceding point and concludes with malicious wit and an untranslatable pun that, "above all, [the prince] must abstain from taking the property of others, for men sooner forget the death of their father [*padre*] than the loss of their patrimony [*patrimonio*]." Machiavelli also scorns the people because, in a confusing world that is dominated by appearances, they are unable to see through those appearances to the realities beneath them. Thus, in chapter 18 of *The Prince*, Machiavelli recommends that the prince be a "great hypocrite and dissembler," and insists that such duplicity will triumph because "men are so simple and so obedient to present necessities, that he who deceives will always find someone who will let himself be deceived." People, in Machiavelli's view, are mired in the present, incapable of imagining alternatives to their immediate situation or of finding alternative explanations for the phenomena they encounter. This is why he claims that it is easier for a hereditary ruler to keep his throne than for a new prince to do so, and why he recommends that when a prince acquires a new state, he should eliminate its old rulers but preserve its customs, laws, and taxes as much as possible. The people, being slaves to custom, cannot stand change.

The people are not all bad, however, in Machiavelli's estimation. In the *Discourses*, for instance, in which he expresses his preference for republican government, he insists that although the people may be deceived by generalities, they are much better than princes at judging particulars. Moreover, he argues that republics live longer than principalities because the latter depend for their survival on the talents of a single individual who may not pass them on to his descendants, whereas the former have the resources provided by the entirety of the people. Even in *The Prince*, however, Machiavelli stresses the value of the people as he rejects what he calls a "trite proverb": "he who builds on the people builds on mud." The prince can build on the people not because he can count on their love, which Machiavelli says is a weak chain that will break apart at the slightest blow from self-interest, but because the prince will have taken pains to shape them and their responses. He does this partly by satisfying, or allowing them to satisfy, their material desires, and partly by creating an image of himself that not only fills them with fear if they should cross him, but also inspires in them feelings of reverence and awe for him. In the *Discourses*, Machiavelli says such shaping was done in ancient Rome by the laws and ordinances and customs of the state, and most fundamentally by Roman religion. By contrast, in Machiavelli's Italy, the people cannot be educated properly because the Church's wickedness has undermined its capacity to inspire faith. Instead, what is required is a charismatic prince who can move his subjects to feel terror and something close to religious awe, as Machiavelli reports Cesare Borgia did for the people of Cesena by having the dismembered body of his dead lieutenant dumped in the town square one morning.

The prince is everything the people are not. Where they are

driven by their appetites, he controls his. Where they are taken in by appearances, he sees through them and cunningly manipulates them to serve his own ends. Where they are the slaves of custom and convention and resistant to change, he has the ability to "think outside the box," and to be good or bad, violent or mild, impetuous or hesitant, as circumstances dictate. And where they can be moved to feel religious awe about him, he works to inspire it in them, all the while paying lip service to conventional religion. What makes the prince different from the vast majority of human beings is summed up in one key term that Machiavelli uses repeatedly in his works: *virtù* (which also appears as an adjective, *virtuoso*, and as an adverb, *virtuosamente*, and even in its Latin form of *virtus* in the title of chapter 6 of *The Prince*). This term is untranslatable, not because there is no English equivalent for it, but rather because there are so many of them, and because more than one is almost always in play. At one extreme is the word's English cognate, "virtue," as when Machiavelli speaks of liberality as a "virtue" in chapter 16 of *The Prince*. However, even in this seemingly unambiguous case, other meanings of the word, such as "ability," "talent," or "skill," are not entirely to be excluded. Indeed, in most cases where the word appears, rendering it as "virtue" in English would be misleading, for the *virtù* of the prince usually involves his setting conventional morality aside in order to do what is politically necessary. *Virtù* also has another set of meanings that define princely action, including "vigor," "valor," and "(martial) prowess," for if *virtù* points to the prince's intellectual and moral flexibility, to his mental agility and craftiness, it also looks back to the meanings of the word's Latin cognate, *virtus*, which identified the skills of the warrior: toughness, endurance, courage, and daring. *Virtus* meant manliness, the qualities that made someone a man—in Latin, a *vir*, the root of the word. These two sets of meanings, then, evoke the two iconic animals with which Machiavelli famously identifies the prince in chapter 18 of his treatise: the prince, he says, "must know well how to use the nature of the beast" and "must choose the lion and the fox from among them, for the lion cannot defend himself from traps, and the fox cannot defend himself from wolves." All of this links the prince to the hero of classical epic, and if Machiavelli himself evokes the figure of Achilles in chapter 18, Odysseus might just as well be named since he, too, as a master of cunning and heroic violence, could be called both fox and lion. Nevertheless, since *virtù*, whenever it appears, cannot help but evoke the traditional, moral notion of "virtue," even if that meaning does not fit the immediate context, this key term will always be, to some degree, contradictory and unstable. It contains within itself, every time it appears, the fundamental opposition between the ethical and the political that lies at the heart of Machiavelli's conception of the prince.

The Prince is a puzzling work for many readers because we know that its creator was wedded to the notion of republican government, yet in his treatise he not only writes about what princes must do in order to gain and maintain their political positions, but he seems to identify so deeply with the figures his text celebrates that it is difficult not to think of him as supporting that sort of rule. Nevertheless, in the *Discourses*, when he states his views of the two sorts of governments, he reveals a decided preference for republicanism. Not surprisingly, modern political thought on republican government harks back to Machiavelli's text, and in the nineteenth century it made Machiavelli a hero to Italians who wanted to unite Italy and make it a republic. His clear preference in the *Discourses* is hard to reconcile with his arguments in *The Prince* for princely rule, a difficulty that has led at least a few scholars to claim that *The Prince* was written tongue-in-cheek, that it depicts a figure whose behavior is so morally reprehensible that Machiavelli must have been speaking ironically. This view, in which the prince turns into an anti-prince, goes too far, for it ignores the crucial fact that in the *Discourses* Machiavelli does not entirely discount princely rule even while he voices his preference for republican government. One of his arguments for Rome's greatness, for instance, is that it allowed for the creation of dictators in times of crisis, since republics, with their complex political deliberations, were often too slow to act. Furthermore, some of the things that the Roman state and its leaders do, such as using religion to inspire and terrify the masses, and ruthlessly punishing those opposed to the political order, are precisely what princes are supposed to do. Most important, perhaps, Machiavelli says very clearly that although republics will last longer than principalities, in order to establish a state or to reestablish one that has degenerated, there must be a single man, a founder or lawgiver—a prince—to take on the task, and thus, in the early chapters of the *Discourses*, he celebrates the first kings of Rome, such as Romulus and Numa, every bit as much as he later celebrates republican heroes such as Brutus.

This last consideration brings us to the crucial question: why should an ardent republican like Machiavelli write *The Prince* at all? One answer is simply that he was writing it for a very specific audience, Giuliano, and then Lorenzo, de' Medici, whose family aspired to something like princely rule over Florence. But at a deeper level, Machiavelli was writing *The Prince* for an Italy in crisis, an Italy that needed a strong leader to create a powerful state, in effect a re-created Rome, that would be able to resist, and perhaps even conquer, the "barbarians," as the Italians dubbed them, who had been invading their country for the past twenty years. Perhaps Machiavelli would have wanted such a ruler to turn this new Rome into a republic eventually. After all, in the "Discourse on Florentine Affairs After the Death of Lorenzo de' Medici the Younger," which he wrote for Pope Leo X in 1520, he tried vainly to persuade the Medici that they could rule Florence best by keeping its republican political system intact while exercising power through it. All of this suggests that although he may well have seen the Medici redeemer envisioned in the last chapter of *The Prince* as a temporary expedient, he was surely not being ironic in that work and really did long for a new prince who would come to save Italy, essentially, from itself.

Machiavelli imagines a world always at war. Since he sees human beings as being driven by insatiable appetites—even princes have them, although they control them better than most people do—and since the means to satisfy those appetites are finite and thus insufficient, conflict and competition are inevitable at every level, from individuals through towns and cities up to nations and empires. Such a world will never know real stability, and its history will be unpredictable, moving forward not as steady progress, but by the irrational leaps and bounds produced by appetite and conflict. Machiavelli sums up this sense of the world by means of the figure of Fortune. The Romans had made Fortune, or Fortuna (from *fors*, meaning "chance, luck, hazard"), a goddess, and they imagined her as a fickle but largely benevolent figure who bestowed goods and possessions on humans—that is, who gave them what we now would call their "fortune." This goddess was kept alive in the Christian Middle Ages and the Renaissance not as a deity to be worshiped, but as a convenient allegorical representation for the uncertain, slippery, unpredictable nature of this world. However, if Fortune was a relatively positive figure for the Romans, she was much less so in later ages; she was an expression of people's anxieties and fears more than their hopes, a foil to their vision of the sure and stable nature of the divine. In a Christian universe, Fortune's acts had to be consistent with God's will, of course, but that did not make them seem any less irrational and unexpected to human beings, who could not share God's divine vision. This is the figure, then, stripped of any association with the divine, that Machiavelli turns to in order to symbolize his sense of the mysteriousness and opacity of the world, the unpredictable movement of history, the fact that events are so often beyond the control of human reason. For example, near the end of chapter 21 of *The Prince*, Machiavelli presents this pessimistic view clearly when he declares that no course of action will ever be completely sure and free of problems, for this is "the nature of things: that one never strives to avoid one difficulty without running into another; but prudence consists in knowing how to recognize the difficulties and choosing the least bad one as good."

Machiavelli devotes the entire twenty-fifth chapter of *The Prince* to the subject of Fortune and uses two different images to depict it. First, he compares it to a raging river or a flood that overwhelms everything in its path. Although this image would seem to suggest that there is little humans can do to oppose such a mighty force, Machiavelli's view is quite different, for he insists that dikes and embankments can be built to channel the river before it floods. In other words, by means of prudence and foresight and rational planning, Fortune can be dealt with, at least to some degree—in fact, Machiavelli speaks in mathematical terms of being able to do so at least fifty percent of the time. This notion of controlling Fortune's power by building dikes fits perfectly the imagery he uses throughout *The Prince* to describe the prince and his activities, for he imagines that figure as a builder or architect whose grand construction is the state. Since Machiavelli is particularly concerned with the *new* prince in his book—that is, with someone who acquires a state and becomes its new ruler—it is not surprising that the verb he uses over and over to describe the prince's activities is *fondare*, "to found" or "to establish," more specifically, "to lay down foundations." In Machiavelli's conception, the prince is clearly an artist, and the state his work of art.

The other image Machiavelli uses for Fortune is more traditional, but he does not mention it until the end of the chapter. Between the two images, in the middle portion of the chapter, he presents the proposition that since the world is constantly changing, people will enjoy success only if they are able to adapt their methods to suit their times and circumstances. This means that two persons can use quite different methods and can both succeed, simply because they live at different times or in different circumstances. It also means that if one person always works in one way, sooner or later that person will fail, because the times will have changed and will no longer harmonize with the methods being employed. In order to illustrate this last statement, Machiavelli devotes a long paragraph to a single, somewhat surprising example, that of Pope Julius II. Julius's nature was such, says Machiavelli, that he always acted impetuously, but since the times were such that impetuosity was necessary, he succeeded in all of his undertakings. What is surprising about this example is that one expects Machiavelli to go on and say that the pope finally failed because the prudence and restraint he lacked became necessary at some point. However, Machiavelli cannot say this simply because, he admits, Julius was always successful. The most he can do to save his generalization is to speak in the conditional and to say that if before Julius's death it had become necessary to proceed otherwise, then he would have failed. One might well wonder why Machiavelli chose an example here that seems an embarrassment for his argument. The answer to this question may be found in the last paragraph of the chapter, which begins with a restatement of his general proposition that people will succeed if their methods and their circumstances are in harmony. He could leave it at that, but instead, he then makes an illogical leap, albeit one that seems to derive from what he has just said about Julius II. "I certainly think this," he proclaims, "that it is better to be impetuous than cautious." Since nothing he has said up to this point could explain such an irrational preference, he quickly goes on to justify it by invoking the other, more traditional image of Fortune. "Fortune is a woman," he says, "and it is necessary, if you wish to keep her down, to beat her and knock her about. And one sees that she lets herself be conquered by men of this sort more than by those who proceed coldly. And therefore, like a woman, she is always the friend of the young, because they are less cautious, fiercer, and command her with more audacity." Fortune here is, of course, a version of the traditional goddess, but what is striking about this passage is Machiavelli's vision of the prince manhandling her in order to make her bow to his wishes, a vision that he uses to validate his preference for impetuosity and violence over caution and restraint. In light of this vision, which concludes the chapter, Machiavelli's earlier use of the example of Julius II does not seem so very strange after all. The only difference is that the clever prince will choose to be violent and impetuous, whereas Julius II could not help but be that way.

This final vision from chapter 25 of *The Prince* is not just striking and original, but disturbing too, for it justifies, albeit at a symbolic level, the use of male violence against women. It testifies to a misogynistic aspect of Machiavelli's thought that complements his selection of *virtù* as the key term for defining the prince's behavior. For no matter what specific meanings of that word may be in play, it always connotes manliness, which realizes itself in martial action and makes equal use of force and fraud. Nevertheless, although he primarily focuses on men in his writings, since men were the chief actors on the stage of history from antiquity to the Renaissance, Machiavelli does not present *virtù* as an exclusively masculine trait. In two of his comedies, his original masterpiece *The Mandrake Root* and *Clizia*, which is a loose translation of Plautus's *Casina*, he presents us with shrewd, calculating women who are unmistakably the equals of the men around them, and in the *Discourses* he offers a memorable example of a woman whose courage and daring and disregard for conventions would make her any prince's equal. In the sixth chapter of book 3 of that work, which is dedicated to conspiracies, Machiavelli discusses the various difficulties conspirators will have after they have succeeded in killing the person they were plotting against, one of which is their mistakenly allowing someone else to live on who might take vengeance on them. To illustrate his point, he recounts how a group of conspirators in Forlì assassinated their ruler, Count Girolamo Riario, and took his wife and children prisoner, but were unable to seize the castle that dominated the town. His wife, Caterina, told them that if they let her go to the castle, she would persuade its defenders to surrender, and that she would leave her children behind as security. Once inside, however, Caterina climbed up on the walls and threatened the conspirators with vengeance for the slaying of her husband. Then, says Machiavelli, "in order to demonstrate that she was not concerned about her children, she showed them her genitalia, saying that she still had the means to make more of them." Her cunning, fierceness, and defiance here are a clear display of princely *virtù*, and they have the desired effect on the conspirators: perceiving their mistake, they wind up suffering "the punishment of perpetual exile because of their lack of prudence."

Machiavelli also qualifies in other ways the optimistic assessment of *virtù* and its power that he made in chapter 25 of *The Prince*. He must have believed in that power to some extent, for if he did not, if he felt that all action was essentially futile, then he would hardly have had any reason to have written what he did. Nevertheless, in other passages the claims he makes about the power of princely action are much more restrained. For instance, in his account of the life of Castruccio Castracani, a condottiere, or mercenary military leader, from the Tuscan town of Lucca who repeatedly beat the Florentines in the early fourteenth century and almost conquered their city, he introduces the story with a statement about the superior power of Fortune, about how Castruccio began life as a foundling, because Fortune, wanting "to demonstrate to the world that she, and not prudence, is the one who makes men great," starts "showing her power at a time when prudence cannot have any part in the matter, but rather, everything has to be acknowledged as coming from her." Machiavelli also acknowledges the superior power of Fortune in the twenty-ninth chapter of book 2 of the *Discourses*, which has the revealing title, "Fortune Blinds Men's Minds When She Does Not Want Them to Oppose Her Designs." There he declares that "men can assist Fortune, but not oppose her; they can weave the warp of her designs, but not break it." Lest this appear too gloomy a prospect, he immediately adds: "They should certainly never abandon the struggle, for, since they do not know her purpose, and since she goes by crooked and unknown roads, they always have hope, and having hope, they should never give up." Thus, although the famous—if not infamous—vision of the prince beating Fortune at the end of chapter 25 of *The Prince* presents masculine *virtù* as more powerful than its feminine opponent, Machiavelli's thought is generally more complicated than that and actually tends to move in the opposite direction. Princes can only do as much as Fortune allows them to do, and although he puts a positive spin on this conclusion in the passage from the *Discourses* cited above, the very fact that he feels the need to put a positive spin on it evokes the very pessimism that he is trying to deny. In this regard, one should not forget that his two most exemplary princes, Cesare Borgia and Castruccio Castracani, both die and wind up being pronounced failures.

One of the reasons princes have such a hard time succeeding is the difficulty they encounter in reading the book of history. One cannot adapt one's methods to changing circumstances unless one understands that they have changed. Machiavelli's entire enterprise in *The Prince*, the *Discourses*, and his other political and historical writings is an attempt to do just what his princes must do—namely, to solve the problem of reading history, of extracting general principles and laws from its vicissitudes that can be applied to one's life in the present. He is, of course, convinced that this can be done, or he would not be writing his works. Moreover, he is quite direct in telling his readers that it is possible, most directly in the preface to the first book of the *Discourses*, although he also tells them there that they must imitate what he is doing in his works if they want to understand the past, in particular the classical past, correctly and in a way that will allow it to help them act in the present. Machiavelli repeatedly stresses the novelty or originality of his enterprise, as he does in that preface in which he compares himself to the contemporary explorers who sailed to Africa, Asia, and the Americas. His originality appears in many other ways as well, such as in his avoiding the conventional pieties usually offered as advice to princes in books like his. And although he clearly reveres the ancients, he asks them to provide "the reasons for their actions." He even dares to disagree, in chapter 58 of book 1 of the *Discourses*, with the Roman historian Livy, on whose history of Rome Machiavelli based his work, over the issue of the wisdom of the people. In general, Machiavelli is asking his readers to abandon their prejudices and preconceptions and to learn to analyze history in the dispassionate way he is doing in his books.

As Machiavelli attempts to extract truth from history to serve as a guide for action in the world, he employs a number of different techniques that are essentially matters of style. For instance, he will sometimes distill the essence of what he has observed into generalizations that have the character of maxims or sayings. Here are a few examples: "all armed prophets have been victorious and the unarmed ones have come to ruin" (*The Prince*, chap. 6) "men sooner forget the death of their father than the loss of their patrimony" (chap. 17); "if men were all good, this precept [about not keeping one's word] would not be good, but since they are sadly wicked and would not keep their word to you, you also do not have to keep it to them" (chap. 18); and "love is held together by a chain of obligation which, because men are sadly wicked, is broken at every opportunity to serve their self-interest, but fear is maintained by a dread of punishment which never abandons you" (chap. 17). This last example reveals another one of Machiavelli's characteristic stylistic practices: the use of binary oppositions in the process of analysis. Here he speaks of love and fear, but there are many other binaries in his works, including armed and unarmed prophets, fathers and patrimonies, one's own arms and the arms of others, liberality and miserliness, cruelty and mercy, and, of course, *virtù* and Fortune. Occasionally those binaries expand into three or four terms, as when he considers the differences among mercenary, auxiliary, and citizen armies, although even here he prefers working with pairs, first pitting citizen armies against the other two and then contrasting mercenaries and auxiliaries. Although his use of binaries might seem at first glance a reductive tendency in his thought, his analysis is seldom so simple as to turn on just one single, bald opposition. Consider, for instance, the following passage that comes from chapter 9 of *The Prince*, in which he has been discussing—by means of another typical binary opposition—how one can become the prince of a state either with the aid of the people or with that of the nobility. Focusing on the latter, he then says that they "should be considered principally in two different ways. Either they govern themselves in their proceedings in such a manner that they are entirely dependent on your fortunes, or they do not." In the next sentence Machiavelli then offers yet another binary: "those [noblemen] who are bound to you and are not greedy must be honored and loved; those who are not bound have to be examined in two ways." Those "not bound" to the prince are further divided into the cowardly and the ambitious, and Machiavelli concludes that while the prince can choose useful counselors from the first, "because in prosperity you will gain honor from them and in adversity you do not have to fear them," he cannot use, indeed has to fear, those in the second, "because in adversity they will always help to ruin him." Passages like this one are an artful juggling trick: they offer clarity through the binary oppositions that structure them at every turn, while doing justice to the complicated way real people behave in the real world by multiplying those oppositions so as to account for all sorts of qualifying details.

Another important stylistic technique Machiavelli uses to formulate general rules about history while still doing justice to its complexities is what might be called the supplemental observation or the supplemental generalization. What he does, in essence, is to develop an argument, and then, just when you think he is reaching a conclusion, to offer another observation or generalization that leads to a new and unexpected conclusion that provides a more complicated, and sometimes more comprehensive, explanation for things. A good example of this technique can be found near the end of chapter 7 of *The Prince* where he is reviewing the career of his model prince Cesare Borgia. Since Borgia depended on the armies of his father, Pope Alexander VI, to expand his domain, he had to worry about the possibility that his father could die and the next pope might be hostile to him. Machiavelli specifies that Borgia had to do four things to guarantee his future, of which he had accomplished three before Alexander died. The fourth was to secure a power base large enough to let him withstand any sort of assault, a power base that would have included Tuscany as well as the Romagna. Machiavelli notes that Borgia was well on his way to success on this front, but then his father died, leaving "him with only the state of the Romagna consolidated, and with all the others up in the air." Thus far, Machiavelli seems to be moving toward this conclusion: Borgia had to accomplish four things, and since he did only three of the four, his failure was inevitable. However, Machiavelli complicates things by observing that at his father's death, Borgia was left "between two very powerful enemy armies, and deathly ill." The fact that Borgia had not consolidated his power base turns out not to have been the only cause of his failure. Instead, Machiavelli argues that Borgia had so much *virtù* and had done everything so well, "that if he had not had those two armies on top of him, or if he had been healthy, he would have held out against every difficulty." Machiavelli then revises even this explanation one last time, ignoring the issue of the French and Spanish armies, perhaps to get at what he sees as the ultimate truth: "if at the death of Alexander [Borgia] had been healthy, everything would have been easy." By adding more and more explanatory material, Machiavelli really offers a series of conclusions, all of which have some validity, although the final one seems to be the most satisfactory. Ironically, in this specific case, the final explanation—that Borgia was deathly ill— cannot really be some sort of "effectual truth," since there is no way to make it into a generalization that can actually be put to work in the real world.

The particular conclusions Machiavelli reaches are less important than the process he goes through to reach them, for it is that process that teaches readers how to interpret the book of the past. Despite Machiavelli's penchant for pithy sayings and dramatic binary oppositions, it is this complex sorting out, and re-sorting out, of arguments and evidence that really serves as a model for the reader's own appropriation of history for use in the present. Machiavelli even manages this teaching process at the level of the individual sentence. For the most part in his political writings, he composes relatively lengthy, elaborate, Latinate sentences, some of whose length and elaborateness get lost as they make their way into English. Italian has more inflections than English, an inheritance from its Latin ancestor, and Italian prose writers of the Renaissance, including Machiavelli, who sought to imitate the density and complexity of Latin style, used them to that end. Consider the following sentence from chapter 19 of *The Prince* in which Machiavelli explains why the emperor Septimius Severus was able to survive despite treating the Roman people badly: "for in Severus there was so much ability [*virtù*] that by keeping the soldiers his friends, even though the people were oppressed by him, he was always able to rule happily, for those abilities [*virtù*] of his made him so admirable in the sight of the soldiers and the people that the latter were, to some degree, astonished and stupefied, and the former, respectful and satisfied." What is noteworthy about this sentence is the way that Machiavelli inserts a phrase (in Italian, a participial phrase) and a clause in between the beginning of his thought and its completion. All he really needed to write in order to explain why Severus survived is this: "in Severus there was so much ability [*virtù*] that he was always able to rule happily." Instead, he deliberately interrupts the syntax with the phrase about keeping the friendship of the soldiers and the clause noting that Severus oppressed the people. This interruption, however, accomplishes two important things. First, it presents aspects of the historical situation within which Severus exercised his *virtù*, and since it does this before completing the thought, the result is that the syntax forces the reader to see Severus's behavior in context; in other words, he does not simply exercise *virtù*, but he does so in the real world in relation to other people and in a particular historical time and place. Machiavelli's syntax thus presents individual action as both constrained and enabled by its social context. Second, by placing "he was able" (a single word, *possé*, in Italian) after the inserted phrase and clause, Machiavelli forces the reader to take those circumstances into account *before* reaching the subject and verb of the clause, thus determining the order or succession of the ideas by means of which readers will think through the situation. In essence, then, Machiavelli teaches his readers to read the past by using his style to force them to think like him.

Surprisingly, despite his use of style to coerce the reader's responses, Machiavelli's texts also appear to register the presence of other voices and points of view. Indeed, one of the most striking features of his works is the fact that he frequently addresses a "you" (either the singular *tu* or the plural—or polite—*voi* in Italian), and sometimes associates that "you" with a position different than his own. What is more, he will even slide from speaking of a third person ("the prince," "he") into addressing a "you" in the midst of a single sentence. Note this shift in the following example from chapter 19 of *The Prince*: "a prince who wants to hold onto his state is often forced not to be good, for when that group, whether it be the people, the soldiers, or the nobles, whose support you believe you need in order to rule, is corrupt, you must follow its humor and satisfy it." The inclusion of a "you" here may be explained in part, of course, by the fact that Machiavelli's works are generally addressed to specific individuals. Or the "you" may be a reflection—perhaps a recollection—of the actual discussions that Machiavelli had with his friends in such places as the gardens of Cosimo Rucellai's palace. In either case, however, although this technique might seem to give Machiavelli's works a dialogic dimension, portraying them as exchanges among people with different viewpoints, ironically the "you" is never allowed to articulate a viable alternative to Machiavelli's opinions, but is instead resoundingly refuted by him. Even more typically, the "you" has no opinion, no character; it is a kind of blank slate for the hand of Machiavelli the teacher to write his lessons on. In essence, the "you" who appears in Machiavelli's works is reduced to being his "yes-man." If Machiavelli may be said to employ a rhetoric in his works, then it is a rhetoric of power, for insofar as readers identify with the "you" Machiavelli addresses, that rhetoric strives to make them into his "yes-men," too.

Machiavelli's rhetorical style creates a powerful impression of Machiavelli himself as a distinct and distinctive human being. By writing as he does, he artfully manufactures an identity for himself, thus participating in one of the defining activities of the European Renaissance. One of the most important legacies of the Renaissance to the modern world is the notion that identity is not a given, not something one inherits from one's family or acquires from a profession or derives from participation in the social life of one's local community. Rather, to use a memorable phrase from an educational treatise by the Dutch humanist Erasmus, "men are not born, but made": they are the children not of their parents, but of their own works and deeds. One expression of this new ideology of self-creation, or "self-fashioning," as it is called by contemporary scholars, and the social mobility it enabled and reflected, is the Renaissance myth of Faustus, the man who, having achieved fame through learning and magic, is willing to sell his soul to the devil in exchange for infinite wealth and power. The period also gave birth to the picaresque novel, whose protagonist changes his identity from one episode to the next, moving up and down the social hierarchy with complete ease. It gave birth to countless player-kings— and to players of every stripe—in the theater that took as its motto Shakespeare's famous lines from *As You Like It*: "All the world's a stage, / And all the men and women merely players." And, of course, it gave birth to Machiavelli's prince, that new ruler who rises to the top by means of his *virtù*, displaying prowess and daring as a military leader, prudence and ruthlessness as a political one. His prince is even willing to murder people to whom one might expect him to feel some sort of loyalty or obligation, as Cesare Borgia does to his lieutenant Remirro de Orco, as Oliverotto da Fermo does to his maternal uncle Giovanni Fogliani, and as Machiavelli's Romans do to brothers and sons and other family members. For Machiavelli's princes, family ties and traditional bonds are much less important than the creation of one's identity through the acquisition and maintenance of power achieved by the ruthless exercise of one's *virtù*.

Nowhere is Machiavelli's embrace of the ideology of self-fashioning clearer than in his brief biography of the condottiere from Lucca, Castruccio Castracani. Having read Niccolò Tegrimi's Latin account of Castruccio's life, he doubtless thought that his writing a successful biography in the vernacular would be a useful credential for him to have as he pursued the post of historiographer of Florence, a post the Medici, in fact, awarded him on November 8, 1520. But his reasons for writing the biography ran deeper, and they can be glimpsed in the striking ways that he deliberately distorts and falsifies the biographical record. Biographers as well as historians in the Renaissance felt less of a need to stick to the facts than their modern counterparts do; nevertheless, Machiavelli's distortions are extreme, and they are very revealing as a result. For through them he essentially transforms Castruccio into an almost mythical version of the ideal prince.

Machiavelli makes two quite serious changes in the historical record of Castruccio's life. First, although the real Castruccio was married and had a large number of children, Machiavelli's Castruccio does not marry, and claims he did not do so specifically so that he could adopt as his heir the son of his former patron. One could read this gesture as an attempt on Machiavelli's part to make Castruccio a figure possessing the traditional virtue of loyalty to his patron, a loyalty that transcends even the natural instinct to reproduce. However, it could also be read as Machiavelli's attempt to make Castruccio a figure of *virtù*, for not only has Castruccio made himself the prince of Lucca by means of his deeds alone, but in adopting the son of its former ruler, he thereby becomes the symbolic progenitor of its future rulers, while at the same time he appropriates the identity of his former patron, his surrogate "father," and thus makes himself, in a way, into his own father. The other change Machiavelli makes is that his Castruccio starts off life as a foundling. Not only does this allow Machiavelli to put him in the same category as such mythical lawgivers and founders of states as Moses and Romulus, but it also makes him a perfect example of self-fashioning. For if the notion that people make their own identities may imply that they are denying their parents (at least metaphorically or symbolically), being a foundling eliminates the issue of parents, or at least biological parents, altogether. Moreover, although the baby Castruccio is indeed found and initially raised by a priest and his sister, as soon as he is able, he leaves them behind, after which point they simply disappear from his world—and from Machiavelli's text—and he attaches himself instead to the patron whom he eventually manages to replace. From foundling to prince of Lucca: Castruccio's story of creating an identity for himself by means of his talents, his *virtù*, constitutes the most radical version of self-fashioning the Renaissance could imagine.

Machiavelli was also deeply attracted to the fourteenth-century condottiere because he mirrored the circumstances of Machiavelli's own life. When he wrote the biography in the summer of 1520, he had been in exile from Florence for almost eight years, and he must have felt a fair amount of resentment at how he had been treated. Consequently, he chose to write about Castruccio, who was not, after all, a great Florentine hero, but one of the city's worst enemies. Even more profoundly, Castruccio spoke to Machiavelli because Castruccio's story, especially after Machiavelli got through retouching it, was really his own. Machiavelli, too, had begun in relative obscurity and had become, if not a great general and the prince of a city, then at least the Head of the Second Chancery, the man responsible for creating the Florentine citizen militia, and Soderini's confidential adviser. And he, too, had achieved these things not through family contacts or by dint of social rank, but because of his enormous talent, hard work, and energy—in other words, because of his *virtù*. But if both Castruccio and Machiavelli were Renaissance success stories, both were also failures. Despite the repeated defeats he inflicted on the Florentines, Castruccio never became the ruler of Tuscany, not because of anything his enemies could do to him, but simply because Fortune struck him down on the eve of his greatest triumph. Although this looks simply like bad luck, Castruccio actually blamed himself for not having done better. If Castruccio's rise to power represents the optimistic side of Machiavelli's thought, his sudden fall speaks to Machiavelli's pessimism, a pessimism that was surely shaped by his own fall from power in 1512 and all the difficulties he had in getting back into the city he loved more dearly than his soul. Since he wrote the life of Castruccio while still in exile, its final sentence may really be an assessment of Machiavelli's own lot: "while living [Castruccio] was not inferior either to Philip of Macedonia, the father of Alexander, nor to Scipio of Rome, . . . and without doubt he would have surpassed both if, in exchange for Lucca, he had had Macedonia or Rome as his native land." "In my life," Machiavelli might have said of himself, "I have not been inferior to the great rulers of antiquity, and I would have surpassed them, if I had not had Florence—which could not truly appreciate my talents or summon up the courage and discipline to fight off the barbarian invaders—but rather had Macedonia or Rome as my country." To be sure, in the last seven years of his life Machiavelli did regain some portion of the power and prestige he once enjoyed, but he never achieved again the centrality he had had during the days of the republic. And he died in bitterness, having been passed over by the leaders of the newly re-created republic in 1527, just after the Sack of Rome, which destroyed any hope that Italy might have had to preserve its independence from the larger nation-states whose fatal invasions had begun some thirty-three years before.

*   *   *   *   *

The Prince was not published during Machiavelli's lifetime—it appeared only in 1531 at Rome in an edition together with *The Life of Castruccio Castracani*. Indeed, the two works were printed together frequently during the Renaissance in a clear sign that they were understood to be closely connected to one another, *The Life* offering a full-scale example of the ideal prince described more theoretically and incompletely in Machiavelli's treatise. That connection is also being honored in this translation of the works, which brings the two of them together. In addition, this volume includes the remarkable letter Machiavelli wrote to Francesco Vettori in which he describes his life in exile and reveals that he has been at work writing what was to become his masterpiece. Finally, it also includes a number of excerpts from the *Discourses*, which are generally intended to supplement what Machiavelli says in *The Prince*. In some cases, those excerpts show him thinking about many of the themes of *The Prince*, such as the relationship between force and fraud and that between *virtù* and the power of Fortune. In other cases, they provide a glimpse of Machiavelli's republican sympathies, even though they also show that his preference for republicanism was no simple matter.

The translations of *The Prince* and of Machiavelli's other works are entirely my own. In all cases I have taken pains to turn Machiavelli's Italian into fluent English, although I have also tried to keep something of the syntactical complexity of his sentences. Nevertheless, since English does not use participial phrases to the same extent that Machiavelli does in Italian, and since English lacks the resources of inflection that permitted him to create complicated syntactical structures, I have frequently replaced participial phrases with subordinate clauses, and I have often chosen to break one sentence into two or even three. I have commented earlier in this introduction on the difficulty of translating the key word *virtù*, and because of its basic importance in Machiavelli's thought, I have retained it, as well as related adjectives and adverbs, whenever they occur in the text, putting them in brackets after their English equivalents. I have also elected to capitalize Fortune whenever I detected even a hint of personification, even though the word is not capitalized in Italian, both because Machiavelli says that "Fortune is a woman," and because the word's being gendered as feminine suggests personification in and of itself. Unfortunately, there is a very long list of key terms in Machiavelli's lexicon that are untranslatable either because there is no English equivalent for them or because several different English words could work equally well whenever one of them appears. For instance, *ordini* means literally "orders," but as Machiavelli uses it, the word could mean habits or customs, rules, ordinances, laws, constitution, institutions, and something like the entire social system. Forced to choose, I have opted in each individual case for the English word I think best captures the meaning of Machiavelli's original Italian word in context, although at times, I confess, the context actually allowed for multiple meanings so that I wound up having to choose one English word rather than another on quite arbitrary grounds. Because of all these syntactical and lexical complexities, a reader who consults different translations of Machiavelli's works will find that they differ quite a lot from one another. I offer mine as yet one more, in full awareness of the truth caught in the Italian saying *traduttore traditore*: "the translator is always a traitor."

Wayne A. Rebhorn is the Celanese Centennial Professor of English at the University of Texas at Austin. A graduate of the University of Pennsylvania and Yale University, he has also taught at the Bread Loaf School of English, the Université Paul Valéry in Montpellier, and the Université de Paris, and he has won many awards, including a Fulbright and fellowships from the American Council of Learned Societies and the Guggenheim Foundation. He has written extensively on Renaissance literature in English, Italian, French, Spanish, and Latin on authors from Boccaccio through More and Shakespeare down to Milton. Among his recent books are *The Emperor of Men's Minds: Literature and the Renaissance Discourse of Rhetoric* (1995) and *Renaissance Debates on Rhetoric* (2000), both published by Cornell University Press. His *Foxes and Lions: Machiavelli's Confidence Men* (Cornell University Press, 1988) won the Howard R. Marraro Prize of the Modern Language Association of America in 1990.

The Prince
and Other Writings

The Prince

Chapter

Dedicatory Letter: Niccolò Machiavelli to Lorenzo the Magnificent de' Medici[1]

MOST OF THE TIME, it is customary for those who wish to gain the favor of a prince to approach him with things they hold most dear, or in which they know he takes delight. In this way princes are often presented with horses, arms, cloth of gold, precious stones, and similar ornaments worthy of their grandeur. In my desire thus to offer Your Magnificence some testimony of my devotion, I have not found among my possessions anything which I hold so dear or esteem so highly as the knowledge of the deeds of great men which I have acquired through a long experience of modern events and constant study of antiquity. The results of my long observations and reflections are condensed in one little volume that I am now sending to Your Magnificence.

And although I deem this work unworthy to be presented to you, nevertheless, my confidence in your humanity assures me that you will accept it, knowing that I could not make you a greater gift than that of enabling you to understand in the shortest time that which I have learned through hardships and danger in the course of many years. I have not adorned and padded my work with long periods or bombastic and high-sounding words or any other rhetorical and unessential ornaments with which many writers are accustomed to arrange and embellish their books, for I desire either that nothing should honor my work, or that only the variety of its contents and the gravity of its subject should make it pleasing. Nor do I wish it to be deemed presumptuous if a man of low and humble condition should dare to discuss and direct the government of princes; for in the same way that landscape painters place themselves down in the plain in order to study the nature of mountains and elevated sites, and place themselves on mountains in order to study the nature of the plains, so, in order to know well the nature of the people, it is necessary to be a prince, and to know well the nature of princes, one must be one of the people.

Accept, therefore, Your Magnificence, this little gift in the spirit in which I send it to you. If you will deign to read and study it diligently, you will recognize in it my ardent desire that you may attain that grandeur which Fortune and your own qualities presage for you. And should Your Magnificence gaze down from the summit of your eminence toward this lowly place, you will recognize how I, undeservedly, suffer from the continual malice of Fortune.

Note to the Dedicatory Letter

1. Machiavelli originally dedicated *The Prince* to Giuliano de' Medici, the duke of Nemours (1479–1516), but when he died, Machiavelli replaced him with Lorenzo de' Medici, the duke of Urbino (1492–1519). Although addressed as "the Magnificent," this Lorenzo was actually the grandson of the famous Lorenzo the Magnificent (1449–1492). It is sadly ironic that Machiavelli dedicated his book to members of the very family whose seizure of Florence in 1512 was the source of the personal troubles to which he obliquely refers in the last sentence of the dedication.

Chapter 1

How Many Kinds of States There Are and in What Ways They Are Acquired

ALL STATES AND DOMINIONS that hold or have held sway over men are either republics or principalities. Principalities are either hereditary ones, in which the family of their rulers has been in power for many years, or they are new. The new ones are either entirely new, as was Milan to Francesco Sforza, or they are like new members added on to the hereditary state of the prince who acquires them, as is the Kingdom of Naples for the king of Spain.[1] The dominions thus acquired have either been accustomed to the rule of a prince, or else they are used to being free states, and they are acquired either with the arms of others, or with one's own, either by Fortune or by prowess [*virtù*].

Note to Chapter 1

1. Francesco Sforza (1401–1466) was a professional soldier who served initially the Visconti family that ruled Milan and later the republic that was created when the Visconti line died out in 1447; he made himself the ruler of the city-state in 1450. The Kingdom of Naples, which included southern Italy and Sicily, was captured by King Ferdinand II of Aragon (1452–1516) in 1503.

Chapter 2

On Hereditary Principalities

I WILL NOT SPEAK here of republics, because I have discussed them fully elsewhere.[1] I will deal only with principalities, and following the order described above, I will show how those principalities can be governed and maintained.

I say, then, that in hereditary states accustomed to the family of their prince, there are far fewer difficulties in maintaining them than in new ones, for it is sufficient merely not to neglect ancient customs and to accommodate oneself to unexpected events. In this way, if such a prince is ordinarily industrious, he will always be able to maintain his state unless a very extraordinary and excessive force deprives him of it, and even if he is deprived of it, when the slightest misfortune happens to the occupier, he will be able to regain it.

We have in Italy, for example, the Duke of Ferrara, who was able to withstand the assaults of the Venetians in 1484 and those of Pope Julius in 1510 for no other reason than because of the antiquity of his family in that state.[2] Inasmuch as the legitimate prince has fewer reasons and less need to harm his subjects, it follows that they would love him more, and if no extraordinary vices make him hated, it stands to reason that they would be naturally well-disposed toward him. In the long and continuous course of his reign, the memories and causes of innovations will disappear, because one change always creates a projecting stone[3] for attaching another.

Notes to Chapter 2

1. That is, in the first book of the *Discourses*.
2. Machiavelli conflates two dukes of Ferrara here. The first, Ercole d'Este (1471–1505), resisted the Venetians but had to yield them some of his territory. The second, Alfonso I d'Este (1486–1534), was attacked in 1510

by Pope Julius II and briefly driven out of his territories. When Machiavelli was writing, the Este family had ruled Ferrara for 400 years.

3. A projecting stone, or *addentellato*, is a stone that projects from the end of a wall like a tooth (*dente*); stones for a new wall may be attached to it.

Chapter 3

On Mixed Principalities

BUT IT IS IN the new principality that one has real difficulties. First, if it is not entirely new, but like a member of another state, so that the whole can be called a mixed state, its disorders spring at first from a natural difficulty which exists in all new principalities: this is that men change rulers willingly, hoping to better their lot, and this belief makes them take arms against their ruler, but in this they are deceived, as their experience shows that things have become worse. This is the result of another very natural and ordinary necessity, which is that a new prince must always inflict harm on those over whom he rules, both with his men-at-arms and with countless other injuries his new conquest entails. Thus you will find enemies in all those whom you have injured by occupying that principality, and you cannot maintain the friendship of those who have helped put you there, since you will not be able to satisfy them as they expected, nor can you treat them with strong medicine, since you are obligated to them. For this reason, however strong one's armies may be, one will always need the favor of the inhabitants to gain possession of a country. It was for these reasons that Louis XII of France swiftly occupied Milan and just as swiftly lost it, and Ludovico's own forces were sufficient to take it from him the first time, for the inhabitants who had willingly opened their gates to him, finding themselves deceived about him and about those benefits that they anticipated, could not bear the offenses of their new prince.[1]

It is indeed true that when lands that have rebelled are re-taken, they are not lost again so easily, for the ruler, now using the rebellion as a pretext, is less averse to secure his position by punishing offenders, clarifying suspicions, and strengthening himself in his weakest places. Thus, if the mere rampaging of a Duke Ludovico on the borders was sufficient to cause France to lose Milan the first time, to make her lose it the second time, she had to have all the world against her and to have her armies wiped out or driven out of Italy, which was the result of the causes mentioned above.[2] Nevertheless, it was taken from her both the first and the second time. The general causes of the first loss have already been discussed; it remains now to be seen what the causes of the second were and what remedies France had available, or what measures might have been taken by another ruler to maintain his conquest more securely than the king of France did. Therefore, I say that those states which, being conquered, are added onto an old state of the conqueror's may or may not be of the same nationality and language. If they are, it is very easy to hold them, especially when they are not accustomed to freedom, and to possess them securely it suffices to have extinguished the line of the princes who formerly governed them, for with regard to other matters, if their old way of life is maintained, and there is no change in customs, the people will live peacefully, as we have seen in the cases of Burgundy, Brittany, Gascony, and Normandy, which have been united to France for such a long time; and although there may be some slight differences of language, the customs of the people are nevertheless similar, and they are able to get along with one another easily.[3] And whoever obtains possession of such states and wishes to retain them must bear in mind two things: first, that the family of their old rulers should be extinct; second, to make no alteration either in their laws or in their taxes. In this way, in a very short space of time, they will all form a single body with the old principality.

But when states are acquired in a country differing in language, laws, and customs, this is where the difficulties arise, and it requires good fortune as well as great industriousness to hold onto them; and one of the best and most effective remedies would be for the person who has acquired them to take up his residence there. This would render their possession more secure and durable, as the Turk has done in Greece; in spite of all the other measures taken by him to hold onto that state, it would not have been possible to keep it, had he not gone there to live. For, by being on the spot, one can see disorders as they arise, and you can quickly remedy them, but when you do not live there, they are only heard about when they have increased, and then they are beyond remedy. Besides this, the province will not be plundered by your officials; the subjects will be pleased with having direct recourse to their prince; and wanting to be good, they will have more reason to love him, and wanting to be otherwise, they will have more reason to fear him. Any outsider who might want to attack that state would be more hesitant, so that as long as the ruler resides there, he will lose it only with the greatest difficulty.

The other and better remedy is to send colonies into one or two places which would be, as it were, the shackles of the state, for it is necessary either to do this or to keep a large force of men-at-arms and infantry there. The colonies will not cost much, so that with little or no expense on his part, the prince can send them out and maintain them, and he only injures those whose lands and houses are taken to give to the new inhabitants, and they constitute but a small part of the state; and those who are injured, remaining poor and disunited, can never do him any harm, while all the others, on the one hand, are uninjured and therefore should be easily pacified, and on the other, are fearful of doing wrong lest they should be treated like those who have been stripped of their property. I conclude that these colonies cost nothing, are more loyal, and give less offense; and the injured parties are unable to do harm, being poor and disunited, as I have said. For it must be noted that men must either be caressed or else destroyed, because they will revenge themselves for small injuries, but cannot do so for serious ones. Thus, the injury done to a man must be such that there is no need to fear his vengeance. But by keeping troops there instead of colonists, one will spend a great deal more, being obliged to consume all the revenues of the state in order to guard it, so that the acquisition turns into a loss, and much greater harm is done, since the entire state is injured by the army's having to move its quarters from place to place. This inconvenience is felt by all, and everyone becomes an enemy, and these are enemies who can do harm, because, though beaten, they remain in their own homes. In every way, then, a garrison is as useless as colonies are useful.

Furthermore, the ruler of a country that is unlike his own, as I have said, should make himself the leader and defender of his less powerful neighbors and do his best to weaken the stronger ones, and he should take care that some outsider, who is as powerful as he is, does not get in by accident. And it always happens that the outsider will be brought in by those who are discontented either because of excessive ambition or because of fear, as was seen when the Aetolians brought the Romans into Greece, and no matter what country the Romans entered, it was always at the request of the inhabitants.[4] The general rule is that as soon as a powerful outsider enters a country, all the less powerful inhabitants become his adherents, moved by the hatred they bear toward the person who used to rule them, so that with respect to these less powerful people, he will not have to put up with any trouble whatever in winning them over, for they will instantly all become part of the state that he acquired there. He merely has to be careful that they do not acquire too much strength and authority; then he can easily, with his own forces and with the favor of the people, put down those who are powerful, so that he will become, in everything, the arbiter of that country. And he who does not govern well in this way will soon lose what he has acquired, and while he holds it, will meet with countless difficulties and annoyances.

The Romans always followed these procedures in the countries they seized: they sent in colonies, provided for the less powerful without increasing their strength, put down the powerful, and did not allow powerful foreigners to gain prestige there. I will let the country of Greece alone suffice as an example: the Romans provided for the Achaeans and the Aetolians, put down the kingdom of the Macedonians, and drove out Antiochus.[5] They did not allow the merits of the Achaeans or the Aetolians to gain them any increase of territory, nor did the blandishments of Philip induce them to be his friends until they had first humbled him, nor could the power of Antiochus make them consent to his having a state in that country. For in these instances the Romans did what all wise princes should do: they have to look not only to present dangers but also to future ones, and make every effort to forestall them. For, if they are seen from afar, they can easily be remedied, but if you wait until they present themselves, there is no longer time to use medicine, since the malady has become incurable. What doctors say about consumption applies here: at the beginning the disease is easy to cure but difficult to diagnose, but in the course of time, when it was not diagnosed at first and treated, it becomes easy to diagnose but difficult to cure. Thus it happens in the affairs of state: if the evils that are developing are diagnosed from afar (which only the prudent man can do), they are quickly cured, but when they have not been diagnosed and are allowed to grow so that everyone recognizes them, then there is no longer any remedy for them.

Thus, the Romans, observing troubles from afar, always found remedies for them and never allowed them to develop in order to avoid a war, for they knew that war does not go away, but is merely deferred to the advantage of others. For this reason they wanted to wage war with Philip and Antiochus in Greece so as not to have to deal with them in Italy, though at the time they could have avoided both wars, something they did not wish to do. Nor did they ever like that saying which now is always on the lips of the wise men of our time, "to enjoy the benefit of time," but they trusted in their own prowess [*virtù*] and prudence, since time drives all things on and may bring in with it the good as well as the bad and the bad as well as the good.

But let us return to France and examine whether she did any of the things just mentioned, and I shall speak not of Charles, but of Louis since his mode of proceeding has been better observed, because he has held territory in Italy for a longer time, and you will see how he did the opposite of all those things which must be done to hold onto a state in a foreign country.[6]

King Louis was brought into Italy by the ambition of the Venetians, who wished by his coming to gain half of Lombardy. I will not blame the king for the action he took, because, wishing to get an initial foothold in Italy and not having friends in this country—on the contrary, the conduct of King Charles had caused all doors to be locked against him—he was forced to take what friendships he could. And his well-considered undertaking would have led to success for him if he had made no error in his other actions. Having acquired Lombardy, therefore, the king immediately regained the prestige taken from him by Charles: Genoa gave in, and the Florentines became his friends; the marquis of Mantua, the duke of Ferrara, the Bentivogli, the lady of Forlì, the lords of Faenza, Pesaro, Rimini, Camerino, Piombino, the Lucchesi, the Pisans, the Sienese—all approached him to become his friends.[7] And then the Venetians could see the foolhardiness of the decision they had made: in order to gain two towns in Lombardy, they had made the king the master of one-third of Italy.[8]

Now consider with how little difficulty the king could have maintained his reputation in Italy if he had observed the rules given above and kept all those friends of his secure and well-defended. For there was a great number of them, and they were weak and afraid, some of the Church, some of the Venetians, so that they would always have been obliged to stick by him, and by their means he could have easily protected himself from the remaining powers. But no sooner was he in Milan than he did the opposite, giving aid to Pope Alexander so that he could occupy the Romagna.[9] Nor did he perceive that by this decision he was weakening himself, casting off his friends and those who had thrown themselves into his lap, and making the Church great by adding enormous temporal power to the spiritual power which gives it so much authority. And having made this first error, he was forced to follow it up, so that to put a stop to the ambition of Alexander and prevent him from becoming lord of Tuscany, he was forced to come to Italy.[10] It was not enough for him to have made the Church powerful and deprived himself of his friends, but, desiring to have the Kingdom of Naples, he divided it with the king of Spain.[11] And where before he alone was the arbiter of Italy, now he brought in a partner to whom those in that country who were ambitious and dissatisfied with him might have recourse; and where he could have left a king in that kingdom who was his tributary, he expelled him in order to bring in another who was capable of driving Louis out himself.[12]

The desire to acquire things is truly very natural and ordinary, and when men who can do so are successful, they will always be praised and not blamed, but when they cannot and want to do so at all costs, here there is error and blame. If France, therefore, could have attacked Naples with her own forces, she should have done so; if she could not, she should not have shared it. And if the division of Lombardy she made with the Venetians deserved to be excused, as having been the means of allowing her to get a foothold in Italy, this other division deserves blame, since it cannot be excused by such a necessity.

Louis had thus made these five errors: he destroyed the minor powers; he increased the power in Italy of one who was already powerful; he brought a very powerful foreigner into that country; he did not come to live there himself; and he did not send colonies there. Still, if he had lived, these errors would not have harmed him, had he not made the sixth one of taking their state from the Venetians.[13] For, if he had not strengthened the Church and brought Spain into Italy, it would have been reasonable and necessary to put the Venetians down, but having once taken those steps, he should never have consented to their ruin, because as long as they were strong, they would have always kept the others from trying to take Lombardy, partly because the Venetians would not have consented to it unless they could become the masters there themselves, and partly because the others would not have wanted to take it from France in order to give it to the Venetians, and they would not have had the courage to attack both of them together. And if anyone should say that King Louis gave up the Romagna to Alexander and the Kingdom of Naples to Spain in order to escape a war, I would reply with the arguments given above: that one should never allow disorders to develop in order to avoid a war, for war is not avoided, but only deferred to your disadvantage. And if others allege the promise that the king had given to the pope to undertake that enterprise for him, in return for the dissolution of the king's marriage and a cardinal's hat for Rouen, I would reply with what I shall say later about the word of princes and how they are to keep it.[14]

Thus King Louis lost Lombardy by not observing any of the rules which have been observed by others who have taken countries and sought to hold onto them. Nor is this some sort of miracle, but something very ordinary and reasonable. And I spoke of this subject with Cardinal Rouen at Nantes, when Valentino (as Cesare Borgia, son of Pope Alexander, was commonly called) was occupying the Romagna. For when Cardinal Rouen said to me that the Italians did not understand anything about war, I replied that the French did not understand anything about statecraft, for if they had, they would never allow the Church to become so powerful. And experience has shown that the power of the Church and of Spain in Italy has been caused by France, and her ruin was caused by them. From this may be drawn a general rule which never, or rarely, fails: that whoever is the cause of another's becoming powerful will come to ruin himself, because that power is created by him through either his industriousness or his force, and both of these qualities are suspect to the one who has become powerful.

Notes to Chapter 3

1. Louis XII, king of France (1462–1515; ruled from 1498), invaded Italy in 1499 and captured Milan on October 5. It was recaptured by Ludovico Sforza, Il Moro, duke of Milan (1452–1508), on February 5, 1500; soon after that he was betrayed to the French by his own troops and spent the rest of his days in prison in France.

2. The French retook Milan a second time in April 1500 and held it for more than ten years until they were driven out of Italy by the Holy League of Julius II, which included the armies of Spain and Venice and, on paper at least, the Holy Roman Empire and England.

3. Although Normandy was incorporated into France in 1204, the other three independent duchies were added only in the second half of the fifteenth century.

4. The Romans invaded Greece in 211 B.C.E. in order to attack Philip V (238–179 B.C.E.) of Macedonia, who was an ally of Hannibal. The Aetolians, a confederacy of states in northern and central Greece, did not literally invite them in, although they did seek an alliance with the Romans.

5. The Achaeans were a league like the Aetolians. Allied to Philip V, they were defeated by the Romans at the battle of Cynoscephalae in 197 B.C.E. Seven years later, the Aetolian League was also defeated, together with their allies the Syrians, who were led by Antiochus III, also known as "the Great," from 223 to 187 B.C.E.

6. Although Charles VIII made the first French invasion of Italy in 1494 in order to claim the Kingdom of Naples, his occupation was short-lived. His successor, Louis XII, invaded Italy again in 1499 and captured Milan. He partitioned Naples with Spain in 1500, fought with Spain over Naples from 1502 to 1505, joined with Julius II in a league against the Venetians in 1508, and was finally expelled from the peninsula in 1513.

7. The rulers mentioned here, many of whom had quite tiny states, were, respectively: Francesco Gonzaga, marquis of Mantua; Ercole I d'Este, duke of Ferrara; Giovanni Bentivogli, lord of Bologna; Caterina Riario Sforza, lady of Forlì; Astorre Manfredi, lord of Faenza; Giovanni Sforza, lord of Pesaro; Pandolfo Malatesta, lord of Rimini, Giulio Cesare da Varano, lord of Camerino; and Jacopo IV d'Appiano, lord of Piombino.

8. Venice had been promised the towns of Brescia, Bergamo, Crema, and Cremona.

9. Pope Alexander was Alexander VI, born Rodrigo Borgia (1431–1503); he was pope from 1492 on. He got the support of Charles by granting him

a dispensation to divorce his wife. The Romagna is a region in north-central Italy bordering on the Adriatic Sea; included within it are the towns of Ravenna, Forlì, Arezzo, Pesaro, and Urbino.

10. In August 1502 Cesare Borgia was preparing to assault Florence. However, Charles actually came to Italy to fight Spain for control of Naples.

11. Louis and Ferdinand II of Aragon signed the Treaty of Granada on November 11, 1500, according to which the French were to get Campania and the Abruzzi, while the Spanish got Puglia, Calabria, and Sicily.

12. He could have left Federico I of Aragon (1431–1501), the original ruler, in Naples but instead brought in Ferdinand II of Aragon, who promptly drove Louis out.

13. Louis joined the League of Cambrai in 1508 under the leadership of Julius II in order to make war on the Venetians. When the latter were defeated the next year, Julius formed the Holy League, which included the Venetians as well as Spain, in order to drive the French out of Italy.

14. Because he wanted to marry Anne of Brittany, who had been the wife of Charles VIII, Louis had to receive a dispensation in order to divorce his first wife. He also wanted his favorite, Georges d'Amboise, archbishop of Rouen, to be made a cardinal. To obtain these things, Louis agreed to help the pope, Alexander VI, gain the Romagna and attack Naples, a promise he felt obliged to keep to the pope's successor, Julius II.

Chapter 4

Why the Kingdom of Darius, Conquered by Alexander, Did Not Rebel Against Alexander's Successors After His Death

CONSIDERING THE DIFFICULTIES THERE are in holding onto a newly acquired state, someone may wonder how it happened that Alexander the Great became the master of Asia in a few years and having hardly occupied it, died, from which it would have seemed reasonable for the whole state to have rebelled; nevertheless, Alexander's successors maintained their hold on it and had no other difficulty in keeping it than that which arose among themselves from their own ambition.[1] I would reply that all principalities known throughout history are governed in two different ways: either by a prince with all the others as his servants who, by his grace and permission, help govern the realm as his ministers; or by a prince and barons who hold that rank not by virtue of the grace of their lord, but by virtue of the antiquity of their family. Such barons have dominions and subjects of their own, who recognize them as their lords and have a natural affection for them. In those states which are governed by a prince and his servants, the prince has more authority, because in the entire country no one is regarded as a superior except him, and if they obey another, they do so as his minister and officer, and do not feel any particular love for him.

Examples of these two different kinds of governments in our own times are the Turk and the king of France. The entire Turkish monarchy is governed by one lord; the others are his servants; and dividing his realm into districts,[2] he sends to them various administrators, and changes and moves them around at his pleasure. But the king of France is surrounded by a multitude of nobles of long standing who are recognized in that state by their subjects and loved by them. They have their hereditary privileges, which the king cannot take away except at his peril. Whoever considers these two states, then, will find it difficult to conquer the state of the Turk, but once it is conquered, will find it easy to hold. And so, on the contrary, you will find that in some respects it is easier to conquer the state of France, but very difficult to hold it.

The causes of the difficulties involved in conquering the kingdom of the Turk are that one cannot be invited in by the princes of that realm, nor hope to facilitate the enterprise by means of a rebellion of those the ruler has around him. This happens because of the reasons given above: because they are all slaves and dependent on their lord, it will be more difficult to corrupt them, and even if they were corrupted, one should not hope they will be very useful, since they would not be able to bring the people with them, for the reasons given. Therefore, whoever attacks the Turks must realize that he will find them united, and he should base his hopes more on his own strength than on others' lack of unity. But once they are beaten and routed in battle so that they can no longer regroup their armies, one has nothing else to worry about except the family of the prince, and once that is extinguished, there is no one left to be feared, since the others have no credit with the people, and just as the conqueror, before his victory, had nothing to hope for from them, so, afterwards, he has no need to fear them.

The contrary occurs with realms governed like that of France, because you can enter them with ease by winning over some of the barons in the kingdom, since there will always be malcontents and those who desire changes. For the reasons mentioned, these men can open the way to that state for you and facilitate your victory, but this, if you then wish to hold onto your power, leads to countless difficulties both with those who helped you and with those you suppressed. Nor is it sufficient for you to wipe out the family of the prince, because the lords who remain will make themselves the heads of new rebellions, and being unable either to content or to exterminate them, you will lose that state whenever the possibility presents itself.

Now, if you consider the nature of the government of Darius, you will find it similar to the kingdom of the Turk.[3] And therefore Alexander first had to strike him down and defeat him in battle; after this victory, with Darius dead, the state remained secure in Alexander's possession for the reasons discussed above. And his suc-

cessors, if they had been united, might have enjoyed it at their lei-
sure, for no tumults arose in the kingdom except those that they
themselves provoked. But it is impossible to hold onto states like
that of France with such ease. Hence, the frequent rebellions of
Spain, France, and Greece against the Romans occurred because of
the numerous principalities contained in those states; as long as the
memory of them lasted, the Romans were always unsure of their
hold, but when that memory had been extinguished, they became
the secure possessors of those states, thanks to the power and the
long duration of the empire. And later, when the Romans were
fighting among themselves, each one of them could draw a following
from those provinces, depending on the authority he had acquired
there, and since the families of their ancient lords were extinct, they
recognized no one except the Romans. Having considered all these
things, therefore, no one should marvel at the ease with which Alexander held the state of Asia and at the difficulties that others have
had in preserving what they acquired, like Pyrrhus and many others.[4] This was not caused by the greater or lesser ability [*virtù*] of
the conqueror, but by the dissimilarities among the conquered.

Notes to Chapter 4

1. When Alexander died in 323 B.C.E., his realm was divided among his
   generals who were already exercising governmental powers. They did wage
   savage wars among themselves; Machiavelli's "no other difficulty" is something of an understatement.
2. *Sangiachi*, which is Machiavelli's italianized form of the Turkish *sanjak*.
3. Machiavelli is referring to Darius III Codomanus, the last king of Persia,
   who reigned from 336 to 331 B.C.E.
4. Pyrrhus of Epirus (307–272 B.C.E.) invaded Italy on several occasions in
   order to aid the Greek colonies that had been established there. He defeated the Romans in battle but failed to acquire a permanent state in the
   peninsula.

Chapter 5

How Cities or Principalities Are to Be Administered That Used to Live Under Their Own Laws Before They Were Conquered

As I HAVE SAID, when those states that are acquired are used to living under their own laws and freedom, there are three ways of holding onto them: the first is to destroy them; the second, to go and live there in person; the third, to allow them to live under their own laws, exacting tribute from them and creating a government there within the state composed of a few people who will keep it friendly toward you. For this government, being created by the prince, knows that it cannot stand without his friendship and power, and has to do all it can to keep them. And a city used to living in freedom can be held more easily by means of its citizens than in any other way—if you want to keep it.

As examples, there are the Spartans and the Romans. The Spartans held Athens and Thebes by creating within them a government consisting of a few people; nevertheless, they lost them.[1] In order to hold Capua, Carthage, and Numantia, the Romans destroyed them, and they did not lose them.[2] They wanted to hold Greece in almost the same way as the Spartans held it, making it free and leaving it under its own laws, and they did not succeed, so that they were compelled to destroy many cities in that country in order to keep it. For, in truth, there is no sure method of holding them except by destroying them. And whoever becomes the master of a city accustomed to living in freedom and does not destroy it may expect to be destroyed by it, for during a rebellion it always takes refuge in the name of liberty and its ancient institutions, which are not forgotten either with the passage of time or because of benefits received. And no matter what one does or foresees, if the inhabitants are not separated or scattered, they will not forget that name and those institutions, and they will have recourse to them instantly at every opportunity, as Pisa did after one hundred years of being held in servitude by the Florentines.[3] But when cities or countries are used to living under a prince and his family is extinguished, they, being on the one hand used to obeying and, on the other, not having their old prince, cannot unite to choose a prince from among themselves, nor do they know how to live as free men. Thus, they are slower to take up arms, and a prince can win them over and assure himself of them with greater ease. But in republics there is greater life, greater hatred, and more desire for vengeance; the memory of their ancient liberty does not and cannot allow them to rest, so that the most secure way is either to destroy them or to go there to live.

Notes to Chapter 5

1. After the fall of Athens to Sparta in 405 B.C.E., the city was ruled by the Thirty Tyrants until 403, when it was liberated by Thrasybulus. Thebes had an oligarchy imposed on it by the Spartans between 389 and 382 B.C.E.
2. Capua, Carthage, and Numantia were completely destroyed and their populations scattered in 211, 146, and 133 B.C.E., respectively.
3. Pisa was purchased by Florence in 1405 and was mistreated throughout the fifteenth century. It liberated itself in 1494 when Charles VIII invaded Italy. Florence regained it in 1509.

Chapter 6

On New Principalities That Have Been Acquired by One's Own Arms and Prowess[1]

NO ONE SHOULD MARVEL if in speaking about principalities that are completely new with regard to their prince and their institutions, I will adduce the greatest examples. Since men almost always walk in the paths beaten by others and proceed in their actions by imitation, and since they cannot always keep on the others' paths or attain the level of skill [*virtù*] of those you imitate, a prudent man should always enter by the paths beaten by great men and imitate those who have been most excellent, so that, if his own skill [*virtù*] does not come up to theirs, at least it will give off something of the odor of theirs. And he will do what prudent archers do when the place they wish to hit appears very distant: knowing the strength [*virtù*] of their bow, they aim much higher than the target they want to hit, not in order to reach such a height with their arrow, but with the aid of such a high aim to be able to hit their target.

I say, then, that in completely new principalities where there is a new prince, one encounters more or less difficulty in holding onto them depending on whether the one who acquires them is more or less skillful [*virtuoso*]. And because the transition from private individual to prince presupposes either skill [*virtù*] or Fortune, it appears that either the one or the other of these two would, in part, mitigate many difficulties; nevertheless, he who has depended less on Fortune has maintained his position better. It also makes things easier if the prince, because he has no other state, is forced to come and live there in person. But to come to those who have become princes through their own skill [*virtù*] and not because of Fortune, I say that the most outstanding are Moses, Cyrus, Romulus, Theseus, and the like. And although one should not discuss Moses, since he was a mere executor of the things he was ordered to do by God, nevertheless he must be admired, if only for the grace that made

24

him worthy of talking with God. But let us consider Cyrus and the others who have acquired or founded realms: you will find them all admirable, and if their particular actions and decrees are considered, they will not appear different from those of Moses, who had so great a teacher. And in examining their actions and their lives, it will be seen that they received nothing from Fortune but an opportunity, which gave them matter into which they could introduce whatever form they thought fit, and that without that opportunity the strength [*virtù*] of their spirit would have been extinguished, and that without that strength [*virtù*] the opportunity would have come in vain.[2]

It was thus necessary that Moses should find the people of Israel enslaved in Egypt and oppressed by the Egyptians, so that they would be disposed to follow him in order to escape from servitude.[3] It was necessary that Romulus should not remain in Alba and should have been exposed at birth, so that he might become king of Rome and founder of that nation. It was necessary that Cyrus should find the Persians discontented with the rule of the Medes, and the Medes soft and effeminate because of a long peace. Theseus could not have displayed his ability [*virtù*] if he had not found the Athenians scattered. These opportunities, therefore, made these men prosper, and their own outstanding ability [*virtù*] enabled them to spot their opportunities, with the result that their nations were ennobled and became most prosperous.

Like these men, those who become princes through their prowess,[4] obtain their principality with difficulty, but hold onto it with ease, and the difficulties they have in acquiring the principality arise in part from the new rules and measures that they are forced to introduce in order to found their state and make themselves secure. It should be borne in mind that there is nothing more difficult to manage, or more doubtful of success, or more dangerous to handle than to take the lead in introducing a new order of things. For the innovator has enemies in all those who are doing well under the old order, and he has only lukewarm defenders in all those who would do well under the new order. This lukewarmness arises partly from fear of their adversaries who have the laws on their side, and partly from the incredulity of men who do not truly believe in new things until they have had a solid experience of them. Thus it happens that whenever his enemies have the opportunity to attack the innovator, they do so with the zeal of partisans, and the others only defend him tepidly, so that he, together with them, is put in danger.

It is necessary, however, in order to treat this matter thoroughly, to determine whether these innovators are standing on their own or depend on others; that is, whether they have to beg or are able to use force in order to conduct their affairs. In the first case they always end up badly and do not accomplish anything, but when they depend on their own resources and are able to use force, then they are rarely in danger. From this comes the fact that all armed prophets have been victorious and the unarmed ones have come to ruin. For, beside what has already been said, people are by nature fickle, and it is easy to persuade them of something, but difficult to keep them persuaded. And therefore, it is necessary to arrange things so that when they no longer believe, they can be made to believe by force. Moses, Cyrus, Theseus, and Romulus would not have been able to have kept their laws respected for so long if they had been unarmed, as was the case in our time with Fra Girolamo Savonarola, who came to ruin, together with his new institutions, as soon as the people began to disbelieve in him, and he had no means of holding steady those who had believed or of making disbelievers into believers.[5] Therefore, such men as these have great difficulty conducting their affairs, and all their dangers are met along the way, and they must overcome them by their skill [*virtù*]; but once they have overcome them and have begun to be held in veneration, having destroyed those who were envious of their abilities, they remain powerful, secure, honored, and prosperous.

To such lofty examples I want to add a lesser one, but one that will certainly be in some measure comparable to them, and I would like it to suffice for all similar cases. And this is the example of Hieron of Syracuse.[6] From being a private citizen this man became the prince of Syracuse, nor did he get anything from Fortune except the opportunity, for the Syracusans, being oppressed, elected him their captain, from which he earned the right to be made their prince. And he was a man of such ability [*virtù*], even as a private citizen, that someone who wrote about him said "that he lacked nothing to reign except a realm."[7] He abolished the old army and established a new one, abandoned old alliances and formed new ones, and as he thus had allies and soldiers of his own, he was able to build on such a foundation whatever edifice he wanted. He thus had great difficulty in acquiring his position, but little in maintaining it.

Notes to Chapter 6

1. Machiavelli uses the Latin word *virtus*; *virtù* is the Italian equivalent.

2. Machiavelli's distinction here between matter and form goes back to the Scholastics and ultimately to Aristotle. The distinction was commonly seen in gendered or sexual terms that identified matter as female and form as male. That sexual identification is clear in Machiavelli's Italian, for he speaks of "introducing" form "into" matter (*introdurvi dentro*), rather than, to use the more idiomatic English expression, of "imposing" form "on" matter.

3. For the story of Moses and the bondage of the Hebrews in Egypt, see the Bible, Exodus 2–6. The story of Romulus's founding of Rome, alluded to in the next sentence, was recounted by Livy (*The History of Rome*, 1.5–1.7), and that of Cyrus and the Medes, alluded to in the following sentence, was told by Herodotus (*Histories*, 1.123–1.130). The "long peace" referred to lasted from 600 to 560 B.C.E. The story of Theseus's unification of Athens is told by Plutarch in his *Life of Theseus*; Plutarch also compares Theseus with Romulus in his *Parallel Lives*. It is noteworthy that these four figures, all of whom founded long-lived states, are mythical or are made to seem so in the stories told of them.

4. *Per vie virtuose*—literally, "through virtuous ways or roads."

5. Girolamo Savonarola (1452–1498) was a religious reformer, a Dominican who preached in the church of San Marco in Florence, denouncing the worldliness of the city. When the Medici were exiled in 1494, he became the spiritual leader of the city, welcomed the French king, Charles VIII, and wanted him to make the city into a republic. Savonarola also attacked the pope, Alexander VI, and was excommunicated by him in 1497. The people of Florence eventually grew tired of his calls for austerity, and at the orders of papal representatives, he and two of his disciples were arrested, tortured, and finally burned in the spring of 1498.

6. Hieron II of Syracuse (ruled c.271–216 B.C.E.) is discussed by the Greek historian Polybius; see *The Histories*, 1.7–9. He was an able general who made himself king of Syracuse. After initially siding with the Carthaginians, he became a dependable ally of the Romans during both of the wars they fought with Carthage.

7. Machiavelli is citing (inaccurately) the Roman historian Marcus Junianus Justinus (*Epitome of the Philippic Histories of Pompeius Trogus*, 23.4).

Chapter 7

On New Principalities Acquired by the Arms of Others and by Fortune

THOSE WHO FROM BEING private citizens become princes solely through Fortune do so with little effort, but they maintain their position with a great deal of it; although they have no difficulty on the way as they go flying along, all their difficulties arise when they have landed. These are the people who are given a state either for money or as a favor conferred by the one who gives it, as happened to many men in Greece, in the cities of Ionia and the Hellespont, who were made princes by Darius in order to hold those places for his security and glory; such were also those who from being private citizens became emperors by bribing the soldiers.[1] These men depend absolutely on the will and fortune of the person who granted them their position, two things which are extremely mutable and unstable, and they do not know how to, and cannot, maintain their position. They do not know how because, unless they are men of great intelligence and ability [*virtù*], it is not reasonable that those who have always lived as private citizens should know how to command others. They cannot maintain their position because they have no forces that are loyal and devoted to them. Moreover, states that spring up quickly, like all the other things in nature which, after being born, grow rapidly, cannot develop roots and all their branchings, so that the first bad weather destroys them, unless, as has been said, those who have become princes have such great ability [*virtù*] that they are able straightway to prepare themselves to preserve what Fortune has thrown in their laps and afterward to lay those foundations that others made before becoming princes.

With regard to these two methods, just described, of becoming a prince by ability [*virtù*] or by Fortune, I want to adduce two examples here which have taken place within recent memory, and these are those of Francesco Sforza and Cesare Borgia. By the appropriate means and with great skill [*virtù*] Francesco, from being a private citizen, became duke of Milan, and what he acquired with a thousand difficulties, he held onto with little effort.[2] On the other hand, Cesare Borgia, called Duke Valentino by the common people, acquired his state through the fortune of his father and lost it in the same manner, and that despite the fact that he used every means and did everything that a prudent and capable [*virtuoso*] man should do to put his roots down in those states that the arms and fortune of others had granted him.[3] Because, as was said above, he who does not lay his foundations beforehand might with great effort [*virtù*] lay them afterward, although he would do so with inconvenience to the architect and danger to the building. If one considers, then, all the duke's proceedings, it will be seen that he had laid firm foundations for his future power, which I do not judge it superfluous to discuss, because I would not know of any better precepts for a new prince than the example of his actions; and if he did not profit from what he established, it was not his fault but resulted from the extraordinary and extreme malice of Fortune.

Alexander VI, in wishing to raise up his son, the duke, had many difficulties, both present and future. First, he saw no way of making him the master of any state that was not a possession of the Church, and if he attempted to take anything for him that belonged to the Church, he knew that the duke of Milan and the Venetians would not consent to it because Faenza and Rimini were already under the protection of the Venetians. He saw, beyond this, that the armies of Italy, and especially of those rulers whom he might have been able to use, were in the hands of people who had reason to fear the pope's power, and therefore he could not depend on them since they all belonged to the Orsini and Colonna families and their confederates.[4] It was, therefore, necessary to disturb the existing order and to unsettle those states in order to make himself the secure master of some of them. This was easy for him to do, for he found that the Venetians, driven by other motives, intended to have the French come back into Italy, something he not only did not oppose, but made easier by dissolving the first marriage of King Louis. Thus, the king came into Italy with the aid of the Venetians and the consent of Alexander, and no sooner was he in Milan than the pope obtained troops from him for the campaign in the Romagna, troops granted to him because of the reputation of the king.

Having then acquired the Romagna and defeated the Colonna,[5] the duke, wishing to hold onto that province and to advance further, was hindered by two things: first, his troops, who did not seem loyal to him; second, the will of France. That is, he feared that the troops of the Orsini, whom he had been using, would fail him and not only keep him from acquiring more territory, but take from him what he had already acquired, and he also feared that the king would do the same thing to him. He had a confirmation of this from the Orsini when, after the storming of Faenza, he assaulted Bologna and observed how coldly they acted in that assault; and as for the king, the duke perceived his intentions when, after he had taken the Duchy of Urbino, he attacked Tuscany, and the king made him desist from that enterprise.[6] As a result, the duke decided to depend no longer on the arms and fortune of others. And first of all, he weakened the Orsini and Colonna factions in Rome by winning over all their followers who were noblemen, making them his own no-blemen and giving them large stipends. And he honored them with military commands and offices, according to their rank, so that in a few months their affection for their factions was extinguished in their hearts and was entirely directed toward the duke. After this he waited for an opportunity to wipe out the Orsini, having already scattered those who belonged to the house of the Colonna, and when a good opportunity arrived, he made even better use of it. For when the Orsini realized, too late, that the greatness of the duke and of the Church meant their ruin, they arranged a meeting at Magione in the territory of Perugia.[7] From this resulted the rebellion of Urbino and tumults in the Romagna and countless dangers for the duke, all of which he overcame with the aid of the French. And when his reputation had been restored, placing no trust either in France or in other outside forces, in order not to have to run the risk of testing them, he turned to deceit. And he knew how to dis-semble his intentions so well that the Orsini were reconciled with him through the mediation of Signor Paolo, whom the duke did not fail to use every sort of courtesy to reassure, giving him money, clothing, and horses, so that their simple-mindedness led them to Sinigaglia and into his hands.[8] Having thus eliminated these leaders and turned their partisans into his friends, the duke had laid down very good foundations for his power, since he held all the Romagna as well as the Duchy of Urbino, and most important, it appeared to him that he had acquired the Romagna as his friend, having won over all those people from the moment they began to taste the benefits of his rule.

And because this part is worthy of note and of being imitated by others, I do not want to leave it out. When the duke had taken the Romagna, and finding it to have been governed by impotent rulers who would have sooner plundered their subjects than governed them, and had given them cause for disunity rather than unity, so that the entire province was full of robberies, fighting, and every other kind of insolence, he decided that, if he wanted to pacify it and make it obedient to its sovereign's power, it would be necessary to give them a good government. For this purpose he put Messer Remirro de Orco in charge, a cruel and decisive man, to whom he gave the fullest authority. In a short time, this man returned the country to peace and unity, enhancing greatly his own reputation as he did so. After that, the duke judged that such excessive authority was not necessary, because he feared it might become odious, and he set up a civil court in the middle of the province with a most excellent presiding judge, in which each city had its own advocate. And because he knew that the rigorous measures of the past had generated a certain amount of hatred toward him, in order to purge the minds of the people of it and to win them over for himself completely, he wanted to show that if any cruelty had taken place, it did not come from him, but from the harsh nature of his minister. And having found the opportunity to do this, one morning he had him put in the piazza at Cesena in two pieces, with a piece of wood and a bloody knife by his side. The ferocity of such a spectacle left those people both satisfied and stunned.[9]

But let us return to the place from which we digressed. I say that the duke now found himself very powerful and partially secure from present dangers, since he had armed himself in the way he wished and had in good measure destroyed those forces which, near by, might have harmed him. Still, he had to take the king of France into account if he wished to proceed with his conquests, because he knew that the king, who had belatedly become aware of his mistake, would not have permitted them. And for this reason he began to seek new alliances and to temporize with France during the expedition that the French were making toward the Kingdom of Naples against the Spaniards, who were besieging Gaeta. And his intention was to secure the support of the latter, which he would soon have succeeded in doing if Alexander had lived.

These were his methods with regard to present matters. As for the future, he had first to fear that a new successor in the Church would not be his friend and might seek to take from him that which Alexander had given him. Responding to this possibility, he thought of four measures to take: first, to eliminate the families of those lords whom he had despoiled in order to take the opportunity of using them away from the pope; second, to win over all the noblemen of Rome, as has been said, so that he might hold the pope in check through them; third, to make the College of Cardinals as much his own as he could; fourth, to acquire so much power before the pope died that he could, on his own, resist a first attack. Of these four things he had achieved three at the death of Alexander; the fourth he had almost achieved. For of the lords whom he had despoiled, he killed as many as he could get hold of, and very few escaped; he had won over the Roman noblemen; and in the College he controlled the greatest number. As to his new conquests, he had intended to become lord of Tuscany, and he was already in possession of Perugia and Piombino, and had placed Pisa under his protection.[10] And as soon as he no longer had to worry about France (for he did not have to do so because the French had been despoiled of the Kingdom of Naples by the Spaniards so that both of them were obliged to buy his friendship), he would have attacked Pisa. After this, partly to spite the Florentines and partly through fear, Lucca and Siena would have yielded at once, for which the Florentines would have had no remedy. If he had succeeded (and he was succeeding the very year that Alexander died), he would have acquired such power and such a reputation that he could have stood alone and would no longer have had to depend on the fortune and forces of others, but on his own power and ability [*virtù*]. But five years after the duke had first drawn his sword, Alexander died, leaving him with only the state of the Romagna consolidated, and with all the others up in the air, between two very powerful enemy armies, and deathly ill. Yet, there was in the duke such great ferocity and so much energy [*virtù*], and so well did he know how men were to be won over or destroyed,[11] and so sturdy were the foundations he had laid in so short a time, that if he had not had those two armies on top of him, or if he had been healthy, he would have held out against every difficulty. And that his foundations were good was evident, for the Romagna waited for him more than a month; in Rome, even though barely half alive, he remained secure; and although the Baglioni, the Vitelli, and the Orsini came to Rome, they roused up none of their followers against him; he was able, if not to make the one he wanted pope, at least to prevent one from being created whom he did not want. But if at the death of Alexander he had been healthy, everything would have been easy. And on the day that Julius II was elected, he himself told me that he had thought of what might happen when his father died and had found a remedy for everything, except that he never thought that at the time of his father's death he would also be about to die himself.[12]

Having reviewed all the actions of the duke, then, I would not know how to reproach him; on the contrary, I feel it is right to hold him up, as I have done, to be imitated by all those who through Fortune and by means of the arms of others have risen to power. For he, having great courage and lofty ambition, could not have conducted himself otherwise, and his designs were frustrated only by the brevity of Alexander's life and his own illness. Whoever, therefore, deems it necessary in his new principality to secure himself against enemies, to win friends, to conquer by force or by fraud, to make himself loved and feared by the people, followed and revered by the soldiers, to destroy those who can or must do you harm, to transform old institutions with new measures, to be severe and gracious, magnanimous and liberal, to eliminate an untrustworthy army, to create a new one, to maintain the friendship of kings and princes in such a way that they must either help you with good grace or offend you with caution—such a person cannot find better examples to imitate than the actions of this man. He can only be blamed for making Julius pope, in which he made a bad decision, for, as has been said, if he could not make a pope to his liking, he could have kept certain ones he did not want from becoming pope, and he should never have agreed that any of those cardinals whom he had offended, or who, having become pope, would have had to fear him, should have been raised to the papacy. For men injure others because of either fear or hate. Those whom he had injured were, among others, San Pietro ad Vincula, Colonna, San Giorgio, Ascanio; all the others, if they had become pope, would have had to fear him except for Rouen and the Spaniards, the latter because of family ties and obligations to him, the former because of his power, since he was closely tied to the king of France.[13] Therefore, the duke, before anything else, should have made a Spaniard pope, and if he could not, he should have agreed to its being Rouen and not San Pietro ad Vincula. And whoever believes that with great men new benefits make them forget old injuries is deceiving himself. The duke, then, erred in his decision, and it was the cause of his ultimate ruin.

Notes to Chapter 7

1. Darius I, king of Persia from 522 to 485 B.C.E., created many satrapies, especially in the Greek city-states of Asia Minor and the Hellespont. By "emperors," Machiavelli means the Roman emperors, such as Septimius Severus, who owed their thrones to the army or the Praetorian Guard; many of these emperors are discussed in chapter 19.

2. On Francesco Sforza, see chapter 1, note 1.

3. Cesare Borgia (c.1476–1507) was the illegitimate son of Rodrigo Borgia, later Pope Alexander VI. He negotiated the treaty in 1498 between his father and Louis XII of France that gave the latter a dispensation to marry the widow of Charles VIII and got his support for the papacy's plan to conquer Naples. In exchange, Borgia was also given the Duchy of Valentinois in France (hence, his name in Italy, "Valentino"), and he gained the king's support for his conquest of the Romagna, which he undertook in 1501, quickly subduing the towns of Fano, Pesaro, Rimini, Cesena, Forlì, Faenza, and Imola. The next year he conquered Camerino and Urbino for the pope, and later in that same year he treacherously and brutally put down a rebellion at Sinigaglia of various lords in the district who had been joined by members of the Orsini, a powerful Roman family. When Alexander died in 1503, however, Borgia's state crumbled, for he could not prevent the election of Giuliano della Rovere, who was an inveterate enemy of the Borgias, as Pope Julius II, and he suffered a series of misfortunes from then until his death in Spain in 1507. Machiavelli met him several times on various diplomatic missions and studied his behavior closely. He idealizes Borgia in *The Prince* but does not distort his actions.

4. The Orsini and the Colonna were long-time rival families in Rome. Machiavelli discusses the difficulties the pope had with them in chapter 9.

5. This occurred between November 1499 and April 1501.

6. Faenza was conquered on April 25, 1501; Bologna was threatened that month and the next but never taken; and Urbino fell in June 1502. Florence bought Borgia off by offering a stipend of 36,000 ducats a year and thus maintained its independence, although it was supposedly under the protection of France.

7. This meeting took place on October 9, 1502.

8. Signor Paolo is Paolo Orsini, the head of the family, who swore allegiance to Borgia on October 25, 1502, at Imola. On December 31, at Sinigaglia, the latter had Vitellozzo Vitelli and Oliverotto da Fermo strangled, and on January 18, 1503, at Castel del Pieve, the same fate befell Paolo Orsini and the Count of Gravina-Orsini.

9. Remirro de Orco—or Ramiro de Lorqua, to use his Spanish name—was Borgia's majordomo. Appointed governor of the Romagna in 1501, he was brought before a civil tribunal presided over by Antonio dal Monte that sat between October and November 1502. Remirro's decapitated body was found in the square of Cesena on December 26 of that year. Note that Machiavelli does not specify in this passage what the "two pieces" of Remirro's body were.

10. Perugia was conquered on January 6, 1503, and Piombino on September 3, 1501. Pisa placed itself under his control in February 1503; it had depended on the French to maintain its independence of Florence, and when the Spanish dislodged the French from Naples and the Pisans could no longer depend on them, they turned to Borgia instead.

11. Machiavelli's Italian for "won over or destroyed" is *guadagnare o perdere*. This second verb can also be translated as "lost," which seems to complement "won over" better than "destroyed." However, in Machiavelli's thought, the true alternative to the prince's winning of people's allegiance is not to lose them—that is, to leave them indifferent—but to destroy them so that they are no longer a potential danger to him.

12. Machiavelli was sent by Florence to Rome for the papal conclave that lasted from October to December 1503. It initially elected Alessandro Piccolomini as Pius III, who died on October 18, just ten days after being chosen, and then elected Borgia's enemy Giuliano della Rovere as Julius II.

13. The four cardinals whom Borgia had injured were, respectively, Giuliano della Rovere, who later became Julius II, Giovanni Colonna, Raffaello Riario, and Ascanio Sforza. Rouen was Georges d'Amboise, the adviser to Louis XII of France.

Chapter 8

On Those Who Became Princes through Crimes

BUT BECAUSE THERE ARE also two other ways of becoming a prince from being a private citizen, which cannot be attributed entirely either to Fortune or to ability [*virtù*], it does not seem to me that I should leave them out, although I will discuss one of them more fully when I consider republics.[1] These are: when one ascends to princely rule by some wicked and nefarious means; or when a private citizen becomes the prince of his native country by the favor of his fellow-citizens. And in speaking of the first method, I will give two examples, one ancient, the other modern, without otherwise entering into the merits of this method, because I judge them to be sufficient for anyone forced to imitate them.

Agathocles the Sicilian, not only from a private life, but from a low and abject position, became king of Syracuse.[2] The son of a potter, he led a wicked life through all the stages of his career; nevertheless, he coupled with his wickedness such vigor [*virtù*] of mind and body that, after joining the army, he rose through its ranks to become military governor of Syracuse. Once established in this position, and having decided to become prince and to hold through violence and without any obligation to others that which had been granted to him by common consent, he reached an understanding about his plan with Hamilcar the Carthaginian, who with his armies was waging war in Sicily. One morning he called together the people and the senate of Syracuse, as if he had things concerning the state to deliberate about, and at a prearranged signal, he had all the senators and the richest of the people killed by his soldiers. After their murders he seized the city and ruled over it as prince without any civil dissension. And although he was defeated twice by the Carthaginians and ultimately besieged, not only was he able to defend his city, but leaving part of his troops to defend against the siege, he attacked Africa with the others, and in a short time he liberated Syracuse from the siege and placed Carthage in dire straits, so that they were obliged to come to terms with him and to be content with the possession of Africa while leaving Sicily to him.

Whoever examines, therefore, the actions and ability [*virtù*] of this man will not see anything, or very little, that can be attributed to Fortune, in that, as was said above, it was not with the favor of any person, but by rising through the ranks of the army, which he had achieved with a thousand hardships and dangers, that he ascended to princely rule, and he afterward maintained it by many courageous and perilous efforts. Still, it cannot be called virtue [*virtù*] to kill one's fellow-citizens, to betray one's friends, to be without loyalty, without mercy, without religion; by such methods one can acquire power, but not glory. For if the ability [*virtù*] of Agathocles displayed when encountering and escaping from perils and his greatness of spirit in supporting and overcoming adversities are considered, there is no reason why he should be judged inferior to any of the most excellent captains. Nevertheless, his ferocious cruelty and inhumanity, together with his countless crimes, do not permit him to be celebrated as being among the most excellent men. One cannot, therefore, attribute to Fortune or ability [*virtù*] that which he achieved without one or the other.

In our own times during the reign of Alexander VI, Oliverotto da Fermo, who many years before had been left fatherless as a child, was raised by one of his maternal uncles, named Giovanni Fogliani, and in the early days of his youth he was sent to serve as a soldier under Paolo Vitelli, so that once he had mastered that discipline, he might attain an excellent position in the army.[3] Then, after the death of Paolo, he fought under his brother Vitellozzo, and in a very short time, because of his intelligence and his vigor of body and mind, he became the leader of his army. But, as it seemed to him servile to be under others, he decided to seize Fermo both with the help of some of its citizens, who preferred servitude to the liberty of their native city, and with the favor of Vitelli. And he wrote to Giovanni Fogliani how, having been away from home for many years, he wanted to come to see him and his city, and to survey portions of his inheritance; and because he had not exerted himself for anything other than to acquire honor, he wanted to come in honorable fashion, accompanied by one hundred of his friends and followers on horseback, so that his fellow citizens might see that he had not spent his time in vain; and he begged his uncle to be so kind to order an honorable reception for him by the citizens of Fermo, which would confer honor not only on him, Oliverotto, but also on himself, since Oliverotto had been his pupil. Giovanni therefore did not fail in any courtesy due to his nephew, and having had him honorably received by the people of Fermo, he lodged him in his own houses. There, after several days had passed, during which he was waiting to put into place secretly that which was necessary for his future wickedness, Oliverotto arranged for a most solemn banquet to which he invited Giovanni Fogliani and all the principal men of Fermo. And when the food had been consumed and all the other entertainments usual at such feasts were done, Oliverotto artfully introduced certain serious matters for discussion, speaking of the greatness of Pope Alexander, and of his son Cesare, and of their undertakings. After Giovanni and the others had replied to those comments, Oliverotto suddenly arose, saying that these were matters to be spoken of in a more secluded place, and he withdrew into a room into which Giovanni and all the other citizens followed him. No sooner were they seated than out from hiding places in the room came soldiers who killed Giovanni and all the others. After this murder, Oliverotto mounted his horse, took possession of the town, and besieged the chief magistrates in the palace, so that out of fear they were forced to obey him and form a government, of which he made himself prince. And when all those were dead who, if they had been discontented, could have injured him, he strengthened himself with new laws, civil and military, so that within the space of the year that he held the principality, not only was he secure in the city of Fermo, but he had become feared by all his neighbors. And his expulsion would have been difficult, like that of Agathocles, if he had not allowed himself to be tricked by Cesare Borgia, when, as was said above, the latter captured the Orsini and the Vitelli at Sinigaglia, where Oliverotto, too, was captured one year after the parricide he had committed, and where he, together with Vitellozzo, who had been his teacher in cunning [*virtù*] and wickedness, was strangled.

Some may wonder how it happened that Agathocles and others

like him, after countless treacheries and cruelties, could live secure
for so long in their native country, and defend themselves from
external enemies, while never being conspired against by their own
citizens, although many others could not, by means of cruelty, hold
onto their states even in times of peace, not to mention the uncertain times of war. I believe this depends on whether the cruelties
are used well or badly. Those can be called well used (if it is per-
missible to say "well" about evil) which are done at one stroke, out
of the need to make oneself secure, and which afterwards are not
persisted in, but are converted into the greatest benefits possible for
one's subjects. Those are badly used which, although they are few
at first, grow over time rather than being extinguished. Those who
follow the first method can find some remedy for their condition
with God and men, as Agathocles did; it is impossible for those
others to survive. Thus, it is to be noted that in taking a state, its
conqueror must consider all those cruelties he has to do and do
them all at one stroke so as not to have to renew them every day,
and to be able, by not repeating them, to reassure men and win
them over by benefiting them. Whoever acts otherwise, either
through timidity or bad counsel, is always obliged to hold a knife
in his hand, nor can he ever make his subjects the foundation of
his rule, since they, because of their fresh and continual injuries, are
unable to feel secure with him. Therefore, injuries should be done
all together, so that the less they are tasted, the less they will offend,
and benefits should be granted little by little, so that they may be
better savored. And above all, a prince must live with his subjects
in such a way that no accident, either bad or good, could make him
vary his behavior, for, when emergencies arise because of adverse
conditions, you cannot use evil in time, and the good that you do
will not help you, since it is judged to be forced, and you will get
no thanks whatsoever for it.

Notes to Chapter 8

1. Machiavelli alludes here to his own *Discourses*.
2. Agathocles of Syracuse (361–289 B.C.E.) came to power in 316, thanks to
   a military coup, and then fought a series of wars against the Carthaginians
   for control of Sicily. He was defeated in battle twice by them, first when

he invaded their territory in Sicily at Himera in 311. After this, the Carthaginians besieged Syracuse for a period, but Agathocles broke through the siege with part of his army in 310 and went to attack them in Africa, where he was ultimately defeated in 307. Agathocles returned to Syracuse and consolidated his power base there, and he finally turned his attention to southern Italy, which he sought to bring under his control, although his efforts were cut short when he was assassinated in 289. Machiavelli misrepresents Agathocles's humble origins: his father was the wealthy owner of a pottery factory. The Hamilcar with whom he formed an alliance in order to seize power in Syracuse was a Carthaginian general who was tried by the Carthaginians for having aided Agathocles, and who died during his trial in 313 B.C.E. He is not to be confused with Hamilcar, usually referred to as Hamilcar Barca, who was also a Carthaginian general and was the father of Hannibal.

3. Oliverotto Effreducci da Fermo killed his uncle, his uncle's son, and several others on December 26, 1501. He was himself killed by Cesare Borgia the following year on December 31. Paolo Vitelli was the condottiere in charge of the Florentine army; he was beheaded in 1499 on suspicion of colluding with the Pisans in a campaign against them.

Chapter 9

On the Civil Principality

BUT, COMING TO THE other alternative, when a private citizen becomes prince of his native city, not through wickedness or some other intolerable violence, but by the favor of his fellow citizens (this may be called a civil principality, since its acquisition does not necessarily depend either entirely on ability [*virtù*] or entirely on Fortune, but rather on a cleverness assisted by Fortune), I say that one ascends to that position either through the favor of the people or through the favor of the nobility. For in every city these two different humors are found, and this arises from the fact that the people desire not to be commanded or oppressed by the great, while the great desire to command and oppress the people.[1] And from these two opposed appetites there arises in cities one of three effects: either princely rule, or liberty, or license.

Princely rule is created either by the people or by the nobility, depending on which one of these parties has the opportunity to create it. For, when the nobility see that they cannot resist the people, they start directing their support toward one of their own and make him prince, so that, under his protective shade, they can satisfy their appetite. The people also, seeing that they cannot resist the nobility, start giving their support to one of their own and make him prince in order to be defended by his authority. He who attains princely rule with the help of the great will maintain his position with greater difficulty than he who becomes prince with the help of the people, because he finds himself to be prince amidst many who think themselves his equals, and for this reason, he is unable to command and manage them to his liking. But he who attains princely rule through the favor of the people finds himself there alone and has no one, or very few, around him who are not ready to obey him. Besides this, one cannot satisfy the great with honor and without injuring others, but one can surely do so with the people, because the aim of the people is more honorable than that of the nobility, since the latter desire to oppress others, while the former desire not to be oppressed. Moreover, a prince can never make himself secure against a hostile people because there are too many of them; against the great he can secure himself, because they are few. The worst that a prince can expect from a hostile people is to be abandoned by them, but from hostile noblemen he has to fear not only being abandoned, but also their active opposition, because, having more foresight and more cunning, the people always have time to save themselves and to seek favors from those whom they expect to win. The prince is, moreover, obliged to live always with the same people, but he can easily do without the same noblemen, being able to make and to unmake them every day, and to take away and restore their reputations as he pleases.

And in order to clarify this point better, I say that the nobility should be considered principally in two different ways. Either they govern themselves in their proceedings in such a manner that they are entirely dependent on your fortunes, or they do not. Those who are bound to you and are not greedy must be honored and loved; those who are not bound have to be examined in two ways. If they do this through pusillanimity and a natural lack of courage, then you should especially make use of those who are good counselors, because in prosperity you will gain honor from them and in adversity you do not have to fear them. But when they do not commit themselves to you deliberately and for reasons of ambition, it is a sign that they think more of themselves than of you, and from those men the prince must guard himself and fear them as if they were open enemies, because in adversity they will always help to ruin him.

Therefore, one who becomes prince by means of the favor of the people must maintain their friendship, which will be easy for him, since they ask nothing of him except not to be oppressed. But one who, against the will of the people, becomes prince through the favor of the great should before anything else seek to win over the people, which will be easy for him if he takes them under his protection. And because men, when they receive good from those from whom they expected evil, feel more obligated to their benefactor, the people will quickly become better disposed toward him than if he had achieved princely rule through their favor. And the prince can win them for himself in many ways for which, because they vary according to circumstances, no sure rule can be given, and which will, therefore, be omitted. I will only conclude that it is necessary for a prince to have the friendship of the people; otherwise he has no remedy in times of adversity.

Nabis, prince of the Spartans, sustained a siege by the whole of Greece and by a most victorious Roman army, and defended his city and his country against them; and when danger was near, he needed only to secure himself against a few of his subjects, but if the people had been hostile to him, this would not have been enough.[2] And let no one dispute this opinion of mine with that trite proverb, that "he who builds on the people builds on mud," because that is true when a private citizen lays his foundation on them and lets himself believe that the people would liberate him if he were oppressed by his enemies or by the magistrates. In this case he might often find himself deceived, as happened in Rome to the Gracchi and in Florence to Messer Giorgio Scali.[3] But when it is a prince who builds his foundations on them, a prince who can command and is a man of courage, who is not dismayed in adversity and does not neglect other preparations, and who with his own spirit and orders keeps up the spirits of the entire people, he will never find himself deceived by them, and he will see that he has laid good foundations for himself.

Usually principalities of this sort are endangered when they are about to go from a civil government to an absolute one, because their princes either command by themselves or by means of magistrates. In the latter case their position is weaker and more dangerous, because they depend completely on the will of those citizens who are appointed magistrates, and who can, especially in times of adversity, take their state from them with great ease, either by opposing them or by not obeying them. The prince has no time to seize absolute authority in times of danger, because the citizens and subjects who are accustomed to taking their orders from the magistrates are not about to obey him in these difficulties, and in doubtful times he will always find a scarcity of those he can trust.[4] For such a prince cannot lay his foundations on what he sees in quiet times, when the citizens have need of the state, because then everyone comes running, everyone makes promises, and each one is willing to die for him when death is far away; but in times of adversity, when the state has need of its citizens, then few of them are found. And this experience is all the more dangerous in that it can only be had once. And therefore, a wise prince must think of a way by which his subjects will always and in all circumstances have need of his state and of him, and then they will always be loyal to him.

Notes to Chapter 9

1. Machiavelli's identification of the people and the nobility as "humors" here implies the notion of the state as a "body politic," a notion that underlies his thinking generally and that he also evokes with his frequent references to "remedies" princes need to apply to sick states. He refers to "humors" in this passage specifically because in Renaissance medicine the body was seen as being composed of four humors (blood, yellow bile or choler, white bile or phlegm, and black bile or melancholy), which should ideally exist in perfect balance but often did not, thereby producing disease. If the humors were thus seen as affecting the physical condition of human beings, they were also seen as simultaneously affecting their mental condition as well, something that is still apparent in the adjectives derived from their names that survive today and that describe attitudes or temperaments: sanguine, choleric, phlegmatic, and melancholic.

2. Nabis was the tyrant of Sparta who ruled from 205 to 192 B.C.E. When Machiavelli speaks of the "few" who were hostile to Nabis, he is probably thinking of the fact that when Nabis was besieged by the Roman general Flaminius in 195, Nabis had eighty Spartan citizens put to death (see Livy, *History of Rome*, 34.27).

3. The Gracchi brothers, Tiberius (162–133 B.C.E.) and Gaius Sempronius (154–121 B.C.E.), were popular reformers who sought to change the Roman constitution to increase the power of the people against that of the senate. The first was elected tribune in 133 and was slain by a senatorial gang in that year, while the second became tribune in 123 and had his slave kill him to avoid capture by his enemies two years later. In 1378 Giorgio Scali was one of the leaders in Florence of what was called the Revolt of the Ciompi ("wool-carders"), one of the guilds that employed the lowest of the people. He dominated the democratic government that

was formed, but because he governed badly, he was tried and beheaded in 1382.

4. For "difficulties" in this sentence, Machiavelli writes *frangenti*, which means "shoals or reefs"; he is possibly thinking of the metaphorical ship of state, in danger of sinking.

Chapter 10

How the Strength of All Principalities Should Be Measured

IN EXAMINING THE CHARACTER of these principalities it is necessary to consider another point, namely, whether a prince has so much power that he can, in case of need, stand on his own, or whether he always needs the defense of others. And to make this part clearer, I say that I judge those princes capable of standing on their own who have an abundance of men or of money, so that they can put together a sufficient army and fight a battle in the field against anyone who comes to attack them; and thus I judge those princes as always being in need of others who cannot take the field against their enemies, but are obliged to seek refuge within their walls and defend them.[1] The first case has already been discussed, and in the future we will say whatever is needed about it.[2] In the second case nothing else can be said except to encourage such princes to fortify and provision their own town and not to take any account of the countryside. And if someone has fortified his town well and, with regard to the governing of his subjects, has conducted himself as has been described above and will be discussed below,[3] he will always be attacked with great caution, for men are always the enemies of undertakings whose difficulty is visible, nor can it ever appear easy to attack one whose town is strong and who is not hated by the people.

The cities of Germany are completely free, have little surrounding countryside, and obey the emperor when they want to, and they do not fear him or any other neighboring power, because they are fortified in such a manner that everyone thinks their conquest must be tedious and difficult.[4] For they all have the necessary moats and walls, have sufficient artillery, always keep in public warehouses enough food and drink and fuel for a year, and beyond this, to keep the lower classes fed, and without loss to the public treasury, they always have in reserve enough to give them work for a year in those trades that are the sinews and lifeblood of the city and of the industries by means of which the lower classes feed themselves. They also hold military exercises in high repute, and beyond this, they have many ordinances to maintain them.

Therefore, a prince, who has a strong city and does not make himself hated, cannot be attacked, and if there were someone who attacked him, he would depart with shame, for in this world things are so changeable that it is almost impossible for anyone to do nothing with his armies for a year but engage in a siege. And should someone reply that if the people have their possessions outside and should see them burning, they will not be patient, and the long siege and their self-interest will make them forget the prince, I respond that a powerful and courageous prince will always overcome all those difficulties, now by giving hope to his subjects that the evil will not last long, now by making them fear the enemy's cruelty, now by skillfully protecting himself against those subjects who appear too ardently opposed to him. Moreover, it stands to reason that the enemy will burn and ruin the country after they arrive, at a time when men's spirits are hot and they are still willing to defend themselves; and therefore, the prince has still less to worry about, for after a few days, when their spirits have cooled down, the damage has already been done, the evils have been suffered, and there is no longer any remedy for them. And then the people will rally around their prince all the more, since he appears to have an obligation to them, their houses having been burned and their possessions destroyed in his defense. And the nature of men is such that they feel obligated as much by the benefits they confer as by those they receive. Thus, if all this is taken into consideration, it will not be difficult for a prudent prince to keep the spirits of his citizens steady, both at first and later on during a siege, so long as he does not lack provisions or the means to defend himself.

Notes to Chapter 10

1. For "battle in the field" Machiavelli has *giornata*, an Italianized version of the French *journée*, which literally meant "day" but had acquired the specialized meaning of "battle in the field (during the course of the day)." In

Discourses 2.17, Machiavelli explains that the normal Italian expression was *fatti d'arme* ("feats of arms").

2. See chapters 6, 12, and 13.
3. See chapters 9 and 19.
4. When Machiavelli had been sent in 1507 by Florence to the court of Maximilian I (1459–1519), the Holy Roman Emperor, he traveled through both Austria and the German-speaking areas of Switzerland, and in 1508 he wrote a short treatise that he called the *Rapporto delle cose della Magna* (*Report on German Affairs*). Since Germany did not exist as a nation in the Renaissance, what he calls Germany is simply the German-speaking area he had visited.

Chapter 11

On Ecclesiastical Principalities

AT PRESENT THE ONLY thing remaining for us to do is to speak of ecclesiastical principalities, concerning which all the difficulties occur before one takes possession of them, for they are acquired either through ability [*virtù*] or through Fortune, and they are maintained without either, since they are sustained by the ancient institutions of religion, which are so powerful and of such a quality that they keep their princes in power no matter what they do or how they live. These princes alone have states and do not defend them, subjects and do not govern them; and their states, though not defended, are not taken from them, and their subjects, though not governed, are not concerned about it, and neither think of, nor are capable of, revolting from them. Only these principalities, therefore, are secure and prosperous. But as they are upheld by a higher cause, which the human mind cannot reach, I shall leave off speaking of them, for it would be the action of a presumptuous and foolhardy man to discuss them, since they are raised up and preserved by God. Nevertheless, if someone inquired of me how it has come about that the Church has reached such greatness in the temporal sphere, considering that prior to Alexander the Italian powers, and not merely those who are called powers, but every baron or lord, however insignificant, used to hold it in little esteem with regard to the temporal sphere, and now a king of France trembles before it, and it has been able to drive him out of Italy and to bring the Venetians to ruin—although this is well known, it does not seem superfluous to me to call a good portion of it to mind.[1]

Before Charles, the king of France, came into Italy, this country was under the rule of the pope, the Venetians, the king of Naples, the duke of Milan, and the Florentines. These powers necessarily had two principal concerns: one, that no foreigner should enter Italy

49

by force of arms; the other, that none of those powers should occupy
more territory. Those they had to worry about most were the pope
and the Venetians. To hold back the Venetians required the union
of all the others, as was the case in the defense of Ferrara, and to
keep the pope down, they made use of the Roman barons, who,
being divided into two factions, the Orsini and the Colonna, always
had some reason for dissension between them, and who, standing
with their arms in their hands right under the pope's eyes, kept the
papacy weak and unstable.[2] And although there arose now and then
a resolute pope, like Sixtus, nevertheless, neither Fortune nor wisdom was ever able to liberate him from these inconveniences. And
the shortness of their lives was the reason for this, because in ten
years, which on average is the life-span of a pope, he might with
difficulty put down one of the factions; and if, for example, one
pope had almost eliminated the Colonna, another one would rise
up who was hostile to the Orsini, which would cause the resurgence
of the Colonna, although he did not have time to eliminate the
Orsini. Consequently, the temporal powers of the pope got little
respect in Italy.

Then came Alexander VI, who, of all the pontiffs who have ever
existed, showed how much a pope with money and troops could
accomplish, for by making Duke Valentino his instrument and seizing the opportunity provided by the French invasion, he did all
those things that I discussed earlier when speaking of the actions of
the duke.[3] And although his intention was to make the duke, not
the Church, great, nevertheless, what he did resulted in the greatness
of the Church, which, after he died and the duke was destroyed,
became the heir of his labors. Then came Pope Julius, and he found
the Church powerful, for it possessed all the Romagna, had eliminated the Roman barons, and had annihilated the factions thanks
to the blows struck by Alexander; and he also found the way open
for accumulating wealth by a method never used before the time of
Alexander.[4] These things Julius not only continued, but intensified,
and he resolved to win Bologna, destroy the Venetians, and chase
the French from Italy. And he succeeded in all these undertakings,
and with all the more praise for him, since he did everything to
increase the power of the Church and not that of any private individual. He also kept the Orsini and Colonna factions in the strait-

ened conditions in which he found them, and although there were some leaders among them who wanted to make changes, nonetheless, there were two things that kept them in line: first, the great power of the Church, which dismayed them; second, their not having cardinals of their own, who are the source of the conflicts between them. For these factions are never at peace when they have cardinals, for the latter nourish factions inside and outside Rome, and those barons are forced to defend them, so that from the ambition of prelates are born the discords and tumults among the barons. Thus, His Holiness, Pope Leo, has found the papacy most powerful. One hopes that if those former popes made it great by force of arms, this one, through his goodness and countless other virtues [*virtù*], will make it very great and worthy of veneration.[5]

Notes to Chapter 11

1. Alexander is Pope Alexander VI (Rodrigo Borgia). The Venetians were defeated by Pope Julius II at the battle of Agnadello on May 14, 1509, and he then drove the French out of Italy in 1513 and was about to have the French king condemned when he died.

2. In 1484 Ferrara was defended from the Venetians by the forces of the pope, the king of Naples, the duke of Milan, and the Florentines in the so-called "War of Salt." The pope in question here is the Sixtus referred to in the next sentence, that is, Sixtus IV, who was pope from 1471 to 1484 and who was a member of the della Rovere family, as was his nephew, Julius II, pope from 1503 to 1513.

3. See chapter 7.

4. In a papal bull of 1500, Alexander taxed all of Christendom, ostensibly to support a crusade against the Turks; he also made cardinals pay for their offices and claimed the right to confiscate the wealth of those cardinals who died. Machiavelli may also be thinking of the general sale of indulgences and ecclesiastical offices practiced by both popes.

5. Pope Leo is Leo X, a member of the Medici family, who was pope from 1513 to 1521. Machiavelli's praise here is complicated, since Leo was a member of the family that had ended the Florentine Republic, ruled the city for most of the rest of Machiavelli's life, and kept him in exile until 1520.

Chapter 12

How Many Kinds of Troops There Are
and on Mercenaries

HAVING DISCUSSED IN DETAIL all the characteristics of those principalities which I proposed to speak of at the beginning, and having
considered some of the causes of their successes and failures, and
having also shown the methods by which many have tried to acquire
and hold onto them, it now remains for me to discuss generally the
methods of attack and defense that can be used by each of the states
I mentioned earlier. We have said above how necessary it is for a
prince to lay good foundations; otherwise, he is certain to come to
ruin. The principal foundations of all states, whether new, old, or
mixed, are good laws and good arms, and because there cannot be
good laws where there are not good arms, and where there are good
arms, there are bound to be good laws, I shall set aside the treatment
of the laws and shall speak of arms.

I say, then, that the arms with which a prince defends his state
are either his own, or they are those of mercenaries, or auxiliaries,
or mixed troops. The mercenaries and auxiliaries are useless and
dangerous, and if anyone has a state founded on the arms of mercenaries, he will never be stable or secure, because they are disunited, ambitious, without discipline, disloyal; bold among friends,
among enemies cowardly; without fear of God, without faith in
men; and your ruin is deferred only as long as the assault is deferred;
and in peace you are plundered by them, in war by the enemy. The
reason for this is that they have no love or any motive that keeps
them in the field other than a little bit of salary, which is not enough
to make them willing to die for you. They are quite willing to be
your soldiers as long as you are not waging war, but when war
comes, then it is: retreat or run away.[1] I should not have to expend
much effort to demonstrate this, since the present ruin of Italy is
caused by nothing other than its having relied for many years on

mercenary armies. These once enabled some men to get ahead, and they did appear courageous among themselves, but when the foreigner arrived, they showed themselves for what they were. In consequence, Charles, king of France, was able to take Italy with a piece of chalk,[2] and he who said that the cause of this was our sins spoke the truth, although they were not the sins he was thinking of, but the ones I have described, and because they were the sins of princes, they too have suffered the punishment for them.

I want to demonstrate more fully the sorry nature of these arms. Mercenary captains are either excellent men, or not: if they are, you cannot trust yourself to them, for they will always aspire to their own greatness, either by oppressing you, who are their employer, or by oppressing others beyond your intentions; but if the captain is not capable [*virtuoso*], ordinarily he will ruin you. And if someone should respond that whoever bears arms will do this, whether mercenary or not, I would reply that armies must be employed either by a prince or by a republic: the prince must go in person and assume the office of captain; the republic has to send its citizens, and when it sends one of them who does not turn out to be capable, it must replace him, and if he is capable, it must keep him by means of the laws from going beyond his proper authority. And one sees from experience that individual princes and armed republics make very great advances, and that mercenary armies do nothing but damage. And it is more difficult to get a republic, armed with its own troops, to submit to the rule of one of its own citizens than one armed with foreign troops.

Rome and Sparta for many centuries stood armed and free. The Swiss are well armed and completely free. As for mercenary armies in antiquity, there is the example of the Carthaginians, who were almost overcome by their mercenary soldiers after the end of the first war with the Romans even though the Carthaginians had their own citizens as leaders.[3] Philip of Macedonia was made captain of the troops of the Thebans after the death of Epaminondas, and after his victory, he took away their liberty from them.[4] The Milanese, after the death of Duke Filippo, hired Francesco Sforza against the Venetians, who, having overcome the enemy at Caravaggio, allied himself with them to oppress the Milanese, his employers.[5] Sforza's father, being a soldier employed by Queen Giovanna of Naples, all of a sudden left her unarmed, so that she was compelled, in order not to lose her kingdom, to throw herself into the lap of the king of Aragon.[6] And if the Venetians and the Florentines have in the past increased their states by means of these forces, and their captains have not made themselves princes of those cities, but have defended them, I reply that the Florentines in this case have been favored by luck, for of the capable [*virtuosi*] captains whom they might have feared, some did not win, some met with opposition, and others directed their ambition elsewhere. The one who did not win was John Hawkwood, whose loyalty could not be known since he did not win, but everyone will confess that, had he won, the Florentines would have been at his mercy.[7] Sforza always had the Bracceschi against him so that they kept an eye on one another. Francesco directed his ambition toward Lombardy; Braccio against the Church and the Kingdom of Naples.[8] But let us come to what occurred a short time ago. The Florentines made Paolo Vitelli their captain, a very prudent man who had risen from private life to achieve the greatest reputation. If he had taken Pisa, there would be no one who would deny that the Florentines would have had to stick with him, because, had he been engaged as a soldier by their enemies, they would have had no remedy for that, and if they had retained him, they would have had to obey him.[9]

As for the Venetians, if one considers the progress they made, it will be seen that they operated safely and gloriously as long as they made war with their own forces (that was before they directed their military operations to the land), and they fought most ably [*virtuosissimamente*] using their nobles and their armed commoners, but when they began to fight on land, they left their prowess [*virtù*] behind and followed the usual customs of Italy. At the beginning of their expansion onto the land, they did not have much to fear from their captains, because they did not have much territory there and enjoyed a substantial reputation, but as they expanded, which they did under Carmagnola, they got a taste of this error. For, seeing that he was most capable [*virtuosissimo*], after they had defeated the duke of Milan under his leadership, and knowing, on the other hand, how he had grown cold in battle, they judged that they could no longer win with him, because he did not want to do so, nor could they dismiss him for fear of losing again what they had acquired, so that they were obliged, in order to make sure of him, to have him killed.[10] They then had as captains Bartolomeo da Bergamo, Roberto da San Severino, the count of Pitigliano, and the like, from whom they had to fear their loss, not their gain, as happened subsequently at Vailà, where in one day they lost what in eight hundred years, with enormous effort, they had acquired.[11] From these armies come only slow, tardy, and weak conquests, but sudden and miraculous losses. And because with these examples I have arrived in Italy, which has now for many years been ruled by mercenary armies, I want to discuss them more in depth, so that when we have seen their origin and development, they can be more easily corrected.

You must, then, understand that in recent times, when the empire began to be driven out of Italy and the pope acquired more prestige there in temporal affairs, Italy was divided into many states, because many of the great cities took up arms against their nobles who had first been favored by the emperor and held them in subjection, while the Church now favored the citizens in order to acquire prestige in temporal affairs; and in many other cities citizens became princes.[12] Thus, since Italy had come almost entirely into the hands of the Church and a few republics, and since those priests and those other citizens were not accustomed to bearing arms, they began to hire foreigners as soldiers. The first to bring prestige to this kind of soldiering was Alberigo da Conio from the Romagna.[13] From the training of this man came, among others, Braccio and Sforza, who were in their time the arbiters of Italy. After these came all the others who up to our own times have led these armies. And the result of their prowess [*virtù*] has been that Italy has been overrun by Charles, preyed on by Louis, raped by Ferdinand, and insulted by the Swiss. The method they have used has been, first, to take away the prestige of the infantry in order to increase their own. They have done this because they had no states of their own and lived by exercising their profession, so that a few foot soldiers would not have increased their reputation and a great many could not be provided for, and therefore they restricted themselves to cavalry, since with a manageable number they could provide for themselves and gain honor. And things have been reduced to such a state that in an army of twenty thousand soldiers, one cannot find two thousand infantry. Beyond this, they had made every effort to spare themselves and the soldiers any hardship and fear by not killing one another in skirmishes, but taking one another prisoner without asking ransom. They would not attack towns at night, nor would those in the towns attack the tents of the besiegers; they made neither stockades nor ditches around the camp; they did not campaign in winter. And all these things were permitted by their military discipline, and were invented by them, as has been said, to escape hardship and dangers, with the result that they have led Italy into slavery and degradation.[14]

Notes to Chapter 12

1. Machiavelli refers to mercenaries here as *soldati* ("soldiers"), using a word that contains a double meaning which runs through this chapter and expresses perfectly Machiavelli's criticism of this sort of army. A *soldato* was, of course, what in modern English (or Italian) we call a soldier, but the word derives from the verb *soldare*, which means to pay someone a salary, a *soldo*, a meaning that was very much alive in Machiavelli's time. It is the basis of his criticism of mercenaries: they serve only for money, whereas a citizen army would fight for love of country.

2. According to the French historian Philippe de Commines, Pope Alexander remarked about the ease with which Charles VIII conquered Italy, saying that he needed just chalk and wooden spurs: chalk to mark the houses where his soldiers would be billeted and spurs to prick on the mules carrying supplies. Savonarola was the one who claimed that the French invasion was due to the sins of the Italians.

3. In 241 B.C.E., after the end of the First Punic War (264–241 B.C.E.), Carthaginian mercenaries turned on their employers in what is called the Servile War.

4. The Thebans asked Philip, Alexander's father, for help against the Phocians, and less than a decade later, in 338 B.C.E., Philip turned on the Thebans and defeated them at the battle of Chaeronea.

5. Filippo Visconti was the last of his line to rule Milan. When he died in 1447, Milan became a republic, but it immediately engaged Francesco Sforza's services as a condottiere, and by 1450 he had made himself the master of the city.

6. The Sforza named here is Giacomuzzo Attendolo Sforza (1369–1424). Giovanna II of Naples had no heir and wanted the French royal family to inherit her kingdom. However, upon her death in 1435, Alfonso of Aragon expelled the French and established the Aragonese house in Naples.

7. Sir John Hawkwood (1320–1394), an English mercenary known as Giovanni Acuto in Italy, served Florence from 1370 to his death. He headed a group of English mercenaries known as the White Company.

8. The Bracceschi were followers of Niccolò Fortebraccio, also known as Braccio da Montone, who was a contemporary of the elder Sforza. In his *Florentine History* (5.2), Machiavelli sees the two as the leading mercenaries of the early fifteenth century; they stood for two opposed schools of military discipline.

9. Paolo Vitelli commanded the Florentine troops against Pisa, but when he did not succeed in capturing the city, he was accused of treason, and was tried and executed in 1499.

10. Francesco Bussone, count of Carmagnola (c.1380–1432), was the victor at the battle of Maclodio (1427), which gave the Venetians Bergamo and Brescia, but because of his dilatory manner in waging war against Milan, the Venetians suspected him of treachery and had him executed in the spring of 1432.

11. Bartolomeo da Bergamo, better known as Bartolomeo Colleoni (1400–1475), was a disciple of Sforza and eventually became the leader of the forces of Venice; he is commemorated by the famous equestrian statue of him by Andrea Verrocchio that stands in front of the church of San Giovanni e Paolo in Venice. Robert da San Severino served Venice in the war against Ferrara (1482–1484). Niccolò Orsini (1442–1510), the count of Pitigliano, was one of the leaders of the Venetian army in the battle of Vailà, also know as Agnadello, which was fought on May 14, 1509, against the forces of Julius and resulted in the Venetians' loss of all of their holdings on land.

12. The developments of which Machiavelli speaks here began in the thirteenth century, especially in northern and central Italy. The empire to which he refers is the Holy Roman Empire, from whose ruler many Italian noblemen, theoretically at least, held their lands as fiefs.

13. Alberigo da Barbiano, count of Conio (d. 1409) founded the first mercenary army in Italy, the Company of St. George, and made the mounted soldier the key fighting figure in the army; he taught both Braccio Montone and Giacomuzzo Attendolo Sforza.

14. This last sentence contains an untranslatable play on words. The somewhat unusual word for "led" in Machiavelli's Italian is *condotta*, the past participle of *condurre* (with a feminine ending). However, the noun *la condotta* meant the "contract" signed by a mercenary to lead (*condurre*) troops into battle; indeed, his signing the *condotta* made him into a *condottiere*, the usual term for a mercenary leader in Renaissance Italy. So what Machiavelli is suggesting here, as he was with his use of the word *soldato* earlier, is that these *condottieri*, men who served only for the money promised by their contract (*la condotta*), have led (*condotta*) Italy into ruin.

Chapter 13

On Auxiliary, Mixed, and Citizen Soldiers

AUXILIARY TROOPS, WHICH ARE the other kind of useless armies, are those of a power whom you have asked to come and defend you with his troops, as was done in recent times by Julius, who, having seen the sad test of his mercenary forces in the Ferrara campaign, turned to auxiliaries and arranged with Ferdinand, king of Spain, to help him with men and arms.[1] These troops can be useful and good in themselves, but they are almost always harmful for the man who calls them in, for if they lose, you are undone; if they win, you remain their prisoner. And although ancient history is full of such examples, nonetheless, I do not want to go beyond this recent example of Pope Julius II, whose decision could not have been more ill-considered, for in wanting to take Ferrara, he put himself entirely in the hands of a foreigner. But his good fortune produced a third factor so that he did not gather the fruit of his bad decision. For when his auxiliaries were beaten at Ravenna, beyond all his expectations and those of others, the Swiss rose up and drove off the victors, so that he was not taken prisoner by the enemy, who had fled, nor by his auxiliaries, since he had won with arms other than theirs.[2] The Florentines, being totally unarmed, hired ten thousand Frenchmen to conquer Pisa, and because of this decision they brought more danger on themselves than in any other period of their troubles.[3] The emperor of Constantinople, in order to oppose his neighbors, brought ten thousand Turks into Greece, who, when the war was over, did not want to go away, which was the beginning of the servitude of Greece to the infidels.[4]

Anyone, therefore, who does not want to conquer, should avail himself of these forces, because they are much more dangerous than mercenaries, for with them defeat is assured, since they are all united, all obedient to others, whereas with mercenaries, once they have won, they still need time and a good opportunity in order to injure you, since they are not a unified group and have been hired and paid by you, and with them, a third party whom you have made their leader cannot quickly acquire enough authority to harm you. To sum up: with mercenaries, their inaction is more dangerous; with auxiliaries, it is their prowess [*virtù*].

A wise prince, therefore, has always avoided these soldiers and has had recourse to his own, and has chosen rather to lose with his own men than to win with those of others, not judging that to be a true victory which is gained by outsiders' arms. I shall never hesitate to cite the example of Cesare Borgia and his actions. This duke entered the Romagna with auxiliary troops, leading an army composed entirely of Frenchmen, and with those he took Imola and Forlì.[5] But as those arms did not then seem reliable to him, he turned to mercenaries, judging them to be less dangerous, and hired the Orsini and Vitelli. When, in using them, he found them to be undependable, unfaithful, and dangerous, he got rid of them and turned to his own men. And it is easy to see the difference between these two sorts of armies if one considers the difference in the reputation of the duke when he had only the French, and when he had the Orsini and Vitelli, and then when he was left with his own soldiers and relied only on himself: his reputation always increased, nor was he ever esteemed so highly as when everyone saw that he was the complete master of his army.

I did not wish to depart from recent Italian examples, but I cannot leave out Hieron of Syracuse, since he is one of those I have previously mentioned. This man, having been made, as I said, head of their armies by the Syracusans, immediately recognized that mercenary forces were useless because they were composed of condottieri like our Italian ones; and because he thought he could neither keep them on nor let them go, he had them all cut into pieces, and from then on he made war with his own arms, not those of others.[6] I also want to call to mind an exemplary figure from the Old Testament that fits this argument. When David offered to Saul to go and fight Goliath, the Philistine challenger, Saul, in order to give him courage, armed him with his own arms, which David, when he had tried them on, refused, saying that with them he could not demonstrate his real worth, and for that reason he wanted to meet the enemy with his own sling and his own knife.

In short, the arms of others either slip off your back, or weigh you down, or tie you up. Charles VII, father of King Louis XI, having by means of his good fortune and ability [*virtù*] liberated France from the English, recognized this necessity of arming oneself with one's own arms and established in his kingdom an ordinance for training cavalry and infantry.[7] Afterward, King Louis, his son, abolished the one concerning the infantry and began to hire the Swiss, which error, followed by others, is, as can now be seen in fact, the cause of the dangers that kingdom faces. By giving such prestige to the Swiss, he degraded all his own troops, for he got rid of the infantry and forced his cavalry to depend on the arms of others, for being accustomed to fighting with the Swiss, they do not think they can win without them. The result is that the French are no match for the Swiss, and without the Swiss, they will not test themselves against others. The armies of France have thus been mixed, partly mercenary and partly her own citizens; taken together, they are much better than armies composed purely of mercenaries or auxiliaries, but much inferior to having one's own troops. And the example already given should suffice, for the kingdom of France would be unconquerable if the ordinances of Charles had been preserved or augmented. But because they are insufficiently prudent, men will start something, and because it then tastes good to them, the poison within it is not perceived, as I said above about consumptive fevers.[8]

Thus, he who does not recognize the ills in a principality when they arise does not have true wisdom—which is something given to few. And, if the initial fall of the Roman Empire were analyzed, one will find it started with the hiring of the Goths as soldiers, because from that beginning the forces of the Roman Empire began to weaken, and all that energy [*virtù*] which was taken from it was given to the Goths. I conclude, therefore, that no principality is secure without having its own armies; on the contrary, it is completely dependent on Fortune, because it does not have the valor [*virtù*] which loyally defends it in the midst of adversity. And it was always the opinion and saying of wise men "that there is nothing so weak and unstable as a reputation for power not based on one's own strength."[9] And one's own troops are those that are composed of subjects, or citizens, or your own dependents; all the others are either mercenaries or auxiliaries. And it will be easy to find the method for organizing one's own troops if one will consider the methods of the four men I cited above,[10] and if one notes how Philip, the father of Alexander the Great, and how many republics and princes, have been armed and organized; to those methods I defer absolutely.

Notes to Chapter 13

1. In September 1510, Julius II launched a war against Bologna and Ferrara. Initially victorious, he was driven out of Ferrara by its duke, Alfonso d'Este, in the spring of 1511 and lost Bologna as well.

2. The French defeated the troops of Julius II at Ravenna on April 11, 1512, but they lost many men to the Spaniards, including their leader Gaston de Foix, and the next month 20,000 Swiss troops came to the aid of the pope and defeated them. The French were decisively expelled from Italy by the next year after the battle of Novara.

3. Florence got Gascon and Swiss troops from their ally, the king of France, for use against Pisa in 1500, but the troops mutinied, and the campaign was terminated.

4. In 1353 the Byzantine emperor John Cantacuzene (1291–1380) hired Turkish troops to fight for him against the Paleologue dynasty, thus giving the Turks their first foothold in Europe.

5. Borgia led an army of French, Gascon, and Swiss troops into the Romagna in the late spring of 1499 and captured Imola on November 24 and Forlì on December 17. In a second campaign there from October 1500 to June 1501, he led a larger army that included mercenaries.

6. Machiavelli mentioned Hieron at the end of chapter 6 (see note 6 in that chapter). The mercenaries he hired had originally been engaged by Agathocles, but they were eliminated because they threatened Hieron's rule. For Hieron, see Polybius, *The Histories*, 1.7–9. For the next story, of Saul and David, see the Bible, 1 Samuel 17: 38–40.

7. In the 1440s, Charles VII (1403–1461) replaced the mercenary companies that had fought the English previously during the Hundred Years' War with a civic militia and finally drove the English out of France in 1453. His son, Louis XI (1423–1483), repealed the ordinance and reorganized the French armies in 1474, replacing the citizen troops with Swiss and German mercenaries.

8. See chapter 3.

9. Machiavelli is citing Tacitus, *Annals*, 13.19; the quotation is slightly inaccurate.

10. The "four men" to whom Machiavelli refers are Cesare Borgia, Hieron of Syracuse, David, and Charles VIII.

Chapter 14

What the Duties of the Prince Are with Regard to the Military

A PRINCE, THEREFORE, MUST have no other object or thought, or take up anything as his profession, except war and its rules and discipline, for that is the only art that befits one who commands. And it has such power [*virtù*] that it not only maintains those who are born princes, but often enables men of private station to rise up to that rank; and one sees, on the other hand, that when princes have thought more of luxurious living than of arms, they have lost their state. The chief cause which makes you lose it is to neglect this art, and the way to acquire it is to be an expert in this art.

From being a private citizen Francesco Sforza became duke of Milan because he was armed; his sons, in order to avoid the hardships of war, from being dukes became private citizens.[1] For among the other bad effects that being unarmed has on you is that it makes you despised, which is one of those infamies which a prince must guard himself against, as will be explained later.[2] For, between an armed man and an unarmed one there is no comparison whatsoever, and it is not reasonable that one who is armed should willingly obey one who is unarmed, or that an unarmed one would be safe among armed servants. For the latter being disdainful and the former suspicious, it is not possible for them to work well together. And therefore, a prince who does not understand military matters, in addition to the other misfortunes already mentioned, cannot be esteemed by his soldiers, nor can he place any trust in them.

He must, therefore, never take his thoughts away from this exercise of war, and in peace he must train himself more than in war, which he can do in two ways, one through activities and the other with the mind. And as for activities, aside from keeping his soldiers well disciplined and exercised, he must always be out hunting, and by means of that, accustoming his body to hardships, and at the

63

same time, learning the nature of the terrain, and getting to know how the mountains rise, how the valleys open out, how the plains lie, and understanding the nature of the rivers and the swamps—and on this he should lavish the greatest care. This knowledge is useful in two ways. First, one gets to know one's country and can understand better how to defend it. Then, with knowledge and experience of the terrain, one can easily understand any other terrain it may be necessary to explore for the first time, for the hills, valleys, plains, rivers, and swamps that are in Tuscany, for instance, have a certain resemblance to those of other countries, so that from a knowledge of the terrain in one country one can easily arrive at a knowledge of it in others. And that prince who lacks this experience lacks the primary thing a captain needs to have, for this teaches you how to find the enemy, choose quarters, lead armies, arrange them for battle, and besiege towns to your advantage.

Philopoemon, prince of the Achaeans, among the other praises that have been given to him by writers, is celebrated because in times of peace he never thought of anything but the methods of war, and when he was in the country with his friends, he would often stop and reason with them: "If the enemy were up on that hill, and we found ourselves here with our army, which one of us would have the advantage? How could we safely go to attack them while maintaining our formation? If we wanted to retreat, how would we do it? If they retreated, how would we pursue them?"[3] And he would put before them, as they were going along, all the contingencies that could occur in an army; he would hear their opinions, give his own, fortify it with arguments, so that through these continual deliberations, no incident whatsoever could occur when he was leading his armies, for which he did not have a remedy.

But as for exercising the mind, the prince must read histories and in them consider the actions of eminent men, see how they conducted themselves, examine the reasons for their victories and defeats in order to be able to avoid the latter and imitate the former; and above all, he must do as some eminent man has done in the past who chose to imitate someone who before him had been praised and glorified, and has always kept his deeds and actions in mind, as it is said Alexander the Great imitated Achilles; Caesar, Alexander; and Scipio, Cyrus.[4] And whoever reads the life of Cyrus written by Xenophon will then perceive in the life of Scipio how that imitation contributed to his glory, and how, in chastity, affability, humanity, and liberality, Scipio conformed to what Xenophon wrote about Cyrus.

A wise prince must follow similar methods and in peaceful times never remain idle, but by being industrious he must make capital out of them in order to be able to avail himself of them in times of adversity, so that when Fortune changes, she may find him prepared to resist her.

Notes to Chapter 14

1. The descendants of Francesco Sforza were his son Ludovico il Moro, duke of Milan from 1494 to 1508, who was defeated twice by the French and the second time sent to France where he remained in prison from 1500 until his death; and Ludovico's son Massimiliano, who regained the dukedom in 1512 but was removed from it definitively in 1515. Machiavelli's reference to Francesco Sforza's "sons" is slightly misleading here.

2. See chapters 15 and 19.

3. Philopoemon (c.253–182 B.C.E.) of Megalopolis was a Greek statesman and general who led the Achaean Confederacy, which was made up of a number of Greek city-states, including Athens, and which conquered Sparta and most of the Peloponnese during his lifetime. Machiavelli's sources here include Livy, *History of Rome*, 35.28 and Plutarch, *Life of Philopoemon*, 4.

4. Machiavelli's sources here are, in order: Plutarch, *Life of Alexander*, 8; Suetonius, *The Deified Julius*, 7; and Cicero, *Letters to his Brother Quintus*, 1.8–23. Scipio was Publius Cornelius Scipio Africanus (236–183 B.C.E.), a Roman general and statesman who defeated the Carthaginians in Spain and then carried the war to Africa, where he decisively defeated Hannibal at the battle of Zama in 202. Cyrus was Cyrus the Great (ruled 557–530 B.C.E.), who initially ruled a small state in central Asia, but conquered a number of others, including the Babylonian Empire, and founded the Persian Empire. His life, heavily fictionalized, is recounted by Xenophon (c.430–c.360 B.C.E.), a pupil of Socrates who was a soldier and a writer of historical and philosophical works, among which was his *Cyropaedia*, or *Life of Cyrus*.

Chapter 15

On the Things for Which Men, and Especially Princes, Are Praised or Blamed

IT REMAINS NOW TO be seen what the methods and procedures must be for a prince with regard to his subjects and friends. And because I know that many have written about this, I fear that if I write about it again, I may be deemed presumptuous, since I depart, especially in discussing this matter, from the rules given by others. But since my intention is to write something of use for those who understand it, it seemed more suitable to me to go after the effectual truth of the matter than after an imaginary one.[1] And many have imagined republics and principalities for themselves which have never been seen or known to exist in reality, for the distance is so great between how we live and how we ought to live that he who abandons what is done for what ought to be done learns his ruin rather than his preservation; because a man who wants to make a profession of goodness in everything is bound to come to ruin among so many who are not good.[2] Therefore, it is necessary for a prince, if he wants to preserve himself, to learn how not to be good, and to use this knowledge and not use it as necessity dictates.

Leaving aside, then, the things that have been imagined about the prince, and discussing those that are true, I say that all men, when they are spoken of, and especially princes, because they are placed at a greater height, are judged for some of those qualities which bring them either blame or praise. And this is why one is considered liberal, another miserly (using a Tuscan term, because avaricious [*avaro*] in our language still means someone who deceives to gain things by theft; miserly [*misero*] we call that man who abstains excessively from making use of what is his own); one is considered a giver, another rapacious; one cruel, another merciful; one treacherous, the other loyal; one effeminate and cowardly, the other fierce and courageous; one humane, the other haughty; one lascivious, the other chaste; one straightforward, the other cunning; one hard, the other easy; one serious, the other frivolous; one religious, the other incredulous; and so on. And I know that everyone will admit that it would be a most praiseworthy thing for a prince to have, of all the qualities mentioned above, those that are held to be good, but since it is impossible to have all of them and to practice any of them completely, because the human condition does not permit it, it is necessary for him to be sufficiently prudent so as to know how to avoid the infamy of those vices which would lose him the state, and, if he can, to guard himself against those which might not lose it for him, although, if he cannot, he can indulge them with less concern. And further, he need not worry about incurring the disgrace of those vices without which it would be difficult for him to save the state, for if everything is carefully considered, it will be found that something which seems a virtue [*virtù*] would, if practiced, become his ruin, and some other thing, which seems a vice, would, if practiced, result in his security and well-being.

Notes to Chapter 15

1. Machiavelli speaks of "effectual truth" (*verità effetuale*) because he is interested in a truth that has an *effect*—that is, leads to action in the world—rather than a truth that is more purely speculative or contemplative and is thus impractical.

2. Machiavelli is thinking here of books such as Plato's *Republic* as well as of traditional books of advice for princes, which always stressed the necessity of following the dictates of conventional morality. More's *Utopia* might also seem to be the kind of book Machiavelli is aiming at in this passage, but it was actually composed several years after *The Prince*.

Chapter 16

Of Liberality and Miserliness

BEGINNING, THEREFORE, WITH THE first qualities mentioned above, I say that it would be good to be considered generous; nevertheless, generosity used in such a way as to give you a reputation for it will harm you, because if it is used virtuously [*virtuosamente*] and as it is supposed to be used, it will not be recognized, and you will not avoid the infamy of its opposite. And therefore, if someone wants to maintain a reputation among men for liberality, it is necessary to avoid omitting any kind of sumptuous display, with the result that a prince so disposed will consume all his wealth in such activities, and he will at last be compelled, if he wants to maintain his reputation for liberality, to impose a heavy tax burden on the people, and become an extortionist, and do everything that can be done to get money. This will begin to make him hateful to his subjects, and being poor, he will not be much esteemed by anyone, so that having by this liberality harmed many and benefited few, he will feel every little disturbance and will be ruined at the first appearance of danger. When he recognizes this and wants to extricate himself from it, he immediately becomes infamous as a miser.

Therefore, since a prince cannot practice this virtue [*virtù*] of liberality so that he gets a reputation for it without harming himself, he must not, if he is prudent, care about being called a miser, because over time he will always be considered more generous when it is seen that because of his miserliness his income is sufficient, he can defend himself from anyone who makes war on him, and he can undertake enterprises without burdening his people. The result will be that he will come to appear generous to all those from whom he takes nothing—who are numberless—and miserly to all those to whom he gives nothing—who are few. In our times we have not seen great things done except by those who have been considered miserly; the others have come to ruin. Pope Julius II, although he had made use of a reputation for liberality in order to attain the papacy, decided not to maintain it afterward, so that he could wage wars. The present king of France has waged many wars without imposing an extra tax on his people, because his additional expenses were taken care of by his long-practiced parsimony. The present king of Spain, if he had had a reputation for generosity, would not have engaged in and won so many campaigns.[1]

Therefore, in order to avoid robbing his subjects, to be able to defend himself, to avoid becoming poor and contemptible, and to avoid being forced to become rapacious, a prince must not be greatly concerned about acquiring a reputation for miserliness, for this is one of those vices that enable him to reign. And if someone should say that Caesar attained imperial rule through liberality, and many others have reached the highest ranks through having been generous, and having had a reputation for liberality, I reply: you are either a prince already, or you are on the way to acquiring that rank; in the first case, this liberality is harmful; in the second, it is indeed necessary to be considered generous. And Caesar was one of those who wanted to attain princely rule over Rome, but if, after having achieved it, he had survived and he had not moderated those expenditures, he would have destroyed his empire. And should someone reply that there have been many princes, who have done great things with their armies and have been reputed to be extremely generous, I reply to you: the prince may either spend his own wealth and that of his subjects, or the wealth of others; in the first case he must be frugal; in the second, he must not omit any aspect of liberality. And that prince who marches with his armies and lives by looting, sacking, and extortion is making use of what belongs to others. For him this generosity is necessary; otherwise, he would not be followed by his soldiers. And with what does not belong to you or your subjects, it is possible to be a more liberal giver, as were Cyrus, Caesar, and Alexander, for spending what belongs to others does not take away from your reputation, but adds to it; only by spending your own do you harm yourself. And there is nothing that consumes itself so much as liberality: while you are using it, you are losing the possibility of using it, and you are becoming either poor and contemptible, or, to escape poverty, rapacious and hated. And above all the things that a prince must guard himself against is being despised and hated, and liberality will lead you to both. Therefore, there is more wisdom in having the reputation of a miser, which begets infamy without hatred, than, because you want to be considered generous, to be forced to acquire a reputation for rapacity, which begets infamy and hatred.

Note to Chapter 16

1. Machiavelli's remarks about Julius II, Louis XII of France, and Ferdinand of Spain are accurate: all were as fiscally prudent as they were committed to warfare.

Chapter 17

On Cruelty and Mercy, and Whether It Is Better to Be Loved or Feared, or the Contrary

PROCEEDING TO THE OTHER qualities mentioned before, I say that every prince should desire to be considered merciful and not cruel; nevertheless, he must take care not to use this mercy badly.[1] Cesare Borgia was considered cruel; still, his cruelty brought order to the Romagna, united it, and restored it to peace and loyalty. If this is considered carefully, it will be seen that he was much more merciful than the Florentine people, who, to avoid a reputation for cruelty, allowed Pistoia to be destroyed.[2] A prince, therefore, must not mind acquiring a bad reputation for cruelty in order to keep his subjects united and loyal, for, with very few examples of cruelty, he will be more merciful than those who, because of too much mercy, allow disorders to continue, from which spring killing and plundering, for these usually harm the whole community, while the executions that come from the prince just harm particular individuals. And more than all other princes, a new prince cannot avoid a reputation for cruelty, because new states are always full of dangers. And Vergil, speaking through Dido's mouth, says:

> Res dura, et regni novitas me talia cogunt
> Moliri, et late fines custode tueri.[3]

Nonetheless, he must be slow to believe and act, although he should not make himself afraid of his own shadow, and he must proceed in such a way, tempered with prudence and humanity, that too much confidence does not make him rash, and too much distrust does not render him unbearable.

From this there arises a dispute: whether it is better to be loved than feared, or the contrary. The reply is that one should like to be both the one and the other, but as it is difficult to bring them

71

together, it is much safer to be feared than to be loved if one of the two has to be lacking. For this can be said of men in general: that they are ungrateful, fickle, hypocrites and dissemblers, avoiders of dangers, greedy for gain; and while you benefit them, they are entirely yours, offering you their blood, their goods, their life, their children, as I said above, when need is far away, but when you actually become needy, they turn away. And the prince who has made their word his entire foundation, finding himself stripped of other preparations, will be ruined, for friendships which are acquired for a price and not through grandeur and nobility of spirit are bought, but are not truly owned, and when the time arrives, they cannot be spent. And men have less hesitation about offending one who makes himself loved than one who makes himself feared, for love is held together by a chain of obligation which, because men are sadly wicked, is broken at every opportunity to serve their self-interest, but fear is maintained by a dread of punishment which never abandons you. Nevertheless, a prince must make himself feared in such a way that if he does not gain love, he does avoid hatred, for to be feared and not to be hated can go very well together, and this he will always achieve if he does not touch the goods and the women of his citizens and subjects. And when he is obliged to shed someone's blood, he should do so when there is proper justification and manifest cause, but above all, he must abstain from taking the property of others, for men sooner forget the death of their father than the loss of their patrimony. Besides, reasons for taking property are never lacking, and he who begins to live by stealing always finds a reason for taking what belongs to others, whereas reasons for shedding blood are rarer and are exhausted sooner.

But when the prince is with his army and has under his command a multitude of soldiers, then it is absolutely necessary not to care about being thought cruel, for without this reputation, no one has ever kept an army united or ready for any feat of arms. Among the marvelous accomplishments of Hannibal there is reckoned this one: that although he had an enormous army composed of countless races and nations of men, and led it to fight in foreign lands, there never arose any dissension either among the rank and file or against the prince, no more when his fortune was bad than when it was good.[4] This could not have arisen from anything other than that inhuman cruelty of his, which, together with his countless abilities [*virtù*], always made him a figure of awe and terror in the sight of his soldiers, and without that, his other abilities [*virtù*] would not have sufficed to produce that effect. And less thoughtful writers admire this accomplishment of his, on the one hand, and on the other, condemn the principal reason for it. And that it is true that his other abilities [*virtù*] would not have sufficed can be seen from the case of Scipio, a most rare man not only in his own times, but in all of recorded history, whose armies in Spain rebelled against him.[5] This arose from nothing other than his excessive mercifulness, which gave more license to his soldiers than was fitting for military discipline. He was reproached with this in the senate by Fabius Maximus and was called the corrupter of the Roman army. The Locrians, having been savaged by one of Scipio's officers, were not avenged by him, nor was the insolence of that officer corrected, all of which arose from his easy-going nature, so that someone in the senate who wanted to excuse him said that there were many men who knew how not to err better than how to correct errors in others.[6] Over time this disposition would have damaged Scipio's fame and glory, if he had persevered in it while supreme military commander, but since he lived under the rule of the senate, this harmful quality of his was not only concealed, but brought him glory.

I conclude, therefore, returning to the question of being feared and loved, that since men love at their own will and fear at the will of the prince, a wise prince must build his foundation on what is his own and not on what belongs to others; he must only contrive to escape hatred, as was said.

Notes to Chapter 17

1. Machiavelli's word for "mercy" here is *pietà*, which no single English word can translate, for it means both "piety," in the sense of religious devotion, and "pity" or "mercy," in the sense of feeling sorrow for the suffering of others. I have used "mercy" here and generally throughout the translation, but the other meaning is never to be excluded when the word appears.
2. Pistoia was divided into two factions, the Panciatichi and the Cancellieri, and in 1501 and 1502, when conflict broke out between them, the Flor-

entines, who controlled the city, refused to intervene, allowing the two factions to tear the city apart.

3. *Aeneid*, 2.563–64: "Harsh necessity and the newness of my reign force me to take such measures and to watch over my borders with a widespread guard."

4. Hannibal (247–183 B.C.E.) was a Carthaginian general who repeatedly beat the Romans during the Second Punic War (219–201), until he was defeated by Scipio in 202 and fled to Syria and then to Bithnia, where he finally poisoned himself lest he fall into the hands of his enemies. Machiavelli's chief source for information on him is Livy. His reference to Hannibal's "inhuman cruelty" is a direct translation of the phrase in Livy; see *History of Rome*, 21.4.

5. On Scipio, see chapter 14, note 4. His troops rebelled in Spain in 206 B.C.E.; see Livy, *History of Rome*, 28.24. Fabius Maximus, mentioned below, was Quintus Fabius Maximus Cunctator (d. 203 B.C.E.). He was the great opponent of Hannibal in the first, defensive phases of the Second Punic War, and his policy of cautiously refusing to engage in battles he knew he would lose earned him the sobriquet of Cunctator, "the hesitator." He was also an opponent of Scipio in the senate. For his accusation that Scipio was the "corrupter of the Roman army," see Livy, *History of Rome*, 29.19.

6. Scipio took the southern Italian city of Locri in 205 B.C.E. and placed it under the control of Quintus Pleminius, who proceeded to pillage it. Never rebuked for his actions by Scipio, he was eventually arrested and punished by the senate. For this material, see Livy, *History of Rome*, 29.21.

Chapter 18

How Princes Must Keep Their Word

How LAUDABLE IT IS for a prince to keep his word and to live with integrity and not by means of cunning, everyone knows; nevertheless, one sees from experience in our times that those princes have done great things who have had little regard for keeping their word and who have been able to confuse men's brains by cunning, and in the end, they have overcome those who made loyalty their foundation.[1]

You must know, then, that there are two methods of fighting, one with laws, the other with force: the first one is proper to man, the second to beasts; but because the first one often does not suffice, one has to have recourse to the second. Therefore, it is necessary for a prince to know well how to use the beast and the man. This procedure was taught to princes allegorically by ancient writers, who relate how Achilles and many other ancient princes were given to Chiron the centaur to be reared so that he might train them in his discipline.[2] Having for a teacher one who was half-beast and half-man means nothing other than that a prince must know how to use both natures, and that the one without the other cannot endure.

Since a prince must know well how to use the nature of the beast, he must choose the fox and the lion from among them, for the lion cannot defend himself from traps, and the fox cannot defend himself from wolves.[3] It is therefore necessary to be a fox to recognize traps and a lion to frighten the wolves. Those who live simply by the lion do not understand this. Therefore, a prudent ruler cannot, must not, keep his word, when keeping it would work against him, and when the reasons which made him promise it have been removed. And if men were all good, this precept would not be good, but since they are sadly wicked and would not keep their word to you, you also do not have to keep it to them. Nor does a prince ever lack reasons to color over his failure to keep it. Of this one could furnish countless modern examples to show how many peace treaties, how many promises, have been rendered null and void by the disloyalty of princes, and how the one who has known best how to use the fox has turned out best. But it is necessary to be able to color over this character well, and to be a great hypocrite and dissembler; and men are so simple and so obedient to present necessities, that he who deceives will always find someone who will let himself be deceived.

I do not want to remain silent about one of these recent examples. Alexander VI never did anything, never thought of anything, other than deceiving men, and he always found material so that he could do it. And there was never a man who was more effective in swearing oaths and in affirming a thing with greater promises who kept his word less. Nevertheless, his deceptions always succeeded for him according to his wishes, since he really knew this aspect of the world.

Therefore, it is not necessary for a prince to have all the qualities mentioned above, but it is certainly necessary to seem to have them. Indeed, I will even be so bold as to say this: that having them and always practicing them are dangerous, but appearing to have them is useful; for instance, to appear—and to be—merciful, loyal, humane, forthright, and religious, but to have your mind disposed so that, when it is necessary not to be that way, you will be ready and able to change to the opposite. And this must be understood: that a prince, and especially a new prince, cannot practice all those things because of which men are considered good, since he is often obliged, in order to maintain the state, to act against loyalty, against charity, against humanity, against religion. And, therefore, it is necessary for him to have a mind disposed to turn itself about as the winds and variations of Fortune dictate, and as I said above, he should not deviate from what is good, if possible, but he should know how to enter into evil when necessity commands.

A prince must therefore take great care that nothing slips from his lips which is not full of the five qualities mentioned above, and when one sees or hears him, he should seem to be all mercy, all loyalty, all sincerity, all humanity, all religion. And nothing is more necessary to seem to have than this last quality. And men in general judge more by the eyes than by the hands, for everyone can see, but few can feel. Everyone sees what you appear to be, few feel what you are, and those few do not dare to oppose themselves to the opinion of the many, who have the majesty of the state to defend them; and in the actions of all men, and especially of princes, where there is no court of appeal, one looks at the outcome.[4] A prince should, therefore, conquer and maintain his state: his means will always be judged honorable and praised by everyone, for ordinary people will always be taken by appearances and by the outcome of an action; and in the world there is nothing but ordinary people, nor is there any place for the few when the many have something to lean on for support. A certain prince of the present time, whom it is not good to name, never preaches anything but peace and loyalty, and is the greatest enemy of both; and both of those things, had he practiced them, would on many occasions have deprived him of either his reputation or his state.[5]

Notes to Chapter 18

1. Machiavelli speaks here of keeping one's *fede*, or "faith," which I have translated as keeping one's "word," the more idiomatic English equivalent of his Italian expression. Later in the chapter he will speak of *fede* as one of the virtues a prince should appear to have; I have translated this *fede* as "loyalty" rather than "faith," especially since Machiavelli also identifies *religione* as another virtue the prince should put on display. The religious meaning of *fede* is, of course, never to be excluded when the term appears.

2. Centaurs were mythological beasts who had the upper portion of a man and the lower of a horse. Chiron is said to have taught not just Achilles, but Aesculapius and Jason. Although Chiron is mentioned in the *Iliad* and centaurs are discussed in Xenophon's *Cyropaedia*, which was clearly one of Machiavelli's favorite books, it is not clear to which "ancient writers" he is referring who supposedly allegorized Chiron in the way he explains in his text.

3. Machiavelli has derived these two allegorical beasts—as well as the notion that the prince must know how to fight like a man, using laws, and like a beast, using force—from Cicero's *On Duties*, 1.11.34 and 1.13.41; needless to say, Machiavelli's perspective on "using the beast" is not Cicero's.

4. "One looks at the outcome": *si guarda al fine*. Machiavelli's statement here concerns the way human psychology works and offers an ironic and satirical perspective on people who are less concerned about the morality

of the prince's methods than about the outcome of his actions since the latter may either benefit or harm them. Machiavelli's statement here is not the equivalent of his saying "the ends justify the means," nor could such a statement be derived from what he says elsewhere in *The Prince*.

5. Machiavelli is alluding to Ferdinand II of Aragon, also called Ferdinand the Catholic.

Chapter 19

On Avoiding Contempt and Hatred

BUT SINCE, WITH REGARD to the qualities which were mentioned above, I have now spoken of the most important, I want to discuss the others briefly in relation to this generalization: the prince, as was partly noted above, must think about avoiding those things which would make him hated or despised, and whenever he has avoided this, he will have done his part and will not be endangered whatsoever by the other vices. He will become hated, above all, as I said, by being rapacious and usurping the property and women of his subjects, from which he must refrain; and whenever the majority of men are not deprived of their property or honor, they live contentedly, and one only has to combat the ambition of a few, which can easily be held in check in many ways. He is rendered contemptible by being thought changeable, frivolous, effeminate, cowardly, irresolute, against which a prince must guard himself as against a reef, and he must do his best so that in his actions one recognizes greatness, courage, dignity, and strength, and concerning the private affairs of his subjects, he should want his sentence to be irrevocable and should maintain such a reputation that no one would think to deceive him or try to get around him.

The prince who creates this opinion about himself will enjoy great prestige, and it is difficult to conspire against and difficult to attack someone who has such a reputation, provided that he is considered to be exceptional and is revered by his people. For a prince must have two fears: one internal, on account of his subjects; the other external, on account of foreign powers. From the latter he can defend himself with good arms and good friends, and he will always have good friends if he has good arms. And internal affairs will always remain stable, when external ones are stable, unless they have already been disturbed by a conspiracy. But even if external conditions should change, if he has ruled and lived as I have said, and does not lose control, he will always be able to withstand every assault, just as I have said Nabis the Spartan did.[1] But as for his subjects, when external conditions do not change, he has to fear that they may conspire in secret, from which the prince will be sufficiently secure if he avoids being hated or despised, and keeps the people satisfied with him, something which it is necessary for him to do, as I said above at length. And one of the most potent remedies a prince has for conspiracies is not to be hated by the masses, for whoever conspires always believes that he will satisfy the people with the death of the prince, but if he believes he would offend them, he will not pluck up the courage to make such a move, because the difficulties on the side of the conspirators are infinite. And experience shows that there have been very many conspiracies, but few have had a successful outcome. For whoever conspires cannot act alone, nor can he find companions except among those he believes to be discontented, and as soon as you have uncovered your intention to a malcontent, you give him the means to make himself content, for by revealing your plot he can hope to gain everything he wants. Thus, seeing a certain gain on the one side and a doubtful one full of danger on the other, if he keeps his word to you, he must either be a rare friend or an absolutely determined enemy of the prince. And to reduce the matter to a few words, I say that on the part of the conspirator there is nothing but fear, jealousy, and the prospect of punishment which terrifies him, but on the part of the prince there is the majesty of the principality, the laws, and the protection of friends and of the state which defend him, so that when the good will of the people is added to these things, it is impossible for anyone to be so rash as to engage in a conspiracy. For whereas ordinarily a conspirator must be afraid before executing his evil deed, in this case he must also fear afterward, since he will have the people as his enemy once his crime has been done, nor can he hope for any sort of refuge.

Numberless examples might be given of this subject, but I will content myself with just one which took place within the memory of our fathers. Messer Annibale Bentivogli, prince of Bologna, grandfather of the present Messer Annibale, was killed by the Canneschi, who conspired against him, and he left no one to succeed him but Messer Giovanni, who was in swaddling bands. Immediately after that murder, the people rose up and killed all the Canneschi. This came about because of the good will that the house of Bentivogli had at that time with the people, which was so great that, since there was no one left in Bologna after the death of Annibale who could govern the state, the Bolognese people, having information that a member of the Bentivogli family was in Florence who had till then been considered the son of a blacksmith, came to fetch him in Florence and gave him control of the city, which was governed by him until Messer Giovanni reached the age to rule.[2]

I conclude, therefore, that a prince should not be greatly concerned about conspiracies when the people are well disposed toward him, but when they are his enemies and hate him, he must fear everything and everyone. And well-ordered states and wise princes have, with great diligence, taken care not to drive the nobility to desperation and to satisfy the people and keep them contented, for this is one of the most important concerns that a prince has.

Among the kingdoms that are well ordered and well governed in our time is that of France, and in it are found countless good institutions on which depend the liberty and security of the king, of which the chief is the parliament and its authority. For the one who organized that kingdom, knowing the ambition of the nobles and their insolence, and judging it necessary to put a bit in their mouths to hold them in check, and on the other hand, knowing the hatred of the people for the great, a hatred based on fear, and desiring to reassure them, did not want these things to be the particular concern of the king in order to relieve him of the dissatisfaction that he might incur among the nobles by favoring the people and among the people by favoring the nobles; and therefore, he established a third judicial body that, without placing any burden on the king, might keep down the great and favor the lesser people.[3] This arrangement could not be better or more prudent, nor is there a greater source of security for the king and the kingdom. From this another notable rule can be drawn: that princes ought to have others carry out unpopular tasks and keep pleasing ones for themselves. Again I conclude that a prince must respect his nobles, but not make himself hated by the people.

It could perhaps seem to many who have pondered the lives and

deaths of a number of Roman emperors that they provide examples
contrary to this opinion of mine, finding that some who always lived
nobly and showed great strength [*virtù*] of character nevertheless
lost their empire or were killed by their own people who conspired
against them. Wishing therefore to respond to these objections, I
will discuss the traits of a number of emperors, showing the causes
of their ruin, which are not different from what I have deduced,
and in addition I will offer things worthy of note to be pondered
by anyone reading about the deeds done in those times. And I will
content myself with taking all those emperors who succeeded to the
imperial throne from Marcus the philosopher to Maximinus: these
were Marcus, his son Commodus, Pertinax, Julian, Severus, his son
Antoninus Caracalla, Macrinus, Heliogabalus, Alexander, and Maximinus.[4] And the first thing to note is that whereas in other principalities one only has to contend with the ambition of the great
and the insolence of the people, the Roman emperors had a third
difficulty, that of having to endure the cruelty and avarice of the
soldiers. This was such a difficulty that it was the cause of the downfall of many of them. For it was difficult to satisfy the soldiers as
well as the people, since the people loved peace and quiet, and because of this they loved princes who were moderate, while the soldiers preferred a prince who had a martial spirit and who was
insolent, cruel, and rapacious, and they wanted him to practice these
qualities on the people in order to get double pay and give vent to
their avarice and cruelty. The result of this was that those emperors
who did not have, by nature or by art, a great reputation, such that
they could use it to rein in both groups, always came to grief, and
most of them who came to power as new princes, knowing the
difficulties created by these two different humors,[5] turned to satisfying the soldiers and thought little about injuring the people. This
choice was necessary because princes, who cannot avoid being hated
by somebody, must first strive to avoid being hated by the vast
majority of people, and if they cannot accomplish this, they must
try with all their might to escape the hatred of the classes that are
the most powerful. And therefore these emperors, who as new
princes had need of extraordinary support, stuck to the soldiers
more willingly than to the people; nevertheless, this turned out to

be useful to them, or not, depending on whether the prince knew how to maintain his reputation with the soldiers.

For the reasons mentioned above, it turned out that Marcus, Pertinax, and Alexander, all of whom lived lives of moderation and were lovers of justice, enemies of cruelty, humane, and mild, had all, except for Marcus, a sad end. Marcus alone lived and died with the greatest honor, because he succeeded to the empire by hereditary right and did not have to acknowledge that he owed it either to the soldiers or to the people; besides, being endowed with many virtues [*virtù*] which made him revered, he kept both parties within their proper bounds as long as he lived and was never either hated or despised.[6] But Pertinax was created emperor against the will of the soldiers, who, being accustomed to living licentiously under Commodus, could not tolerate that honest life to which Pertinax wanted to return them, so that having made himself hated, and contempt being added to this hatred because he was old, he came to grief at the very beginning of his rule.

And here one must note that hatred is acquired as much by good deeds as by evil ones, and therefore, as I said above, a prince who wants to hold onto his state is often forced not to be good, for when that group, whether it be the people, the soldiers, or the nobles, whose support you believe you need in order to rule, is corrupt, you must follow its humor and satisfy it, and then good deeds are your enemies. But let us come to Alexander: he was so good that among the other praises that have been given to him is this one, that in the fourteen years of his reign, no one was put to death by him without a trial; nevertheless, since he was considered effeminate and a man who allowed himself to be ruled by his mother, and since he came to be despised because of this, the army conspired against him and killed him.

Considering now, by contrast, the qualities of Commodus, Severus, Antoninus Caracalla, and Maximinus, you will find them extremely cruel and rapacious. To satisfy the soldiers, they did not spare any sort of injury which could be inflicted on the people, and all except Severus had a sad end. For in Severus there was so much ability [*virtù*] that by keeping the soldiers his friends, even though the people were oppressed by him, he was always able to rule happily, for those abilities [*virtù*] of his made him so admirable in the sight of the soldiers and the people that the latter were, to some degree, astonished and stupefied, and the former, respectful and satisfied. And because the deeds of this man were great for a new prince, I want to show briefly how well he knew how to use the characters of the fox and the lion, whose natures, as I say above, a prince must imitate. Knowing the indolence of the emperor Julian, Severus persuaded his army, which he was leading in Slavonia,[7] that it would be good to go to Rome to avenge the death of Pertinax, who had been killed by the Praetorian Guards, and under this pretext, without revealing his aspirations to imperial rule, he moved his army against Rome and was in Italy before his departure was known. On his arrival in Rome, he was elected emperor by the senate out of fear, and he had Julian killed. After this beginning, there remained two difficulties for Severus if he wanted to make himself master of the entire empire: one in Asia, where Niger,[8] head of the Asiatic armies, had had himself named emperor; and the other in the west, where Albinus also aspired to imperial rule. And since he judged it dangerous to show himself the enemy of both, he decided to attack Niger and to deceive Albinus. To the latter he wrote that, having been elected emperor by the senate, he wanted to share that dignity with him, and he sent him the title of Caesar and, by a resolution of the senate, made him his colleague, which things were accepted as true by Albinus. But when Severus had defeated and killed Niger, pacified things in the east, and returned to Rome, he complained to the senate that Albinus, hardly acknowledging the benefits received from him, had treacherously sought to kill him, and for this it was necessary for him to go and punish Albinus's ingratitude. He then went to find him in France, and there he took away from him both his state and his life.

Whoever examines in detail, then, the actions of this man will find him a most ferocious lion and a most cunning fox, and will see him to have been feared and revered by everyone, and not hated by his armies, and will not marvel that he, a new man, should have been able to hold onto so great an empire, for his immense reputation always protected him from the hatred that the people might have conceived because of his plundering. But his son Antoninus was also a man of the most excellent parts that made him admirable in the sight of the people and pleasing to the soldiers, for he was a military man, most capable of enduring every hardship, a despiser of all delicate foods and every other luxury, which made him loved by all the armies. Nevertheless, his ferocity and cruelty were so great and so unheard of—because, after countless individual murders, he put to death a large part of the populace of Rome and all that of Alexandria—that he came to be hated by all the world, and he began to be feared even by those whom he had about him, with the result that he was murdered by a centurion in the midst of his army. From this it is to be noted that murders such as these, which result from the deliberation of a determined man, cannot be avoided by princes, since anyone who does not care about dying can harm him; however, the prince need not fear such attacks much since they are extremely rare. He must only guard against inflicting serious injury on anyone who serves him and whom he keeps about him in the service of the state, as Antoninus had done, for he had shamefully put to death a brother of that centurion, and also threatened him every day, although he kept him in his bodyguard, which was a foolhardy decision and one bound to cause his ruin, just as it did.

But let us come to Commodus, for whom it would have been very easy to hold onto the empire, because he held it by hereditary right, being the son of Marcus, and it would have sufficed for him merely to have followed in the steps of his father and to have satisfied the soldiers and the people. But being of a cruel and bestial disposition, in order to be able to exercise his rapacity on the people, he turned to indulging the soldiers and making them licentious. On the other hand, by not maintaining his dignity, often descending into the theater to fight with the gladiators, and doing other things that were very base and scarcely worthy of his imperial majesty, he became contemptible in the sight of the soldiers. And being hated on the one hand and despised on the other, he was conspired against and killed.

The only thing remaining for us to do is to describe the traits of Maximinus. He was an extremely warlike man, and since the armies were disgusted with the softness of Alexander, which I have discussed above, he was elected to rule the empire after Alexander's death. He did not possess it for very long, since two things made him hated and despised: the one was his very base origin, for he had formerly herded sheep in Thrace (which was well known ev-

erywhere and made him an object of great scorn in everyone's sight);
the other was that at the commencement of his rule he had deferred
going to Rome to take possession of the imperial seat, and he had
given himself a reputation for great cruelty since he had, through
his prefects, committed many cruelties in Rome and in other parts
of the empire. Consequently, the whole world was moved by contempt because of the baseness of his blood and by hatred caused by
fear of his ferocity, so that first Africa rebelled, then the senate with
all the people of Rome, and then all of Italy conspired against him.
To this was added his own army: besieging Aquileia and finding it
difficult to capture, disgusted by his cruelty, and fearing him less
because they saw he had so many enemies, they murdered him.

I do not want to speak of Heliogabalus, Macrinus, or Julian, who,
being universally despised, were quickly eliminated, but I shall come
to the conclusion of this discourse. And I say that the princes of
our times have to deal less with this difficulty of satisfying the soldiers under their command by extraordinary means, for although
some consideration has to be given to them, nevertheless things are
quickly resolved, since none of these princes have standing armies
that are entrenched in the government and administration of provinces, as were the armies of the Roman empire. And therefore, if it
was necessary to satisfy the soldiers then more than the people, that
was because the soldiers could do more than the people; now, it is
necessary for all princes, except the Turk and the Sultan,[9] to satisfy
the people more than the soldiers, for the people can do more than
the soldiers can. I except the Turk because he always keeps about
him twelve thousand infantry and fifteen thousand cavalry, on
which depend the security and strength of his rule, and it is necessary for that lord, having set aside every other consideration, to
keep them his friends. Similarly, since the realm of the Sultan is
entirely in the hands of the soldiers, he, too, must keep them his
friends, without any regard for the people. And you should note
that this state of the Sultan is different from all other principalities,
for it is similar to the Christian pontificate, which cannot be called
either an hereditary principality or a new principality, because the
sons of the sitting prince are not his heirs and do not succeed him
as rulers, but the one who does is elected to that rank by those who
have the authority to do so. And as this system is ancient, it cannot

be called a new principality, because in it there are none of those difficulties that exist in new ones, for although the prince really is new, the institutions of that state are old and are set up to receive him as if he were their hereditary lord.

But let us return to our subject. I say that whoever will consider the preceding discussion will see that either hatred or contempt has been the cause of the ruin of those previously mentioned emperors, and he will also recognize how it happens that, although some of them proceeded in one way and some in the opposite way, in each of those groups one man had a happy end and the others an unhappy one. Because for Pertinax and Alexander, being new princes, it was useless and harmful for them to try to imitate Marcus, who ruled the state by hereditary right; and similarly, for Caracalla, Commodus, and Maximinus, it was fatal for them to imitate Severus, because they did not have sufficient ability [*virtù*] to follow in his footsteps. Thus, a new prince in a new principality cannot imitate the deeds of Marcus, nor is it necessary for him to imitate those of Severus either, but he must take from Severus those qualities that are necessary to found his state, and from Marcus those that are useful and glorious for preserving a state that is already established and secure.

Notes to Chapter 19

1. See chapter 9.
2. After Annibale Bentivogli was killed in 1445 by Battista Canneschi, Santi Bentivogli, the illegitimate son of Annibale's cousin, ruled until 1462, when Giovanni came of age. Giovanni was succeeded by his son, the "present Annibale," who ruled for just two years, 1510–1512.
3. The initial French parliament was that of Paris; it grew out of the king's court during the reign (1226–1270) of Louis IX. Provincial parliaments developed in and after the fifteenth century. These parliaments, unlike the one in England, were primarily judicial, not legislative, bodies.
4. Marcus the philosopher is Marcus Aurelius Antoninus, who ruled from 161 to 180. Lucius Aelius Aurelius Commodus, his son, was assassinated in 193, a year that saw no fewer than four emperors, since he was succeeded by Publius Helvius Pertinax, who ruled from January to March; by Marcus Didius Julianus, who ruled from March until he was assassinated in June; and finally by Septimius Severus, who died a natural death in 211. Severus's successor, Marcus Aurelius Antoninus Caracalla, was

assassinated in 217 by Marcus Opellius Macrinus, who took the throne but was himself put to death the next year. Heliogabalus (Varius Avitus Bassianus) followed him and was assassinated in 222. He was succeeded by Marcus Aurelius Severus Alexander, who ruled as Alexianus and was assassinated in 235. Finally, Alexianus was followed by Caius Julius Verus Maximinus, who was killed in 238. It is noteworthy that the reign of Marcus Aurelius is seen as one of the high points of the Roman Empire, a view Machiavelli endorses in the *Discourses* (see 1.10); the emperors he focuses on thus represent a steep decline after Marcus Aurelius's reign. Machiavelli's likely source for all this information is the Greek historian Herodian, whose *Histories* had been translated into Latin by the Italian humanist Angelo Poliziano.

5. Machiavelli's reference to "humors" here is based on the idea of the state as a body politic, and the citizens who inhabit it as the substances, the "humors," that make the body function. On this subject, see chapter 9, note 1.

6. Marcus Aurelius was adopted as heir by the preceding emperor, Antoninus Pius.

7. Slavonia is the modern Slovenia; Severus's army was actually not far from Vienna when he decided to move against Julian in Rome.

8. Niger was Pescennius Niger, who was proclaimed emperor by the legions in Antioch in 193; he was beaten by Severus at Nicaea in that year and killed by his own soldiers. Albinus was Decius Claudius Septimius Albinus, head of the legions in Gaul; he was beaten by Severus in 198 and led to Rome, where he was executed.

9. The Turk is possibly Selim I (1465–1520). The Sultan is the Sultan of Egypt, whose state was the caliphate, established by Muhammad as an elective monarchy. In 1517 Selim captured Egypt and became its Sultan.

Chapter 20

Whether Fortresses and Many Other Things Which Are Employed Every Day by Princes Are Useful, or Not

SOME PRINCES, IN ORDER to hold onto their states securely, have disarmed their subjects; some others have kept their subject lands divided; some have nourished hostilities against themselves; some others have devoted themselves to winning over those who were suspect at the start of their rule; some have constructed fortresses; some have torn them down and destroyed them. And although a definite judgment cannot be given about all these things without going into the particular details about those states in which some such deliberation had to be made, nevertheless I will speak in as general a way as the subject matter itself will allow.

It has never been the case, then, that a new prince has disarmed his subjects; on the contrary, when he found them disarmed, he has always armed them, for when they are armed, those arms become yours, those who were suspect to you become loyal, and those who were loyal remain so and from being subjects make themselves your partisans. And since all subjects cannot be armed, when the ones whom you do arm receive benefits, you can deal more securely with the others; and this difference in treatment that the armed ones recognize toward themselves makes them feel more obligated to you; the others excuse you, judging it necessary that those who face more danger and have more responsibilities get greater rewards. But when you disarm them, you begin to offend them, and you show that you distrust them either because of their cowardice or lack of loyalty, and both of these judgments generate hatred against you. And because you cannot remain unarmed, you are obliged to turn to a mercenary army, whose character was discussed above; and even if it were good, it could not be so strong that it could defend you from powerful enemies and suspect subjects. But as I have said, a new prince in a new principality has always ordered that his state should be armed. Histories are full of these examples. But when a prince acquires a new state, which, like a member, is attached to his old one, then it is necessary to disarm that state, except for those who, when you were acquiring it, were your partisans, and even those, when time and opportunity serve, must be made weak and effeminate, and it is necessary to arrange things so that all the armed power of your state is concentrated in your own soldiers who live near you in your original state.

Our forefathers and those who were considered wise used to say that it was necessary to hold Pistoia by means of factions and Pisa by means of fortresses, and for this purpose they nurtured disagreements in some of their subject towns in order to hold onto them more easily. In those times when Italy had, to a certain degree, a balance of power, this wisdom may have served well, but I do not believe it can be given as a rule today, for I do not believe that factions have ever done any good. On the contrary, when the enemy approaches, divided cities will necessarily be lost immediately, for the weaker party always attaches itself to the forces outside, and the other will not be able to hold out.

The Venetians, moved, as I believe, by the reasons stated above,[1] nourished the Guelf and Ghibelline factions in their subject cities, and although they never allowed them to reach the point of shedding blood, nevertheless they nourished this dissension among them, so that those citizens, being occupied with those disagreements of theirs, would not unite against them. As has been seen, this did not then turn out to their advantage, because, after the defeat at Vailà,[2] one of those factions immediately took courage and seized their entire state from them. Such methods, therefore, argue weakness in a prince, for in a strong principality such divisions will never be permitted, because they are profitable only in time of peace, enabling one by means of them to manage one's subjects more easily, but when war comes, such a procedure reveals its faultiness.

Without doubt, princes become great when they overcome the difficulties and obstacles that confront them, and therefore Fortune, especially when she wants to make a new prince great—someone who has more need of acquiring prestige than does an hereditary prince—causes enemies to appear for him and has them undertake campaigns against him, so that he may have cause to overcome them and to climb up higher on the ladder which his enemies have brought him. Therefore, many think that a wise prince, when he has the opportunity, should cunningly nourish such hostility, so that through its suppression his greatness will be augmented.

Princes, and especially those who are new, have found more loyalty and more usefulness in those men who at the beginning of their rule were considered suspect than in those whom at the beginning they trusted. Pandolfo Petrucci, prince of Siena, ruled his state more with those whom he suspected than with the others.[3] But of this one cannot speak in general terms, as it varies according to the situation. I will only say this: that the prince will always win over those men with the greatest ease who had been his enemies at the founding of the principality, but who are the sort who need his support in order to maintain themselves, and they will be all the more compelled to serve him loyally in that they recognize how really necessary it is for them to cancel by their deeds the bad opinion he had of them. And thus the prince always gets greater use out of them than out of those who, in serving him from positions of too much security, neglect his affairs.

And since the subject requires it, I do not wish to fail to remind princes who have recently taken over a state through the help of those inside it that they should consider well what cause may have moved those who favored them to have done so; and if it is not natural affection for them, but only because those men were not happy with that state, he will be able to keep them his friends only by means of enormous effort and with great difficulty, because it will be impossible for him to satisfy them. And by carefully considering the cause of this, using examples drawn from antiquity and modern times, he will see that it is much easier to win the friendship of those who were content with the state before and were therefore his enemies, than those who, not being content with it, became his friends and supported his occupation of it.

It has been the custom of princes, in order to be able to hold their states more securely, to build fortresses that may serve as the bridle and bit for those who might plan to act against them, and in order to have a secure refuge against an unexpected attack. I praise this procedure because it has been used since antiquity. Nevertheless, in our own times Messer Niccolò Vitelli was seen to demolish two fortresses in Città di Castello in order to hold onto that state.[4] Guido Ubaldo, duke of Urbino, on returning to his dominions from which he had been chased by Cesare Borgia, razed all the fortresses of that country to the ground and concluded that without them it would be more difficult for him to lose that state again. The Bentivogli, returning to Bologna, used similar measures. Thus, fortresses are useful, or not, according to the times, and if they help you in one way, they harm you in another. The question can be considered this way: the prince who fears his own people more than foreigners ought to build fortresses, but the one who has more fear of foreigners than of the people ought to forget about them. The castle of Milan, which Francesco Sforza built there, has brought and will bring more wars upon the house of Sforza than any other disorder in that state.[5] Therefore, the best fortress that exists is not to be hated by the people, for even though you have fortresses, they will not save you if the people hate you, because when once the people have taken up arms, they will never lack outsiders to come to their assistance. In our times no one has seen that a fortress has been profitable to any prince except the countess of Forlì when Count Girolamo, her consort, was killed, for by its means she was able to escape a popular uprising and wait for help from Milan to retake her state.[6] At that moment, the times were such that no outsider could come to the assistance of the people, but later, fortresses were of little value to her when Cesare Borgia attacked her, and the people, being hostile to her, joined with the outsiders. Therefore, at that time, and earlier, it would have been safer for her not to have been hated by the people than to have had fortresses.

Having considered all these things, then, I shall praise the prince who builds fortresses and the prince who does not, and I shall blame anyone who, trusting in fortresses, thinks it of little moment to be hated by the people.

Notes to Chapter 20

1. See chapter 17.
2. After they lost the battle of Vailà, also known as Agnadello, which was

fought against the forces of Julius II on May 14, 1509, the Venetians had to face rebellions in many of their principal cities on land, including Brescia, Verona, Vicenza, and Padua.

3. Pandolfo Petrucci (1450–1512) was the ruler of Siena from 1500 until his death.

4. Niccolò Vitelli, the father of Vitellozzo and Paolo, was chased from his city by Pope Sixtus IV in 1474, but returned with the help of Florence in 1482 and destroyed the castles built there by the pope. In the next sentence, Guido Baldo is Guido Ubaldo, or Guidobaldo, di Montefeltro (1472–1508), duke of Urbino from 1482 on, who was driven out of his state by Cesare Borgia in 1502 but regained it the next year; his court is celebrated in Baldesare Castiglione's classic *Book of the Courtier*. Machiavelli's next example is that of the Bentivogli family of Bologna, who were driven out of their city by Julius II in 1506 but regained it in 1511 and destroyed the castle of Porta Galliera that the pope had erected as a symbol of his power.

5. The Sforza rulers of Milan had relied on the protection of their castle when oppressing the people in the city, and twice in Machiavelli's lifetime Ludovico had lost his state to the French without even a shot being fired. The castle, now known as the Castello Sforzesco, still stands in the heart of the city.

6. The countess of Forlì was Caterina Riario, whose husband Girolamo Riario was killed by plotters in 1488. She took refuge in her castle and waited until her uncle, Ludovico il Moro, came to her rescue from Milan. Cesare Borgia attacked and defeated her in December 1499.

Chapter 21

How a Prince Should Act to Gain Prestige

NOTHING MAKES A PRINCE so esteemed as when he personally accomplishes things rare and exemplary. In our times we have Ferdinand of Aragon, the present king of Spain. He may almost be called a new prince, because from being a weak king he has become, through the fame and glory he has achieved, the first king among Christians, and if you consider his actions, you will find them all very great and some even extraordinary. At the beginning of his reign he attacked Granada, and that undertaking was the foundation of his state.[1] First, he did it when his country was at peace and without a hint of opposition: he kept the minds of the barons of Castile occupied with this undertaking, and they, thinking of that war, did not consider making any political changes; and by this means he acquired prestige and power over them without their becoming aware of it. He was able to maintain his armies with money from the Church and the people, and with that long war he was able to lay a foundation for his own army, which has since brought him honor. Besides this, in order to be able to undertake greater enterprises, always making use of religion, he devoted himself to the pious cruelty of driving the Marranos out of his kingdom and despoiling them—this example could not be more pitiful or rare.[2] Under this same cloak of religion, he attacked Africa, undertook his Italian campaign, and has finally attacked France; and thus he has always done great deeds which he contrived and which have always kept his subjects' minds in suspense and amazed and occupied with their outcome. And these actions of his have sprung one out of the other in such a way that between one and the other he never gave men the space to work in tranquility against him.

It also helps a prince a great deal to give rare examples of his abilities in domestic government, like those which are recounted of

Messer Bernabò of Milan. When it happens that someone does something extraordinary, whether for good or for ill, in civil life, the prince should choose a method of rewarding or punishing him that will be much talked about.[3] And above all, a prince must strive in his every action to give the impression of himself as a great man and one of exceptional intelligence.

A prince is also esteemed when he is a true friend and a true enemy, that is, when he declares himself without any reservation in favor of one person against another. This policy will always be more useful than staying neutral, for if two powerful neighbors of yours come to blows, either they are such that if one of them wins, you will have to fear the victor, or you will not. In either of these two cases, it will be more useful for you to declare yourself and wage an honest war, because in the first case, if you do not declare yourself, you will always be the prey of the one who wins, to the delight and satisfaction of the one who has been defeated, and you will have no excuse or anything else to defend you or offer you a refuge. For whoever wins does not want suspect friends who would not help him in adversity, and whoever loses will not take you in, because you were not willing, with sword in hand, to share the fortunes of war with him.

Antiochus went to Greece, being sent there by the Aetolians to drive out the Romans.[4] He dispatched orators to the Achaeans, who were friends of the Romans, to encourage them to remain neutral, while on the other side, the Romans were urging them to take up arms for them. The matter came up to be deliberated in the council of the Achaeans, where the legate of Antiochus urged them to remain neutral, to which the Roman legate replied: "As to what these men are saying about how you should not get involved in the war, nothing is farther from your interests; without thanks, without dignity, you will be the prize of the victor."

And it always happens that the one who is not your friend will seek your neutrality, and the one who is your friend will ask you to declare yourself by taking up arms. And most of the time, irresolute princes, in order to avoid present dangers, follow the path of neutrality and come to ruin. But when the prince declares himself boldly in favor of one party, if the one whom you adhere to wins, even though he is powerful and you remain at his discretion, he does feel obligated to you and there does exist a bond of friendship contracted between you, and men are never so dishonorable that they will destroy you and make so great a display of ingratitude. Moreover, victories are never so complete that the victor does not have to have some hesitations, especially with regard to justice. But if the one to whom you adhere loses, you will be taken in by him, and while he can, he will aid you, and you will become the ally of one whose fortune may rise again.

In the second case, when those who fight one another are such that you do not have to fear the one who wins, taking sides is still so much more prudent. For you go to defeat one with the help of another who ought to have saved him if he had been wise, since if he wins, he remains at your discretion, and with your help, it is impossible that he should fail to win.

And here it should be noted that a prince must never ally himself with one more powerful than himself in order to attack someone else, unless necessity compels it, as was said above, for if he wins, you remain his prisoner, and princes must avoid as much as possible being at the discretion of others. The Venetians allied themselves with France against the duke of Milan, and they could have avoided making that alliance, which resulted in their ruin.[5] But when one cannot avoid it, as was the case with the Florentines when the pope and Spain took their armies to attack Lombardy, then the prince must join in, for the reasons stated above. Nor should any state ever believe that it can always choose safe courses. Rather, let it think that it has to take only dubious ones, for this is to be found in the nature of things: that one never strives to avoid one difficulty without running into another; but prudence consists in knowing how to recognize the difficulties and choosing the least bad one as good.

A prince must also show himself a lover of virtue [*virtù*], welcoming able [*virtuosi*] men and honoring those who excel in each art. Moreover, he must encourage his citizens quietly to practice their trades, whether in commerce, or agriculture, or any other occupation that men have, in such a way that this man is not afraid to augment his possessions for fear that they might be taken from him, nor that man to start a commercial enterprise for fear of taxes. On the contrary, he must prepare prizes for whoever wants to do these things and for whoever thinks in any way about improving his city or his state. Besides this, he must, at appropriate times during the year, keep the people occupied with festivals and spectacles, and as every city is divided into guilds or clans, he must take account of those groups, meet with them from time to time, and give them examples of his humanity and magnificence, always preserving unshaken, however, the majesty of his position, for this should never fail in any way whatsoever.

Notes to Chapter 21

1. Ferdinand's armies drove the Moors from Spain in 1492 with the capture of their last stronghold in Granada. He was a "new prince" in the sense that he acquired Castile through marriage and ruled it, as well as Aragon, from 1474 to 1504. Since Castile actually belonged to his wife Isabella, it is not surprising that he chose to distract the barons of that kingdom with foreign wars.

2. The Marranos were Jews or Moors who had converted to Christianity but were distrusted by the Spaniards; using religion as a pretext, Ferdinand drove them out of Spain in 1502. Machiavelli's comment on this event as something "pitiful" and "rare" suggests his mixed feelings about it, despite his recognition that such things contributed to the prince's reputation. In the next few sentences, he notes how Ferdinand took the war against the Moors to Africa in 1509; how he had earlier captured Sicily from the French in 1496 and the entire Kingdom of Naples from them in 1504; and how he drove them from Italy between 1511 and 1513. Finally, he notes how Ferdinand attacked France in 1512, obtaining control of Navarre by 1515.

3. Bernabò, or Barnabò, Visconti (1323–1385) was duke of Milan from 1354 until 1385, when he was killed by his nephew Gian Galeazzo, with whom he had ruled jointly. Like his entire family, he was famous for the ingenious cruelty of his punishments.

4. Antiochus III, also known as "the Great" (223–187 B.C.E.), was the king of Syria and was allied to the city-states of northern and central Greece that made up the Aetolian League. The Achaeans were also a confederacy of Greek city-states. The Romans defeated the Achaeans in 197 and the Aetolians, along with Antiochus, in 190. The episode Machiavelli is about to recount can be found in Livy, *History of Rome*, 35.48–49. The quotation he cites is from 35.49 and is slightly inaccurate.

5. They did this in 1499 when Louis XII drove Ludovico Sforza from Milan. In the next sentence, Machiavelli indirectly refers to the fact that Florence maintained its alliance with France in 1512, when Julius II and Ferdinand

of Aragon combined to drive the French out of Italy, one result of which was the destruction of the Florentine Republic. This led to the restoration of the Medici to political power, and it marked the beginning of Machiavelli's own exile from the city.

Chapter 22

On Those Whom Princes Have as Secretaries

THE CHOOSING OF MINISTERS[1] is a matter of no little importance for a prince: they are either good, or not, depending on the prudence of the prince. The first conjecture that one makes of a ruler's intelligence comes from seeing the men he has about him, and when they are capable and loyal, one may always consider him wise because he knew how to recognize their ability and keep them loyal. But when they are otherwise, one may always make a negative judgment of him because the first mistake one makes is made in the choice of ministers.

There was no one who knew Messer Antonio da Venafro, the minister of Pandolfo Petrucci, prince of Siena, who did not judge Pandolfo to be a very worthy man for having him as his minister.[2] And there are three kinds of brains: the one understands things on its own; the other discerns that which others understand; the third understands neither by itself nor through others. That first kind is most excellent, the second excellent, the third useless. Therefore, it necessarily had to be the case that, if Pandolfo was not in the first group, he was in the second. For whenever someone has enough judgment to recognize the good or evil that a person does or says, even if he lacks imaginative power, he will still recognize the bad deeds as well as the good ones of his minister, and he will extol the latter and correct the others; nor can the minister hope to deceive him, and he will therefore be on his best behavior.

But as to how a prince may know his minister, there is this method which never fails. When you see that your minister thinks more of himself than of you, and that in all his actions he pursues his own self-interest, a man such as that will never be a good minister, nor will you ever be able to trust yourself to him. For the man who has the state of another in his hands must never think of himself but always of his prince and must never think about anything except what concerns his prince. And on the other side, the prince must think about how to keep his minister good, honoring him, enriching him, making him feel a sense of obligation, sharing honors and responsibilities with him, so that the minister recognizes that he cannot survive without the prince, and so that his many honors do not make him desire yet more honors, his great riches do not make him desire yet more riches, and his many responsibilities make him fear changes. When, therefore, ministers and princes, with regard to the relationship between them, are made thus, they can have confidence in one another, and when it is otherwise, the outcome will always be harmful for one or the other.

Notes to Chapter 22

1. Machiavelli consistently speaks of the prince's "minister" (*ministro*) in this chapter, rather than his "secretary," although the Latin title of the chapter refers directly to the latter. There Machiavelli's word for "secretaries" is the late Latin phrase *a secretis* (literally, "from or by the secrets"), a phrase which underscores the fact that a secretary was supposedly one who was the keeper of his employer's secrets. From the title to the chapter and from what Machiavelli says in it about the activities of the "minister," it should be clear that by this word he means something like "confidential adviser." In various writings, Machiavelli identified himself as a "secretary."

2. Antonio Giordani da Venafro (1459–1530), a professor in the Studio of Siena, was Pandolfo Petrucci's counselor and widely recognized for his knowledge of the law and his eloquence. The following passage in Machiavelli's chapter about the three types of brains comes from Livy, *History of Rome*, 22.29.

Chapter 23

How Flatterers Are to Be Avoided

I DO NOT WANT to leave out an important subject and an error from which princes have difficulty defending themselves unless they are very prudent and have good judgment, and these are the flatterers of which courts are full. Because men are so pleased with their own affairs, deceiving themselves about them, they defend themselves from this plague with difficulty. But wishing to defend themselves against it, they run the risk of becoming contemptible, for there is no other way to guard oneself against flattery than by making men understand that they will not offend you by telling you the truth, but when every person can tell you the truth, you lose respect. Therefore, a prudent prince must hold to a third course by choosing wise men for his government and giving them alone complete liberty to speak the truth to him, and only of those things that he asks about and of nothing else. But he must ask them about everything and hear their opinions; afterwards, he should deliberate by himself on his own; and with these counsels and with each of these men he should comport himself in such a way that everyone recognizes that the more freely they speak, the more acceptable they will be to him. Aside from these men, he should not desire to hear anyone, should carry out what he has deliberated on, and should be steady in his deliberations. Whoever acts otherwise either throws himself down, exposed to the flatterers, or he changes his mind as often as opinions vary, with the result that he gets little respect.

In this connection I want to adduce a modern example. Father Luca, a servant of Maximilian, the present emperor, speaking of his majesty, said that the emperor never took counsel with anyone, and never did anything in his own way, which arose from his following a method contrary to the one mentioned above.[1] For the emperor is a secretive man, does not communicate his designs to anyone, and does not take advice about them; but when people start to notice and understand those as they are being put into effect, then those whom the emperor has about him begin to criticize them, and he, easily swayed, is diverted from them. As a result of this, what he does one day, he undoes the next, and no one ever understands what he wants or what he plans to do, and one cannot rely on his deliberations.

A prince, therefore, must always take counsel, but when he wants to, not when others want to; on the contrary, he must discourage anyone from advising him on any matter unless he asks him about it. But he must certainly be a great asker of questions, and then, a patient hearer of the truth concerning the things he has asked about; indeed, when he understands that someone, for whatever scruple, is not telling him the truth, he should become angry. And although many think that any prince who creates the impression of being prudent is so reputed not because of his nature, but because of the good counselors he has around him, without a doubt they deceive themselves. For this is a general rule which never fails: a prince who is not wise in his own right cannot be well advised, unless by chance he has put himself entirely in the hands of one single person who, governing him in everything, was a very prudent man. In this case he might do well, but he would not last long, for that governor would in a short time take his state away from him. But by getting counsel from more than one person, a prince who is not wise will never get unanimous advice, nor will he be able to put it all together by himself; among his counselors, each one will think of his own interests, nor will the prince know how either to correct or to understand them. And one cannot find counselors who are otherwise, for men will always turn out badly for you unless by some necessity they are made good. Therefore, to conclude: good counsel, from whomever it may come, must necessarily arise from the prudence of the prince, and not the prince's prudence from good counsel.

Note to Chapter 23

1. Father Luca was Luca Rainaldi, a bishop, counselor, and ambassador who served Maximilian I of Austria, the Holy Roman Emperor. Machiavelli met him during a diplomatic mission to Maximilian in 1507 and 1508.

Chapter 24

Why the Princes of Italy Have Lost Their States

THE THINGS WRITTEN ABOVE, if prudently observed, make a new prince seem an old one and render him immediately more secure and unshakable in his state than if he had been in it a long time. For the actions of a new prince are watched much more than those of an hereditary one, and when they are recognized as virtuous [*virtuose*], they attract men much more and bind them much more to him than ancient blood would do. For men are much more taken by present matters than by past ones, and when they find things good in the present, they enjoy them and seek nothing more; on the contrary, they will seek out every way possible to defend him as long as the prince himself does not fail in other things. And so he will have the double glory of having established a new principality and adorned it and strengthened it with good laws, good arms, good friends, and good examples, just as that other man will be doubly shamed because, having been born a prince, he lost his state because of insufficient prudence.

And if one considers those rulers in Italy who have lost their states in our times, such as the king of Naples, the duke of Milan, and others, one will find in them, first, a common defect with regard to arms, for the reasons that were discussed at length above.[1] Then it will be seen that some of them either had the people as their enemy, or if they had the people as their friends, they did not know how to secure themselves against the nobility; for without these defects, states are not lost that have enough strength to keep an army in the field. Philip of Macedonia, not the father of Alexander the Great, but the one who was conquered by Titus Quintius, did not have much of a state compared to the grandeur of the Romans and of Greece, which attacked him; nevertheless, because he was a military man who knew how to keep his hold on the people and secure himself against the nobility, he sustained the war against the Romans for many years; and if at the end he lost control of several cities, his kingdom nevertheless remained his.[2]

Therefore, these princes of ours, who have been in their principalities for many years and have then lost them, should not blame Fortune, but rather their own indolence, for, never having thought in quiet times that things might change (which is a common defect in men, not to reckon on storms in a calm), when adverse times arrived, they only thought of fleeing and not of defending themselves, and they hoped that the people, tired of the insolence of the conquerors, would recall them. This policy, when others are lacking, is good, but it is truly bad to have abandoned the other remedies for this one, for one should never wish to fall down in the belief that you will find someone to pick you up. This either does not happen, or, if it does, it does not make for your security, since that defense was cowardly and did not depend on your own forces. And only those defenses are good, are certain, are enduring, that depend on you yourself and your ability [*virtù*].

Notes to Chapter 24

1. The king of Naples is Federico of Aragon; the duke of Milan is Ludovico Sforza, also known as Ludovico il Moro. These figures are discussed in chapter 3.
2. Philip V of Macedonia was defeated by the Romans under Titus Quintius Flaminius at the battle of Cynoscephalae (197 B.C.E.) after more than a dozen years of war. Contrary to what Machiavelli claims here, Philip's final defeat was decisive.

Chapter 25

How Much Fortune Can Do in Human Affairs, and How She Is to Be Resisted

IT IS NOT UNKNOWN to me how many have held and hold the opinion that the things of this world are governed by Fortune and by God in such a way that men with their prudence cannot control them, indeed, that there is no remedy for them whatsoever, and for this reason, they would conclude that one should not sweat much about things, but should let oneself be ruled by chance. This opinion has had more credibility in our times because of the great varying of affairs that has been seen and is seen every day, which goes beyond all human conjecture. When I think about this at times, I am inclined to share this opinion of theirs to a certain extent. Nevertheless, so that our free will may not be extinguished, I think it may be true that Fortune is the arbiter of half of our actions, but that she still leaves the other half of them, more or less, to be governed by us. And I compare her to one of these destructive rivers that, when they are raging, flood the plains, destroy trees and buildings, take up earth from this side and place it on the other; everyone flies before them, everyone yields to their onslaught without being able to oppose them in any way. And although this is how they are, it does not follow, therefore, that men, when times are quiet, cannot make provision against them with dikes and embankments, so that when they rise again, either they would go into a canal, or their impetus would not be so wild or so destructive. It happens similarly with Fortune: she shows her power where there is no force [*virtù*] organized to resist her and directs her onslaught there, where she knows that no embankments and dikes have been made to hold her. And if you consider Italy, which is the locus of these changes, and the one who has set them in motion, you will see that it is a countryside without embankments and without any dikes at all; for if it had been defended by the necessary valor [*virtù*], as Germany,

Spain, and France are, this flood would not have caused the great changes that it has, or it would not have come upon us at all. And let this be enough to have said in general about opposing Fortune.

But limiting myself more to particulars, I say that one sees this prince prosperous today and ruined tomorrow without having seen him change his nature or any one of his traits. I believe this arises, first, from the causes that have already been discussed at length; that is, that a prince who relies entirely on Fortune comes to ruin as she changes. I also believe that the man who adapts his mode of proceeding to the nature of the times will prosper, and similarly, that the man whose mode of proceeding is not in accord with the times will not prosper. For one sees that in those affairs which lead men to the end which each one has in view, that is, to glory and riches, they get there in various ways: one with caution, the other with impetuousness; one through violence, the other with cunning; one through patience, the other with its opposite; and each using these diverse means can reach his goal. One also sees that of two cautious men, one succeeds with his designs, the other does not, and in the same way, two men succeed equally with two different procedures, one by being cautious and the other impetuous—this arises from nothing other than the nature of the times, which are, or are not, in conformity with their course of action. From this results that which I have said: that two men, operating differently, obtain the same outcome; and of two men, operating in the same way, one arrives at his goal, and the other does not. On this also depends the variation in what is considered good, for if one governs himself with caution and patience, and if the times and circumstances turn in such a way that his behavior is good, he will prosper, but if the times and circumstances change, he will be ruined, because he does not change his mode of proceeding. Nor can any man be found who is so prudent that he knows how to adapt himself to this, both because he cannot deviate from that to which his nature inclines him, and also because, when he has always prospered by walking in one path, he cannot be persuaded to depart from it. And therefore, the cautious man, when it is time to act impetuously, does not know how to do it, so that he is ruined, for if he changed his nature with the times and circumstances, Fortune would not change.

Pope Julius II acted impetuously in everything he did, and he found the times and circumstances so in conformity with that mode of proceeding of his, that he always achieved a happy outcome. Consider the first campaign he made against Bologna while Messer Giovanni Bentivogli was still living.[1] The Venetians were not pleased with it, nor was the king of Spain; with France, he was in the midst of negotiations about the campaign; and nevertheless, because of his ferocity and impetuosity, he personally set the expedition in motion. This move caused both Spain and the Venetians to stop and hesitate, the latter because of fear and the other because of the desire he had to regain the entire kingdom of Naples; and on the other hand, Julius dragged the king of France along behind him, because, seeing the pope make this move and desiring to make him his ally in order to put down the Venetians, the king felt that he could not refuse the pope troops without obviously harming him.[2] Thus, with his impetuous move Julius achieved that which no other pontiff would have achieved with the utmost human prudence, because, if he had waited until the negotiations were concluded and everything was settled in order to depart from Rome, as any other pontiff would have done, he would never have succeeded, for the king of France would have had a thousand excuses, and the others would have stirred up a thousand fears. I wish to omit the pope's other actions, which were all similar and which all turned out well for him; and the shortness of his life did not allow him to experience the contrary, for if times had come in which it was necessary to proceed with caution, his ruin would have resulted, for he would never have deviated from these methods to which his nature inclined him.

I conclude, therefore, that since Fortune changes and men remain set in their ways, they will prosper as long as the two are in accord with one another, but they will not prosper, when the two are not in accord. I certainly think this: that it is better to be impetuous than cautious, for Fortune is a woman, and it is necessary, if you wish to keep her down, to beat her and knock her about. And one sees that she lets herself be conquered by men of this sort more than by those who proceed coldly. And therefore, like a woman, she is always the friend of the young, because they are less cautious, fiercer, and command her with more audacity.

Notes to Chapter 25

1. Julius II attacked Perugia and Bologna in 1506, conquering the first city on September 13 and the second on November 11. Giovanni Bentivogli (1438–1508) ruled Bologna from 1462 until Julius drove him out in 1506; he died two years later in exile.
2. Ferdinand II of Aragon had ceded several ports in Puglia to the Venetians in 1494; he regained them in 1508.

Chapter 26

An Exhortation to Seize Italy and Liberate Her from the Barbarians

HAVING CONSIDERED, THEREFORE, all the things discussed above, and meditating on whether in Italy at present the times were ripe to honor a new prince, and if there were material which might give a prudent and capable [*virtuoso*] man an opportunity to introduce a form into her that would confer honor on himself and be good for all her people, I think that so many things are coming together to benefit a new prince that I do not know what time was ever more suitable for him. And if, as I said, it was necessary, in order to see the ability [*virtù*] of Moses, that the people of Israel should be slaves in Egypt, and to recognize the greatness of spirit of Cyrus, that the Persians should be oppressed by the Medes, and to recognize the excellence of Theseus, that the Athenians should be dispersed; so, at the present, in order to recognize the ability [*virtù*] of an Italian spirit, it has been necessary that Italy should be reduced to its present condition, and that she should be more enslaved than the Hebrews, more servile than the Persians, and more dispersed than the Athenians, without a head, without order, beaten, despoiled, torn apart, overrun, and having endured every sort of disaster.[1]

And although before now a glimmer of light may have shown itself in someone so that it was possible to think that he was ordained by God for her redemption, nevertheless, it has been seen since then how, at the height of his career, he was cast down by Fortune.[2] Thus, left almost lifeless, she is waiting for the one who can heal her wounds and put a stop to the plundering of Lombardy, to the rapacious taxation of the Kingdom of Naples and of Tuscany, and cure her of those wounds which have been long festering. Behold how she prays to God to send someone to redeem her from these barbarous cruelties and insolence. Behold, as well, how she is ready and willing to follow any banner, provided that there is someone to pick it up. Nor is there anyone in sight at present in whom she can place more hope than in your illustrious house, which, with its fortune and ability [*virtù*], favored by God and the Church, of which it is now the Prince, could make itself the head of this redemption.[3] This will not be very difficult for you if you call up before you the actions and lives of those men named above. And although those men were rare and marvelous, nonetheless, they were men, and each of them had less of an opportunity than the present one, for their enterprise was not more just than this one, nor easier, nor was God more a friend to them than to you. The justice here is great: "that war is just for those people for whom it is necessary, and those arms are pious where there is no hope except in arms."[4] Here there is the greatest willingness, nor can there be great difficulty where there is great willingness, provided that your house adopts the arrangements made by those whom I have proposed for you as a model. Besides this, extraordinary things have been seen here brought about by God: the sea has been opened; a cloud has shown you the road; the rock has poured out water; here it has rained manna; everything has come together for your greatness.[5] The remainder you must do yourself. God does not wish to do everything in order not to deprive us of our free will and of the portion of the glory that belongs to us.

And it is no marvel that none of the Italians mentioned before have been able to do that which it is hoped your illustrious house may do, and if in so many revolutions in Italy and so many military campaigns, it always seems that military ability [*virtù*] is extinguished in her, this has happened because her ancient institutions were not good, and there has been no one who knew how to find out new ones. And nothing confers so much honor on a new man on the rise as do the new laws and the new institutions that he has discovered. These things, when they have good foundations and have greatness in them, make him revered and marveled at, and in Italy there is no lack of matter into which any kind of form can be introduced.[6] Here there is great ability [*virtù*] in the members, were it not for the lack of it in her heads. In duels and in combats involving just a few men, look at how superior the Italians are in strength, in dexterity, in ingenuity. But when it comes to armies, those things are not to be seen. And all of this derives from the weakness of their heads, for those who have the know-how are not obeyed, and with everyone thinking that he knows how, there has not been anyone up to now who, through his ability [*virtù*] and fortune, has been able to make the others yield precedence to him. Hence, it has come about that in so much time, in so many wars waged during the last twenty years, whenever there has been an entirely Italian army, it has always made a bad showing. The first witness to this is Taro, then Alessandria, Capua, Genoa, Vailà, Bologna, Mestre.[7]

If your illustrious house, therefore, wishes to follow those excellent men who redeemed their native lands, it is necessary before all else, as the true foundation of every undertaking, to provide yourself with your own citizen army, for you cannot have more loyal, or truer, or better soldiers. And although each one of them may be good, all together they will become better when they see themselves commanded by their prince and honored and provided for by him. It is necessary, therefore, to prepare oneself with such arms in order to be able to defend oneself from foreigners with Italian prowess [*virtù*]. And although the Swiss and Spanish infantry are deemed terrifying, nonetheless in both there is a defect, so that a third kind of force could not only oppose them, but be confident of overcoming them. For the Spaniards cannot withstand cavalry, and the Swiss have to fear the infantry they encounter in combat who are as resolute as they are. Whence it has been seen—and experience will show—that the Spaniards cannot withstand the French cavalry, and the Swiss can be defeated by Spanish infantry. And although we have not had a complete experience of the latter, still, we have had a hint of it in the battle of Ravenna, when the Spanish infantry confronted the German battalions, who make use of the same formation as the Swiss. There, the Spanish, using their bodily agility and aided by their spiked bucklers, entered between and under the Germans' pikes and were in a safe position to attack them without the Germans being able to find a remedy for it; and if it had not been for the cavalry that charged them, the Spaniards would have annihilated them.[8] Knowing, therefore, the defects of both of these kinds of infantry, a new kind can be organized that will resist cavalry and have no fear of foot soldiers; this will depend on the kind of arms being used and on a change in the system. And these are among the things which, when newly instituted, give reputation and greatness to a new prince.

This opportunity must not, therefore, be allowed to pass, so that Italy, after so much time, may see her liberator. I cannot express with what love he would be received in all those provinces which have suffered because of these foreign inundations, with what thirst for vengeance, with what steadfast loyalty, with what piety, with what tears. What doors would be closed against him? What people would refuse him obedience? What envy would oppose him? What Italian would refuse him homage? To everyone this barbarian domination stinks. May your illustrious house therefore take up the task with that courage and that hope with which just enterprises are taken up, so that under its banner this country may be ennobled, and under its auspices that which Petrarch said may prove true:

> Virtù contro a furore
> prenderà l'arme; e fia el combatter corto:
> ché l'antico valore
> nelli italici cor non è ancor morto.[9]

Notes to Chapter 26

1. See chapter 6.
2. The "someone" in question here is Cesare Borgia.
3. The cardinal Giovanni de' Medici was made Pope Leo X in 1513.
4. Machiavelli is quoting the speech of the Roman leader Gaius Pontius to the Samnites as given in Livy, *History of Rome*, 9.1.
5. All of these "extraordinary things" are the miracles God performed for the Hebrews when they were marching through the wilderness; see the Bible, Exodus 14.21, 13.21–22, 16.13–15, and 17.5–6. It is not clear what contemporary events Machiavelli was thinking of here; he may be speaking ironically.
6. Machiavelli once again uses the Scholastic distinction between matter and form; see chapter 6, note 2. In the next sentence he employs metaphors which imply that the state is like a human body—that is, a body politic.
7. Machiavelli's "twenty years" essentially start with the invasion of Charles VIII in 1494. He then ticks off the series of major Italian defeats during that period, starting with the one at Fornovo on the Taro in 1495, when the army of Francesco Gonzaga met that of Charles in retreat; although the former won the field, Charles really won in that he was able to continue

to withdraw. Alessandria was conquered by the French in 1499, Capua was sacked by them in 1501, and Genoa surrendered to them in 1507. At the battle of Vailà, or Agnadello, in 1509, the Venetians were beaten by the French in league with the Papacy and lost all their holdings on the mainland as a result. Bologna was abandoned to the French by the Holy League in 1511. And Mestre was burned by the Spaniards in 1513, just before the battle of La Motta with the French.

8. The battle of Ravenna was fought on April 11, 1512, between the Spanish and the French; it was the prelude to the decisive expulsion of the French from Italy in the next year.

9. This excerpt come from Petrarch's *canzone* "Italia mia" (*Canzoniere*, 128.93–96): "Valor [*virtù*] against furor / will take up arms; and the combat will be short, / for ancient valor / in Italian hearts is not yet dead."

The Life of Castruccio Castracani of Lucca

WRITTEN BY NICCOLÒ
MACHIAVELLI AND SENT TO
HIS DEAREST FRIENDS,
ZANOBI BUONDELMONTI
AND LUIGI ALAMANNI[1]

FOR THOSE WHO THINK about it, my dearest Zanobi and Luigi, it seems a marvelous fact that all, or the majority, of those who have accomplished truly great things in this world and have been outstanding among the men of their age, have had low and obscure origins and births or have been afflicted by Fortune beyond all measure. For either all of them have been exposed to wild beasts or have had fathers so base that, ashamed of them, they made themselves into sons of Jove or of some other god. Since many of them are known to everyone, it would be tiresome and hardly acceptable to the reader to repeat who they were; therefore, I omit them as superfluous.[2] I certainly believe that this derives from the fact that Fortune, wishing to demonstrate to the world that she, and not prudence, is the one who makes men great, starts showing her power at a time when prudence cannot have any part in the matter, but rather, everything has to be acknowledged as coming from her.[3]

Castruccio Castracani of Lucca was, then, one of those who, considering the times in which he lived and the city in which he was born, did very great things, and like the others, did not have a happier or more renowned birth, as will be seen in the narration of the course of his life. Since I feel I have found many things in his life that are most exemplary concerning both ability [virtù] and Fortune, I thought I would recall it to the memory of men. And I decided to address it to you, as to those who, more than other men whom I know, delight in noble [virtuosi] deeds.

I say, then, that the Castracani family is numbered among the noble families of the city of Lucca, although in these times, in keeping with the law of all earthly things, it has disappeared. Into it was born one Antonio, who, after having become a priest, served as the canon of St. Michael's of Lucca and as a sign of honor was called Messer Antonio.[4] He had no family other than a sister, whom he married to Buonaccorso Cennami, but after Buonaccorso died and she was left a widow, she returned to stay with her brother, with the intention of never marrying again.

Behind the house in which he lived, Messer Antonio had a vineyard, which one could enter from many directions and without much difficulty since it was bordered by a number of vegetable gardens. It happened one morning, a little after sunrise, when Madonna Dianora (for that was the name of Messer Antonio's sister) was walking through the vineyard, picking, as is the custom of women, certain herbs in order to make certain seasonings of hers, that she heard a rustling among the foliage under a vine, and turning her eyes toward it, heard a sound like weeping. Moving toward it, she discovered the hands and face of a baby boy who, wrapped up in the leaves, seemed to ask her for help. As a result, partly amazed, partly frightened, full of compassion and wonder, she picked him up, and having carried him home and washed him and wrapped him up in white swaddling bands, according to the custom, she presented him to Messer Antonio upon his return home. Hearing what had happened and seeing the boy, he was no less filled with wonder and pity than was the woman, and after considering between themselves what course of action they ought to take, they decided to raise him, since he was a priest and she did not have children. Having taken a nurse into the house, then, they took care of him with the same love as if he were their own son, and having had him baptized, they gave him the name of Castruccio in memory of their father.

Castruccio's grace grew with the years,[5] and in everything he showed intelligence and prudence, and depending on his age, he quickly learned those things to which he was directed by Messer Antonio. Intending to make him a priest and eventually to relinquish his canonry and other benefices to him, Antonio taught him accordingly. But he had come upon a subject totally opposed to the priestly temper, for as soon as Castruccio reached the age of fourteen and began to feel a bit of courage in confronting Messer Antonio, and not to fear Madonna Dianora at all, he laid ecclesiastical books aside and began to practice with arms, nor did he take delight in anything other than in handling them or in running, jumping, wrestling, and similar sports with others who were his peers, in which he showed the greatest ability [*virtù*] of mind and body, and far surpassed all others of his age. And if he sometimes did read, no reading pleased him other than that which spoke of war or of things done by the greatest men. Because of this, Messer Antonio suffered inestimable sorrow.

There was in the city of Lucca a gentleman of the Guinigi family named Messer Francesco, who in riches and grace and strength [*virtù*] far exceeded all the other Lucchesi.[6] His profession was war, and he had long fought under the Visconti of Milan, and since he was a Ghibelline, he was esteemed above all the others who belonged to that party in Lucca.[7] Since he was then in Lucca and met every morning and evening with the other citizens under the loggia of the Podestà, which is at the head of the Piazza di San Michele, the main square of Lucca, he often saw Castruccio with the other boys of the neighborhood engaging in those exercises which I spoke of above; and since it seemed to Messer Francesco that, in addition to surpassing them, Castruccio had a kingly authority over them, and that they, in a certain way, loved and revered him, he became very eager to know who he was. Being informed about him by the bystanders, Messer Francesco was inflamed with even greater desire to have him in his service. And one day, having summoned the boy, he asked him where he would rather be, in the house of a gentleman, who would teach him to ride and handle arms, or in the house of a priest, where he would never hear anything other than holy offices and masses. Messer Francesco noticed how happy Castruccio became when he heard horses and arms mentioned, but how he remained reticent, slightly embarrassed, until he was encouraged by Messer Francesco to speak, when he replied that if his guardian was agreeable, nothing would give him greater pleasure than to leave priestly studies behind and to take up those of a soldier. The reply pleased Messer Francesco greatly, and in a very few days, he arranged things so that Messer Antonio gave Castruccio to him. He was impelled to do this more by the boy's nature than by anything else, since he judged that he could not keep him for long as he was.

Once Castruccio had passed thus from the house of Messer Antonio Castracani, the canon, into the house of Messer Francesco Guinigi, the condottiere, it is extraordinary to think in how very little time he came to master all those skills [virtù] and reflexes that are required in a true gentleman. First of all, he became an excellent rider, managing all the wildest horses with the greatest dexterity, and in jousts and tournaments, although quite young, he was worthier of notice than anyone else, for in every feat, whether involving strength or dexterity, no man was found to surpass him. To this were added his manners, in which was seen an incredible modesty, for he was never seen to do a deed or heard to speak a word that was displeasing; and he was respectful to his elders, modest with his equals, and pleasant to his inferiors. These things made him loved not only by the entire Guinigi family, but by the entire city of Lucca.

It happened in those times, when Castruccio had already reached the age of eighteen, that the Ghibellines were driven out of Pavia by the Guelfs, and Messer Francesco Guinigi was sent by the Visconti of Milan to their aid.[8] With him went Castruccio, who was in charge of his whole company. In this expedition, Castruccio showed so many signs of his prudence and courage that no one who took part in that campaign acquired such prestige with everyone as he did, and his name became great and honored not merely in Pavia, but in all Lombardy.

After he returned to Lucca, with much more prestige than he had had at his departure, Castruccio did not fail to make friends for himself as much as it was possible for him to do so, employing all the methods that are necessary to win men over. But Messer Francesco Guinigi, dying and leaving behind his thirteen-year-old son, named Pagolo, made Castruccio the tutor and guardian of his property, having sent for him before he died and begged him to agree to bring up his son with the same devotion with which Castruccio himself had been brought up, and to pay the son those debts of gratitude which he had been unable to pay the father. Messer Francesco thus having died, Castruccio served as the guardian and tutor of Pagolo, and grew so much in reputation and power that the favor he was accustomed to enjoying in Lucca changed into envy, so much so that many slandered him as a suspicious man who had the heart of a tyrant. Among these the chief was Messer Giorgio degli Opizi, head of the Guelf party. Since he was hoping, after the death of Messer Francesco, to become prince of Lucca, he felt that Castruccio, who had retained control through the favor his meritorious qualities obtained for him, had taken away his opportunity, and for this reason he went about spreading rumors to deprive Castruccio of favor. The latter first felt anger at this, to which apprehension was soon added, since he thought that Messer Giorgio would never rest until he had brought him into disfavor with the vicar of king Robert of Naples, who would have him chased out of Lucca.[9]

The lord of Pisa at that time was Uguccione della Faggiuola of Arezzo, who had first been elected by the Pisans as their captain and had then made himself their ruler.[10] In Uguccione's entourage there were several exiles from Lucca of the Ghibelline party, whom Castruccio was plotting to bring back with Uguccione's help; and he also communicated his plan to his friends inside the city who could not stand the power of the Opizi. Having thus arranged what they were supposed to do, Castruccio cautiously fortified the Onesti tower and filled it with munitions and an abundance of provisions, so that if it were necessary, he could hold out in it for several days. And when the night came that had been agreed on with Uguccione, who had descended with many troops into the plain between the mountains and Lucca, Castruccio gave him the signal, and as soon as he saw it, Uguccione advanced on Saint Peter's Gate and set fire to its outer wall. On the other side, Castruccio raised the cry calling the people to arms and forced the gate from the inside, so that, once Uguccione and his troops had entered, they overran the city and killed Messer Giorgio along with all the members of his family and many of his friends and partisans, and drove out the governor.[11] The city's government was reorganized as it pleased Uguccione, with the greatest damage to the place, because it is reported that more than a hundred families were then driven out of Lucca. Of those who fled, one part went to Florence, another to Pistoia; these cities were ruled by the Guelf party and therefore came to be the enemies of Uguccione and the people of Lucca.

Since it seemed to the Florentines and the other Guelfs that the Ghibelline party had gained too much power in Tuscany, they agreed to restore the exiled Lucchesi, and having put together a huge army, they came into Val di Nievole and occupied Montecatini; from there they laid siege to Montecarlo in order to have free passage to Lucca.[12] Meanwhile, Uguccione, having assembled a great many Pisans and Lucchesi, and in addition many German cavalry which he had brought from Lombardy, advanced toward the camp of the Florentines, who, hearing that the enemy were coming, departed from Montecarlo and placed themselves between Montecatini and Pescia, whereas Uguccione situated himself below Montecarlo, two miles away from the enemy. There for several days there were light skirmishes between the cavalry of the two armies, because, Uguccione having become ill, the Pisans and the Lucchesi avoided fighting a battle with the enemy.

But as Uguccione's illness became worse, he retired to Montecarlo in order to get treatment and left Castruccio in charge of the army. This caused the downfall of the Guelfs, for they took heart, since it seemed to them that the enemy's army was left without a leader. Castruccio recognized this and waited for several days in order to strengthen this opinion of theirs, making a show of being afraid by not letting anyone leave the fortifications of their camp. On the other side, the Guelfs, the more they saw this fear, the more arrogant they became, and every day they would present themselves, drawn up in battle formation, before Castruccio's army. The latter, thinking he had fostered enough courage in them and having understood their battle formation, decided to fight the battle with them, but first he made a speech to stiffen the resolve of his soldiers and showed them that victory was certain if they were willing to obey his orders.

Castruccio had seen how the enemy had put all their strongest forces in the center of their formation and the weaker troops on the flanks; consequently, he did the contrary, putting the bravest men on the flanks of his army and those of less value in the middle.[13] He left the camp in this formation, and as soon as he came in sight of the enemy army, which arrogantly, as usual, was coming to confront him, he ordered the squadrons in the middle to advance slowly and those on the flanks to move rapidly. In this way, when he joined battle with the enemy, only the flanks of the two armies fought, and the squadrons in the middle remained inactive because Castruccio's troops there had remained so far behind that those of the enemy did not make contact with them. Thus, the strongest of Castruccio's troops were fighting with the weakest of the enemy, and their strongest were standing still, without being able to do harm to those in front of them or to give any aid to their comrades. Hence, without much difficulty, the enemy on both flanks were put to flight, and those in the middle, seeing themselves stripped of their own troops on their flanks, took to flight without having been able to display any of their prowess [virtù]. Great were the rout and the slaughter, for better than ten thousand men were killed there, together with many captains and great knights of the Guelf party from all over Tuscany, and in addition, many princes who had come to their aid, such as Piero, the brother of King Robert, and Carlo, his nephew, and Filippo, lord of Taranto. And on Castruccio's side, the losses

did not reach three hundred, among whom died Francesco, Uguccione's son, an eager young man who was killed in the first attack.

This rout made Castruccio's name truly great, to such an extent
that Uguccione became so jealous and suspicious of his position
that he could never think of anything except how he could eliminate
him, since it seemed to him that the victory had not given him
power, but had taken it away. And while he went on thinking such
thoughts, waiting for a plausible excuse to put them into effect, it
happened that Pier Agnolo Micheli, a man of worth and highly
regarded, was killed in Lucca, and his killer took refuge in Castruccio's house, where the officers of the chief of police, going to arrest
him, were repulsed by Castruccio, so that by means of his help the
murderer saved himself. Hearing of this and believing he had just
cause to punish him, Uguccione, who was then at Pisa, called his
son Neri, to whom he had earlier given the rule of Lucca, and ordered him, using the pretense of inviting Castruccio to a banquet,
to arrest him and put him to death. Castruccio, therefore, went to
the ruler's palace with easy confidence, not fearing any harm, and
was first detained for supper by Neri and then arrested. But Neri,
fearing that if he put him to death without any justification, the
people would be angered, kept him alive in order to get better in-
structions from Uguccione about how to proceed. The latter, con-
demning his son's tardiness and cowardice, left Pisa with four
hundred cavalry to go to Lucca in order to finish things off. He had
yet not reached Bagni[14] when the Pisans took up arms and killed
Uguccione's lieutenant and the other members of his household
who had remained in Pisa, and made Count Gaddo della Gherardesca their ruler. Before he arrived in Lucca, Uguccione heard what
had happened in Pisa, but he thought that he should not go back,
lest the Lucchesi, after the example of the Pisans, should also close
their gates on him. But the Lucchesi, when they heard of the events
in Pisa, seized the opportunity to liberate Castruccio, despite the
fact that Uguccione had arrived in Lucca. First, they began in groups
to speak disrespectfully around the public squares, then to make
a disturbance, and after that to take up arms, demanding that
Castruccio be set free, so that Uguccione, for fear of worse, took
him out of prison. In response, Castruccio quickly gathered his
friends and, with the help of the people, attacked Uguccione. When

Uguccione saw that he had no remedy for this, he fled with his friends and went to Lombardy to seek service with the lords of the della Scala family, where he died in poverty.[15]

From being a prisoner, Castruccio had become, in effect, the prince of Lucca, and with the help of his friends and the new favor of the people, he managed to have himself made captain of their forces for a year.[16] Having obtained this, in order to make a reputation for himself in war, he set out to regain for the Lucchesi many towns that had rebelled after the departure of Uguccione. And so, with the support of the Pisans, with whom he was allied, he went to besiege Serezana, and in order to assault it, he built a fortress above it—which, subsequently surrounded by walls by the Florentines, is today called Serezanello—and in the space of two months he took the town.[17] Then, thanks to the reputation he gained there, he seized Massa, Carrara, and Lavenza, and in a very short time occupied all of Lunigiana. In order to close the pass that goes from Lombardy to Lunigiana, he attacked Pontremoli and drove out Messer Anastagio Palavisini, who was its lord. Returning to Lucca after this victory, he was met by all the people. Castruccio felt he should not defer making himself prince, and so, with the help of Pazzino dal Poggio, Pucinello dal Portico, Francesco Boccansacchi, and Cecco Guinigi, men with substantial reputations in Lucca who were bribed by him, he made himself the ruler of the city and by a solemn decree of the people was elected prince.

At this time, Frederick of Bavaria, king of the Romans, had come to Italy to take the crown of the Empire.[18] Castruccio allied himself with him and went to visit him with five hundred cavalry, leaving his lieutenant Pagolo Guinigi in Lucca, to whom, because of the memory of his father, Castruccio showed as much consideration as though Pagolo were his own son. Castruccio was received honorably by Frederick, and having been given many privileges, was made his lieutenant in Tuscany. And because the Pisans had driven out Gadda della Gherardesca and for fear of him had gone to Frederick for help, Frederick made Castruccio ruler of Pisa, and the Pisans, out of fear of the Guelfs, and especially of the Florentines, accepted him.[19]

When Frederick returned to Germany, leaving a governor in Rome, all the Ghibellines of Tuscany and Lombardy, who belonged to the Emperor's party, took refuge with Castruccio, and all of them promised him sovereignty over their states, if by means of his aid they could get back into them again. Among them were Matteo Guidi, Nardo Scolari, Lapo Uberti, Gerozzo Nardi, and Piero Buon-accorsi—all Ghibellines and Florentine exiles. And since by using them as well as his own forces, Castruccio planned to make himself ruler of all Tuscany, Castruccio, in order to enhance his reputation, made an alliance with Matteo Visconti, prince of Milan, and called the entire city and its surrounding countryside to arms.[20] And because Lucca had five gates, he divided its territory into five parts and armed it and assigned them leaders and banners, so that he could put together twenty thousand men in a hurry, without counting those who could come to his aid from Pisa. When he had girded himself thus with these forces and these friends, it happened that Messer Matteo Visconti was attacked by the Guelfs of Piacenza, who had driven out the Ghibellines with the help of the Florentines and of King Robert, who had sent them troops. Hence, Messer Matteo asked Castruccio to attack the Florentines so that they, being obliged to defend their homes, would recall their troops from Lombardy. And so, Castruccio attacked the Valdarno with a great many soldiers and occupied Fucecchio and San Miniato, doing a great deal of damage in the countryside, thus compelling the Florentines to recall their troops.[21] Hardly had they returned to Tuscany when Castruccio himself was obliged by another crisis to return to Lucca.

In that city the Poggio family was powerful because it had not merely given Castruccio prominence, but made him prince, and thinking it had not been rewarded according to its merits, it conspired with other families in Lucca to make the city revolt and drive Castruccio out of it. And seizing the opportunity one morning, they rushed, armed, on the lieutenant whom Castruccio kept there in charge of justice, and killed him. But when they wanted to go on to incite the people to riot, Stefano di Poggio, an aged and peaceful man who had not participated in the conspiracy, came before them and with his authority compelled his family to lay down their arms, offering himself as a mediator between them and Castruccio in order to obtain for them what they desired. They therefore put down their arms, with no greater prudence than when they had taken them up, for Castruccio, hearing the news of what happened in

Lucca, lost no time in coming to Lucca with part of his troops, leaving Pagolo Guinigi behind as leader of the rest. And finding that the tumult had subsided, beyond his expectations, and thinking it would be quite easy to make himself secure there, he stationed his armed partisans in all the strategic places. Stefano di Poggio, believing that Castruccio had to feel in his debt, went to find him and did not beg for himself, because he judged that he had no need to, but for the other members of his family, entreating him to pardon some, making allowances for youth, and to pardon others because of the ancient friendship and obligation he had to their house. To this Castruccio replied graciously and encouraged him to be of good cheer, talking as though it was more pleasing to him to have found the disturbances quelled than he had been angry over their outbreak, and he encouraged Stefano to have them all come to him, saying that he thanked God he had an opportunity to show his clemency and kindness. When they came, then, taking the word of Stefano and Castruccio, they were, together with Stefano, imprisoned and put to death.

The Florentines meanwhile had regained San Miniato, whereupon Castruccio decided to put an end to the war, since it seemed to him that until he had made himself secure in Lucca, he could not go far from home. Having sounded out the Florentines about a truce, he found them readily inclined to one because they too were worn out and desired to put an end to their expenditures. They therefore made a truce for two years and such that each one would keep what it was holding. Freed from war, then, Castruccio, in order to avoid running into the dangers he had run into before, used various pretexts and excuses to eliminate all those in Lucca who through ambition might aspire to princely rule. Nor did he pardon anyone, depriving them of their country, their property, and, for those he could lay his hands on, their life, insisting that he had learned through experience that none of them would be loyal to him. And for his greater security he built a fortress in Lucca, making use of material from the towers of those he had driven out or put to death.

While Castruccio had suspended the war with the Florentines and was fortifying himself in Lucca, he did not fail to do those things he could manage to do, short of open war, to enhance his greatness.

And having a great desire to occupy Pistoia, since it seemed to him that if he obtained the possession of that city, he would have a foothold inside Florence, he gained the friendship of the entire mountain region, and with the factions in Pistoia he conducted himself in such a way that each one trusted him.[22] That city was then divided, as it has always been, into Whites and Blacks. The head of the Whites was Bastiano di Possente; of the Blacks, Jacopo da Gia. Each one had very close dealings with Castruccio, and each one desired to drive out the other, with the result that the two of them, after much mutual suspicion, took up arms. Jacopo fortified himself at the Florentine gate, Bastiano at the Lucchese gate, and since both of them trusted Castruccio more than the Florentines, judging him to be more decisive and readier to go to war, each of them sent to him secretly for help. Castruccio promised it to both of them, saying to Jacopo that he would come in person, and to Bastiano that he would send Pagolo Guinigi, his protégé. Having given them precise meeting times, he sent Pagolo by the Pescia road, while he himself went straight to Pistoia, and at midnight, for so Castruccio and Pagolo had agreed, each one arrived at Pistoia, and both were received as friends. Once they were inside, when it seemed right to Castruccio, he gave the signal to Pagolo, after which one killed Jacopo da Gia and the other Bastiano di Possente, and all their partisans were either captured or killed; and they took possession of Pistoia without further opposition. Having expelled the city council from the palace, Castruccio compelled the people to obey him, canceling many of their old debts and making them many promises, and he did the same for everyone in the surrounding countryside, many of whom had run to see the new prince. Thus, everyone, full of hope and swayed in good measure by his abilities [virtù], calmed down.

At this time it happened that the Roman people began to riot on account of the high cost of living, saying its cause was the absence of the pontiff, who was living in Avignon,[23] and blaming the German rulers, so that every day there were murders and other disorders for which Henry, the emperor's lieutenant, could find no remedy. As a result, Henry became very fearful that the Romans would call in King Robert of Naples and drive him out of Rome and give it back to the pope.[24] Not having any friend closer by to whom he could have recourse than Castruccio, he sent to him, begging him to agree not merely to send help, but to come in person to Rome. Castruccio judged that it was not to be put off, both because he wanted to pay a debt of gratitude to the emperor and because he judged that since the emperor was not in Rome, there was no other remedy for the situation. Therefore, leaving Pagolo Guinigi at Lucca, he set off with six hundred horsemen for Rome, where he was received by Henry with the greatest honor, and in a very short time his presence brought so much prestige to the emperor's party that, without bloodshed or other violence, everything calmed down. By having a large amount of grain brought in by sea from the region of Pisa, Castruccio removed the cause of the turmoil; afterward, partly by admonishing, partly by punishing the chief men in Rome, he brought them willingly back under Henry's rule. Castruccio was made a senator of Rome and given many other honors by the Roman people. This office Castruccio assumed with the greatest pomp and put on a brocaded toga with letters on the front that said, "He is that which God wills"; and behind they said, "He shall be that which God shall will."[25]

Meanwhile, the Florentines, who were angry that Castruccio had made himself master of Pistoia during a period of truce, were thinking about how they could make it rebel, something they considered easy to do because of his absence. Among the Pistoian exiles in Florence were Baldo Cecchi and Jacopo Baldini, both men of authority and ready to take any risk. They plotted with their friends inside the city, so that with the aid of the Florentines they entered Pistoia at night and drove out Castruccio's partisans and officials, killing some of them and restoring liberty to the city.[26] This news greatly annoyed and displeased Castruccio, and taking leave of Henry, by forced marches he came to Lucca with his troops. When they heard of Castruccio's return, the Florentines, thinking that he would not likely stand idly by, decided to anticipate him and to enter the Val di Nievole first with their troops, judging that if they occupied that valley, they were going to cut off the road for him to retake Pistoia, and having put together a huge army of all the friends of the Guelf party, they came into Pistoia's territory. On the other side, Castruccio came out to Montecarlo with his troops, and having learned where the Florentine army was, he decided not to go to meet it on the plain of Pistoia, nor to wait for it on the plain of Pescia, but, if he could do so, to confront it in the pass of Serravalle. He thought that if this plan succeeded, he would carry off a sure victory, for he had learned that the Florentines had assembled thirty thousand men altogether, while he had chosen twelve thousand of his own. And although he trusted in his own industriousness and in the prowess [*virtù*] of his troops, still he feared that if he gave battle in a wide-open space, he would be surrounded by the very large number of his enemies.

Serravalle is a castle town between Pescia and Pistoia, placed on a hill that encloses the Val di Nievole, not in the pass itself, but two bowshots above it. The place where one crosses the pass is more narrow than steep, for it slopes up gently on both sides, but it is so narrow, especially on the top of the hill where the waters divide, that twenty men side by side would fill it up. In this place Castruccio planned to confront the enemy, both because his fewer troops would have an advantage and because he did not want them to discover the enemy before the battle, fearing that they would be dismayed, if they saw the very large number of their opponents. The keeper of the castle of Serravalle was Messer Manfredi, a German by birth, who, before Castruccio became the ruler of Pistoia, had been allowed to stay in that castle town as a place where the Lucchesi and the Pistoians had equal rights of access, nor had anyone had cause to attack him after that, since he promised them all to stay neutral and not to attach himself to either one of them. Thus, for this reason, and because he was in a strong location, he had been allowed to stay there. But when the recent events occurred, Castruccio became eager to occupy that place, and having a close friendship with a townsman, he arranged with him that on the night before the battle was to be fought, he should let in four hundred of his men and kill the ruler.

Being thus prepared, he did not move his army from Montecarlo so that the Florentines would be encouraged to cross the pass. Since they wanted to keep the war away from Pistoia and to take it into Val di Nievole, they encamped below Serravalle, with the intention of crossing the hill the next day. But Castruccio, having taken the castle during the night without a sound, left Montecarlo at midnight and arrived in silence with his troops in the morning at the foot of

Serravalle, with the result that the Florentine army and he, each on his own side, began to climb the slope at the same time. Castruccio had directed his infantry to go by the main road and had sent a band of four hundred cavalry toward the castle on the left-hand side. The Florentines, on the other side, had sent four hundred cavalry ahead, and had moved their infantry after that, and behind them, their men-at-arms, nor did they believe they would find Castruccio up on the hill, because they did not know that he had made himself master of the castle. Thus, the Florentine cavalry, having climbed the slope, unexpectedly came upon Castruccio's infantry and found them so close that they hardly had time to lace up their helmets. Since, therefore, the unprepared were being attacked by the prepared and the well-organized, Castruccio's troops drove the Florentines back with high spirits, something they could hardly resist, although some of them fought back. However, by the time the noise reached the rest of the Florentine camp, everything had become completely confused. The cavalry were crowded in by the infantry, the infantry by the cavalry and the baggage train; because of the narrowness of the place, the leaders could move neither forward nor backward, with the result that no one, in so much confusion, knew what could or should be done. Meanwhile the cavalry, who were engaged in hand-to-hand combat with the enemy infantry, were being killed and butchered without being able to defend themselves, because the adverse nature of the terrain did not let them; nevertheless, they were resisting, more out of necessity than because of their prowess [*virtù*], because, having the mountains on their flanks, their friends behind, and their enemies ahead, no way was left open for them to flee.

Meanwhile, Castruccio, seeing that he did not have enough men to make the enemy turn and run, sent a thousand infantry by way of the castle and had them descend with the four hundred cavalry that he had sent earlier. They struck the enemy on the flank with such fury that the Florentine troops, unable to sustain the impetus of the charge, began to flee, defeated more by the place than by the enemy. And the flight began with those in the rear scattering over the plain toward Pistoia, each man providing for his own safety as best he could.

This rout was great and very bloody. Many leaders were captured, among them Bandino de' Rossi, Francesco Brunelleschi, and Giovanni della Tosa, all Florentine noblemen, together with many other Tuscans and men from the Kingdom of Naples, who fought alongside the Florentines, having been sent by King Robert to aid the Guelfs.

As soon as they heard about the defeat, the Pistoians did not delay in chasing out the party friendly to the Guelfs and giving themselves up to Castruccio. Not content with this, the latter took Prato and all the castle towns of the plain on both sides of the Arno, and he stationed himself with his troops on the plain of Peretola, two miles from Florence, where he stayed for many days to divide up the booty and to celebrate the victory he had had. In derision of the Florentines he had money coined and races run by horses, by men, and by whores. Nor did he miss the opportunity to try to bribe some noble citizens to open the gates of Florence to him at night, but when the conspiracy was discovered, Tommaso Lupacci and Lambertuccio Frescobaldi were taken and beheaded.[27]

Terrified, then, by the rout, the Florentines did not see any remedy by which they could save their freedom, and to be more certain of help, they sent ambassadors to Robert, king of Naples, to offer him the city and sovereignty over it.[28] That king accepted it, not so much because of the honor done him by the Florentines, as because he knew of what moment it was for his state that the party of the Guelfs should maintain its control in Tuscany. Having agreed with the Florentines that he should have two hundred thousand florins annually, he sent his son Carlo to Florence with four thousand cavalry.

Meanwhile the Florentines were somewhat relieved of Castruccio's troops, because he had been obliged to leave their territory and go off to Pisa in order to put down a conspiracy formed against him by Benedetto Lanfranchi, one of the first citizens of the city.[29] This man, unable to endure having his native city enslaved to someone from Lucca, plotted against him, planning to occupy the citadel and, after driving out the guards, to kill Castruccio's partisans. But in these affairs, if a small number is sufficient to keep things secret, it is not large enough to carry them out. So, while Benedetto was seeking to draw more men into his plot, he included one who revealed Benedetto's intentions to Castruccio. Nor was this revelation made without incriminating Bonifacio Cerchi and Giovanni Guidi, Florentines who were exiled in Pisa. In response, Castruccio, seized Benedetto and had him killed, sending all the rest of that family into exile and beheading many other noble citizens. And since it seemed to him that Pistoia and Pisa were hardly loyal, he devoted all his industry and energy to making sure of them. This gave the Florentines time to regroup their forces and enabled them to wait for Carlo's arrival. When he came, they decided not to waste time and put together a large force, summoning to their aid almost all the Guelfs of Italy, and forming an immense army of more than thirty thousand infantry and ten thousand cavalry. And after debating which they ought to attack first, Pistoia or Pisa, they decided it was better to attack Pisa, as a plan more likely to succeed because of the recent conspiracy that had taken place there, and one more useful to them, since they thought that once Pisa was taken, Pistoia would surrender of her own accord.

Coming out, then, with their army at the beginning of May of 1328, the Florentines immediately occupied Lastra, Signa, Montelupo, and Empoli, and arrived with it at San Miniato.[30] Castruccio, on the other side, hearing about the large army that the Florentines had sent against him, was not dismayed in any way. He thought that this was the moment Fortune would place the rule of Tuscany in his hands, believing that the enemy would not make a better showing at Pisa than they had at Serravalle, and that they would not have any hope of recovering as they had before. Having gathered together twenty thousand of his foot soldiers and four thousand cavalry, he stationed himself with his army at Fucecchio, and sent Pagolo Guinigi to Pisa with five thousand infantry. Fucecchio is situated in a stronger location than any other castle town in Pisan territory, being between the Gusciana[31] and the Arno and somewhat raised above the plain. If he stayed there, the enemy could not prevent him from getting supplies from Lucca or Pisa unless they divided themselves into two parts, nor could they, except to their disadvantage, either go out to meet him or move toward Pisa, for in the first case they would be caught in between Castruccio's troops and those in Pisa; in the second, they would have to cross the Arno, something they could not do with the enemy on their backs, except by exposing themselves to great danger. In order to encourage them to choose this plan of crossing the river, Castruccio did not place himself with his troops on the banks of the Arno, but next to the walls of Fucecchio, leaving a lot of space between the river and himself.

After occupying San Miniato, the Florentines debated what was to be done, whether to go to Pisa or to meet Castruccio, and having measured the difficulties involved in the alternatives, they resolved to go and attack him. The Arno was so low that it could be forded, but not in such a way that the infantry could avoid being immersed up to their shoulders and the cavalry up to their saddles. When the morning of June 10 arrived, then, the Florentines, drawn up in battle formation, had part of their cavalry and a force of ten thousand infantry begin the crossing. Castruccio, who was ready and eager to do what he had planned, attacked them with a force of five thousand infantry and three thousand cavalry, and did not give them time to get out of the water before he was in hand-to-hand combat with them. He also sent a thousand light infantry downstream along the banks of the Arno and a thousand upstream. The Florentine infantry were weighed down by the water and by their arms, and none of them had yet climbed up the steep bank out of the river. Some of the horses that had crossed had broken up the riverbed, thus making the passage difficult for the others, many of whom, upon encountering the unstable bottom of the river, fell upside-down on their riders, while many others got so stuck in the mud that they could not get out. Hence, the Florentine captains, seeing the difficulty of crossing at that place, made their troops withdraw and go higher upstream in order to find a spot where the bottom was still sound and the bank had a gentler slope and could take their weight. Opposed to these troops were the infantry that Castruccio had sent up along the bank. His men were lightly armed with small, round shields and short spears in their hands, and with loud shouts they wounded the enemy in the face and the chest. The result was that the horses, terrified by the wounds and the shouts, refused to go forward and fell, topsy-turvy, on top of one another. The fight between Castruccio's men and those who had crossed the river was hard and terrible, and a great many fell on each side as each tried with all its might to overcome the other. Castruccio's men wanted to shove the enemy back down into the river; the Florentines wanted to push his men away in order to make more room for the others in their army so that, once they had come out of the water, they would be able to fight. And the tenacity of all the men was reinforced by the exhortations of their captains: Castruccio reminded his men that these were the same enemy soldiers whom they had defeated not long before at Serravalle; and the Florentines reproached theirs that so many should allow themselves to be beaten by so few. Seeing that the battle kept on going and that his men and their adversaries were already worn out, and that everywhere there were many wounded and dead, Castruccio sent forward another force of five thousand infantry, and when he had led them just behind the backs of those who were fighting, he ordered the ones in front to open their ranks and, as if they were turning in flight, to withdraw, one part toward the right and the other toward the left. When this was done, it gave the Florentines space to advance into and to gain some ground. But once Castruccio's fresh troops came to blows with the tired Florentines, it did not take long before they pushed them back into the river. Thus far, the cavalry on either side had had no advantage, because Castruccio, knowing that his were inferior, had ordered his officers merely to hold off the enemy, since he was hoping to defeat their infantry, and when they were defeated, then to beat their cavalry more easily—something which happened according to his plan. For, seeing that the enemy infantry had retreated into the river, he sent the remainder of his infantry against the enemy cavalry, and as his infantry was wounding them with lances and javelins, and his cavalry was pressing upon them with great fury, they took to flight. The Florentine captains, seeing the difficulty their cavalry had in crossing the river, tried to get the infantry across at a place farther downstream in order to attack Castruccio's troops on their flank. But since the banks were steep and occupied at the top by his men, they tried to do so in vain. Thus, the Florentine army was routed, to the great honor and glory of Castruccio, and of such a great multitude not a third escaped. Many leaders were taken, and Carlo, King Robert's son, together with Michelangelo Falconi and Taddeo degli Albizzi, the Florentine commissioners, fled to Empoli. The booty was substantial, the slaughter very substantial, as one would expect in so great a conflict, for of the Florentine army 20,231 died, of Castruccio's men, 1,570.

But Fortune, inimical to his glory, when it was time to give him life, took it from him and broke off those plans that he had thought to put into effect a long time before, nor could anything other than death have impeded them. Castruccio had labored all that day in the battle; then, when it had come to an end, completely exhausted and dripping with sweat, he stopped at the gate of Fucecchio to wait for the troops who were returning from the victory and to receive them in person and thank them, and at the same time, if anything should still be undertaken by the enemy, who in some place might be capable of resisting, to have a ready remedy for that, since he judged it the duty of a good captain to be the first to mount his horse and the last to dismount. Thus, while standing exposed to a wind that usually rises up from the Arno at midday and is almost always unhealthy, he got thoroughly chilled, something to which he paid no attention, since he was used to such discomforts. It was, however, the cause of his death. For the following night he was attacked by a very severe fever, which kept rising, and when Castruccio learned that the illness was deemed mortal by all the doctors, he called for Pagolo Guinigi and spoke these words to him:

"If I had thought, my son, that Fortune had wanted in the middle of my journey to cut off the road toward the glory which I was promising myself I would attain through my many successful deeds, I would have labored less and left you with fewer enemies and less envy, though a smaller state. For, content with ruling Lucca and Pisa, I would not have subjugated the Pistoians and angered the Florentines with so many injuries, but having made each of these peoples my friends, I would have led, if not a longer, then certainly a quieter life, and I would have left you a state, which, though smaller, without doubt would have been more secure and stable. But Fortune, who wants to be the arbiter of all things human, did not give me enough judgment to have understood her early on, nor enough time to overcome her. You have heard—for many have told you, and I have never denied it—how I came into your father's house while still young and lacking all those aspirations that should be found in every noble spirit, and how I was nurtured by him and loved by him much more than if I had been born of his own blood, so that, under his tutelage, I became valorous and was able to obtain that fortune that you yourself have seen and see now. And since, at the point of death, he entrusted you and all his goods to my loyal care, I have brought you up with the same love and have increased your goods with the same loyalty by which I was and still am bound. And so that you should have not merely what was left you by your father, but also what Fortune and my ability [*virtù*] have gained, I decided never to take a wife, lest love of children should have prevented me in any way from showing your father's family the gratitude that I felt myself obligated to show.[32] I leave you, therefore, a large state, something which makes me very content, but because I leave it to you weak and unstable, I am full of grief. Lucca is yours, which will never be truly content under your rule. Pisa is yours, where the men are fickle by nature and full of deceit, a city which, although accustomed at various times to servitude, nevertheless will always disdain having a ruler from Lucca. Pistoia still remains yours, but it is scarcely loyal because of its divisions, and is angry at our family because of its recent injuries. You have as neighbors the Florentines, wounded and injured by us in a thousand ways, yet not destroyed, to whom the news of my death will be more pleasing than the conquest of all of Tuscany would be. You cannot trust the princes of Milan and the emperor, because they are far away, indolent, and their assistance comes late. You must not, therefore, put your hope in anything except your own industriousness and the memory of my prowess [*virtù*], and in the reputation the present victory brings you, which, if you know how to use it with prudence, will help you reach an accord with the Florentines, something with which, since they have been terrified by the present rout, they should eagerly comply. As for them, where I sought to make them my enemies and thought their hostility would bring me power and glory, you have to try with all your might to make them your friends, because their friendship will make you secure and comfortable. In this world it is a matter of great importance to know oneself and to know how to measure the strength of one's spirit and of one's condition, and anyone who knows he is not suited for war should do his best to rule by means of the arts of peace. My counsel is that it would be good for you to apply yourself to them and do your best in this way to enjoy the results of my labors and dangers; in this you will easily succeed if you will take these reflections of mine as truths. And to me you will be doubly obligated: first, because I left you this realm; second, because I have taught you how to keep it."

Then, having summoned those citizens of Lucca, Pisa, and Pistoia who had fought under him, and having commended Pagolo Guinigi to them and made them swear obedience to him, Castruccio died, leaving a happy memory of himself with all those who had heard of him, and with those who had been his friends, as much regret as for any prince who ever died at any other time. His funeral was celebrated most honorably, and he was buried in San Francesco in Lucca. But ability [*virtù*] and Fortune were not so friendly to Pagolo Guinigi as to Castruccio, because not much later he lost Pistoia, and then Pisa, and had real difficulty preserving his rule over Lucca, which remained in his family's control down to the time of Pagolo, his great-grandson.[33]

Thus, Castruccio, judging from what we have shown, was a rare man not only in the context of his own era, but in that of many eras that had come before it. As for his person, he was taller than average, and every limb was proportioned to the others, and he was gracious in his bearing and received men with such humanity that no one ever spoke with him who went away discontent. His hair was reddish, and he wore it cut above the ears, and always and at all times, even when it rained or snowed, he went bare-headed.

He was gracious to his friends, terrible to his enemies, just with his subjects, deceitful with outsiders; when he could win by fraud, he never sought to win by force, for he used to say that the victory, not the manner of the victory, would bring you glory.

No one was ever bolder about entering into dangers, or more wary in getting out of them, and he used to say that men should try everything and not be frightened of anything, and that God loves strong men, because one sees that He always punishes the powerless by means of the powerful.

He was also marvelous with retorts and stinging taunts, both sharp and urbane, and as he did not spare anyone when speaking in this style, so he did not get angry when they did not spare him. Hence, it is recorded that he made many sharp remarks, and that he listened to many with patience.[34]

When he had bought a partridge for a ducat, and a friend reproved him, Castruccio said: "You would not have paid more than a soldo for it." And when his friend answered that he was right, Castruccio replied: "A ducat is worth much less to me."[35]

Once when he had a flatterer in his presence, he spit on him out of scorn, and the flatterer said: "To catch a little fish, fishermen let themselves get completely soaked in the sea; I shall certainly let myself get wet with a little spit in order to land a whale." Castruccio did not merely hear this patiently, but rewarded him for it.

When someone spoke ill of him because he lived in too much splendor, Castruccio said: "If this were a vice, there would not be such splendid banquets on the feast days of our saints."

When he was walking down a street and saw a young man who was coming out of the house of a whore and was completely red-faced because he had been seen by Castruccio, he said to him: "Do not be ashamed when you come out of there, but when you go in."

When a friend gave him a knot to untie that was very carefully entwined, he said: "You fool, do you think I want to untie something which, when it is tied, gives me so much trouble?"[36]

When Castruccio said to one who professed to be a philosopher, "You are all like dogs that always hang around whoever will give them the best food," the man replied: "On the contrary, we are doctors who go to the houses of those who have the greatest need for us."

When he was going from Pisa to Livorno by water and a dangerous storm came up that frightened him greatly, he was rebuked for cowardice by someone in his entourage, who said that he himself was not afraid of anything. In reply, Castruccio said that he did not wonder at it, because each man values his life for what it is worth.

Being asked by someone what he needed to do to gain esteem for himself, Castruccio said: "When you go to a banquet, take care that one block of wood is not sitting on another."

When someone was boasting of having read many things, Castruccio said: "It would be better to boast of having remembered them."

When someone was boasting that, though he drank a great deal, he did not get drunk, Castruccio said: "An ox does the very same thing."

Castruccio had a young woman with whom he was on intimate terms; being blamed for this by a friend who said that it was especially bad for him to let himself be had by a woman: "You are wrong," said Castruccio; "I had her, not she me."

Also, when someone blamed him for eating fancy foods, he said: "You would not spend as much as I do on them." And when the man said that Castruccio spoke the truth, Castruccio added: "Then you are more miserly than I am gluttonous."

Once he was invited to supper by Taddeo Bernardi of Lucca, a very rich and extravagant man, and after he arrived at the house, Taddeo showed him a room entirely decorated with tapestries and with a floor made of precious stones of various colors which were arranged in diverse patterns representing flowers, leafy branches, and similar greenery. Castruccio, having gathered a great deal of saliva in his mouth, spat it all in Taddeo's face. When the latter got angry, Castruccio said: "I did not know where to spit so as to offend you less."[37]

Asked how Caesar died, he said: "May God grant that I might die like him!"[38]

One night at the home of one of his gentlemen, where a large number of ladies had been invited to a party, he was dancing and enjoying himself more than was fitting for one of his station; upon being reproved for it by a friend, he said: "He who is considered wise by day will never be considered foolish by night."[39]

When a man came to ask him a favor, and Castruccio pretended not to hear, the man threw himself on his knees on the ground before him. When Castruccio reproved him for doing so, he said: "You are the reason for it, since you have ears in your feet." As a result, he got double the favor he was asking for.

He used to say that the road to Hell was easy since one went downhill and with one's eyes closed.[40]

When someone asked him a favor with a great many superfluous words, Castruccio said to him: "When you want something more from me, send someone else."

When the same sort of man had bored him with a long oration and had said to him at the end, "I have perhaps tired you by speaking too long," he said, "You have not, for I have not heard a thing you have said."[41]

He used to say of one who had been a beautiful boy and was afterwards a handsome man that he caused too much harm, because before he stole husbands from their wives, and now he was taking wives from their husbands.

To an envious man who was laughing, he said: "Are you laughing because you are faring well or because another is faring badly?"

When he was still under the tutelage of Messer Francesco Guinigi, and one of his peers said to him, "What do you want me to give you for you to let me slap your face?" he replied: "A helmet."[42]

Having had a citizen of Lucca killed who had been the cause of his greatness, and being told that he had done wrong in killing one of his old friends, he replied that they were deceiving themselves, for he had killed a new enemy.[43]

Castruccio used to praise greatly those men who chose wives and then did not marry them, and likewise, those who wanted to travel by sea and then did not do so.

He used to say he marveled at men who, when they buy a vase of earthenware or glass, sound it first to see if it is rings true, but then, when they were taking a wife, were content only to see her.

When someone asked him, just as he was about to die, how he wanted to be buried, he replied: "With my face downward, since I know that when I die, this city will turn upside-down."

Upon being asked if, in order to save his soul, he ever thought to become a friar, he replied that he had not, because it seemed strange to him that Brother Lazarus should go to Paradise and Uguccione della Faggiuola to Hell.[44]

Being asked how much it was good to eat if one wanted to stay healthy, he replied: "If a man is rich, when he is hungry; if a man is poor, when he can."

Seeing one of his gentlemen having his clothing laced up by one of his servants, he said: "I hope to God that you will have him feed you, too."

Seeing that a man had written on his house in Latin that God should guard it from the wicked, he said: "He himself should not go in there."

Walking down a street where there was a little house with a large door, he said: "That house will run away through that door."

Being given to understand that a foreigner had corrupted a young boy, he said: "He must be from Perugia."

When he asked which town was famous for cheaters and grafters, he was answered, "Lucca," where everybody was one by nature, except for Bontura.[45]

When he was arguing with an ambassador of the king of Naples over the property belonging to exiles, he began to get rather angry. The ambassador said to him, "So, you have no fear of the king?" Castruccio replied: "This king of yours, is he good or bad?" And when the ambassador replied that he was good, Castruccio retorted: "Why, then, do you want me to be afraid of good men?"

Many other things said by him could be recounted, in all of which one would see his wit and his gravity, but let these suffice as testimony to his great qualities.

He lived forty-four years, and was princely whether his fortune was good or bad. And as there are a great many memorials to his good fortune, so he also wished that there should be some to his bad fortune. Hence, the manacles with which he had been shackled in prison can still be seen today hung up in the tower of his home, where they were put by him so that they would always bear witness to his adversity. And because while living he was not inferior either to Philip of Macedonia, the father of Alexander, nor to Scipio of Rome, he died at the same age as both of them, and without doubt he would have surpassed both if, in exchange for Lucca, he had had Macedonia or Rome as his native land.[46]

Notes to *The Life of Castruccio Castracani*

1. Zanobi Buondelmonti (1491–1527) came from an old Florentine family and participated in the famous, wide-ranging discussions on politics, history, and literature with Cosimo Rucellai, Machiavelli, and others that took place in the gardens of the Palazzo Rucellai—that is, the Orti Oricellari. An ardent republican, Buondelmonte was one of the dedicatees of the *Discourses*, and he appeared as a character in Machiavelli's dialogue *The Art of War*. A writer from an old Florentine family, Luigi Alamanni (1495–1556) was also one of the participants in the discussions in the Orti Oricellari and a character in *The Art of War*.
2. Machiavelli is thinking of such figures as Moses and Romulus.
3. Contrast what Machiavelli says here about the power of fortune with what he says in chapter 25 of *The Prince*.
4. The entire account of Castruccio's early life and of Messer Antonio and his sister is a complete fabrication on Machiavelli's part.
5. Machiavelli speaks here of Castruccio's *grazia*, which I have translated as

"grace." The word identifies a key set of attributes in him, including charm, affability, the ability to ingratiate oneself with others, and even a kind of charisma or personal magnetism. Francesco Guinigi, who appears in the next paragraph, is also said to have this quality.

6. Francesco Guinigi is also Machiavelli's invention.

7. In the late Middle Ages there were two opposing political factions in Germany identified with two noble families, the Welfs (Guelfs) and the Hohenstaufens (Ghibellines: the word comes from "Waiblingen," the name of a Hohenstaufen castle). The two were rivals for the crown of the Holy Roman Empire. Imported into Italy in the thirteenth century, the two words were initially used to distinguish supporters of the papacy, the Guelfs, from supporters of the Holy Roman Emperor, the Ghibellines. Eventually this distinction disappeared, and the terms were used simply to designate rival local factions in different Italian city-states.

8. Machiavelli alludes to the conflict between Guelfs and Ghibellines in Lombardy at the time of the descent of Henry VII, the Holy Roman Emperor, into the peninsula. Pavia was taken by the Guelfs in July 1315. At that time, Castruccio was not, in fact, residing in Lucca.

9. Robert I of Naples (Robert of Anjou) had become the ruler of Florence at that time, the city having given itself as a fief to the king in June 1315 in order to gain his protection from Henry VII and the Ghibellines.

10. Uguccione became the ruler of Pisa in October 1315.

11. The governor, or chief magistrate of Lucca, was Gerardo da San Lupidio, the vicar of Robert of Anjou; Uguccione replaced him with his own son Francesco.

12. Montecatini is a hill town 6 miles from Pistoia and a mile north of the main road to Lucca. Montecarlo is also a hill town 7 miles east of Lucca. In reality, Uguccione had seized Montecatini, where he later defeated the army of the Florentines and their allies in battle on August 29, 1315. Contrary to what Machiavelli claims, Uguccione, and not Castruccio, was in charge.

13. Castruccio's tactics here, completely invented by Machiavelli, resemble those of the Roman general Scipio Africanus when he fought the Carthaginian general Hasdrupal in Spain; Machiavelli certainly knew of them since they are described in Livy's *History of Rome*, 23.26–29.

14. Bagni, actually Bagni San Giuliano, is only some 5 miles from Pisa. The Pisans revolted in April 1316 and made Gaddo their general; he became their ruler only in 1320.

15. Uguccione took refuge first with Spinetta Malaspina in Garfagnana, then with Cangrande della Scala, who was lord of Verona from 1311 to 1329. Uguccione died in Vicenza in 1319.

16. Castruccio was named *capitano generale* for six months on June 12, 1316; on November 4 his commission was extended for another year.

17. Serezana and the other towns mentioned in the following sentences are all located in northwestern Tuscany; Pontremoli is on its northernmost border. The remains of several fortresses associated with Castruccio can still be found in the area.

18. Machiavelli conflates two historical personages: Frederick of Austria and Louis of Bavaria. In 1314 the former was chosen Holy Roman Emperor by a minority of Electors, whereas the latter was chosen Emperor by a majority. War ensued between them, which Louis eventually won; he was then crowned in 1328. Castruccio was awarded several titles by Frederick and was made a duke by Louis.

19. Castruccio was acclaimed as the ruler of Pisa on April 29, 1328. Louis of Bavaria, not Frederick, had him named imperial vicar of the town the following day; in 1324 he had already made Castruccio imperial vicar of Lucca and Pontremoli.

20. Machiavelli is confusing chronology here. Since Castruccio was made ruler of Pisa in 1328, he could not be seeking an alliance with Matteo Visconti, who ruled Milan from 1313 until his death in 1322. However, Machiavelli's description of how Castruccio organized his own people for war is historically accurate, and since Machiavelli was a strong advocate of a citizen army in both *The Prince* and the *Discourses*, this aspect of Castruccio's activities may have helped to draw Machiavelli to him.

21. One account places these events in the second half of 1323. Fucecchio was a town situated north of the Arno in the direction of Pisa. San Miniato was on the south side of the river and commanded the road between Empoli and Pisa; it is not to be confused with the church of San Miniato in Florence itself.

22. The "mountain region" is the mountainous country west and northwest of Pistoia. The account of the taking of Pistoia that Machiavelli goes on to give is an invention. Castruccio did, in fact, capture the city on May 5, 1525, but thanks to the treachery of one of its citizens, Filippo Tredici.

23. Between 1309 and 1376 the popes were forced to reside in Avignon because Rome was held by the Holy Roman Empire.

24. The "Henry" in this sentence appears to be the Holy Roman Emperor Henry VII himself rather than the "Henry" who appeared in the preceding sentence and who was his lieutenant. Note that Machiavelli is again confusing two historical figures, in this case Henry VII with Louis of Bavaria, who actually held the imperial throne at this time. The "debt of gratitude" that Castruccio felt he owed the emperor, referred to in the next sentence, derived from the fact that the latter had restored territory to Lucca that had been taken by Pisa and had named Castruccio the duke of Lucca, Pistoia, Luni, and Volterra.

25. The mottos on Castruccio's toga contain a small ambiguity that cannot be rendered in English. The initial pronoun *egli* in both would normally

be translated as "he" but could also be rendered as "it," making the mottos a slight bit less self-celebratory than they are as I have translated them. Note that Castruccio was also named a count of the Sacred Lateran Palace while he was in Rome.

26. While Castruccio was at Rome, the Florentines took Pistoia, on January 28, 1328. He returned to Tuscany immediately, took Pisa by April, and reconquered Pistoia on August 3. He defeated the Florentines not at the battle of Serravalle, which is described in the next paragraphs, but at that of Altopascio, in September 1325.

27. This attempt took place in April 1325 and appears to have involved only one man.

28. Machiavelli again confuses people and dates. The city gave itself to Robert, who controlled it from 1313 to 1321. After the defeat at Altopascio in 1325, it gave itself to Carlo, duke of Calabria, who ruled from July 1326 to December 1327.

29. The conspiracy of Lanfranchi occurred in October 1323 and was actually in favor of Castruccio when Pisa was ruled by Ranieri di Donoratico. Lanfranchi was caught by the Pisans and executed.

30. These events occurred in June 1325, not May 1328. In the battle of Fucecchio, which Machiavelli is about to recount, he combines details from Castruccio's victories over the Florentines at Altopascio (September 23, 1325) and at Carmignano (May 14, 1326), while exaggerating the numbers of the soldiers who fought and of those who died in the battle.

31. The Gusciana, or, more properly, the Usciana, is a canal that drains marshy land near Fucecchio and takes the water to the Arno.

32. Castruccio did, in fact, marry a woman named Pina Streghi of the Da Vallecchio family that ruled the town of Corbara. He had as many as nine children with her, plus several illegitimate ones, and spoke his dying words not to Pagolo Guinigi, but to his own son Enrico. Note that neither Moses nor Romulus, who are alluded to at the start of the biography as being like Castruccio, had children.

33. This is the first member of the Guinigi family mentioned by Machiavelli who actually existed. He ruled Lucca from 1400 to 1430. After Castruccio's death, Louis of Bavaria took the city from his children and named as imperial vicar Francesco Castracani, a relative of Castruccio's who was also his opponent.

34. Unless noted otherwise, all of the remarks attributed to Castruccio come from sayings attributed to various ancient philosophers in Diogenes Laertius's *Lives of the Eminent Philosophers*; specific sources in this text are identified in the notes below. Most of the sayings have been adapted in some way by Machiavelli, some quite significantly.

35. See Diogenes Laertius's "Aristippus," 2.66. Aristippus (c.435–350 B.C.E.) was a disciple of Socrates and founder of the Cyrenaic school of philos-

ophy, which believed that all knowledge came through the senses and that sensory pleasure was the highest good. All but one of the next fifteen sayings come from this biography, 2.67–79. Note: a *soldo* was worth considerably less than a ducat.

36. The obscurity of this quip can be clarified by reference to its source in Diogenes Laertius's work, which speaks of an enigma, a "knotty problem," not of an actual knot; see "Aristippus," 2.70.

37. Taddeo Bernardi remain unidentified; in Diogenes Laertius's text the figure is merely a steward (see "Aristippus," 2.75).

38. Machiavelli has substituted Caesar for Socrates in Diogenes Laertius's work; see "Aristippus," 2.76.

39. The source of this saying has not been identified.

40. Diogenes Laertius, "Bion," 4.49. Bion (c.335–c.245 B.C.E.) was an eclectic philosopher who espoused positions embraced by the Cynics as well as by the Cyrenaics. Three of the next four sayings come from this life; see 4.49–51.

41. Diogenes Laertius, "Aristotle," 5.20.

42. Diogenes Laertius, "Diogenes," 6.54. Diogenes was a Greek philosopher (c.238–c.150 B.C.E.), who was the head of the Stoic school in Athens. Ten of the next twelve sayings come from this life; see 6.29–68.

43. This saying appears actually to have been one of Castruccio's; see Niccolò Tegrimi's life of Castruccio, *Castrucci Antelminelli Castracani lucensis ducis vita* (Modena, 1496), p. 64.

44. "Brother Lazarus" is a jocular reference to a character in Christ's parable of Lazarus and the rich man in which the first, who suffered greatly in this life, is saved in the next, whereas the second, who prospered on earth, goes to Hell (see the Bible, Luke 16:19–31). Uguccione della Faggiuola was the ruler of Pisa who initially supported Castruccio, but then turned against him, was defeated by him, and fled to Lombardy where, Machiavelli says, he died in poverty.

45. Machiavelli may be responding here to Dante's gibe at the reputation of Lucca in the *Inferno* (21.41). Bontura is Bontura Dati, who was, according to Dante, the most corrupt grafter of them all.

46. Castruccio actually died at forty-seven, but Machiavelli has him die at the same age as Philip and Scipio for obvious reasons.

A Letter from Niccolò Machiavelli to Francesco Vettori[1]

TO THE MAGNIFICENT
FLORENTINE AMBASSADOR
TO THE SUPREME PONTIFF,
AND HIS BENEFACTOR,
FRANCESCO VETTORI, IN ROME

Magnificent Ambassador,

Divine graces were never late.[2] I say this, because it appeared to me that I had lost—no, rather strayed away from—your favor, since you had gone so long without writing to me, and I was uncertain what the reason for this could be. And I paid little attention to all the reasons that came to mind, except for this: I feared you had stopped writing to me because someone had written to you that I had not been a good guardian of your letters; and I knew that, except for Filippo and Pagolo, no one has seen them because of anything I have done.[3] I found it [i.e., your favor] again, thanks to your last letter of the twenty-third of the past month, in which I am very content to see in how orderly a manner and how calmly you are carrying out your public duties, and I encourage you to continue thus, because he who gives up his own interests for the interests of others, I know loses his own profit and gets no thanks from the others. And since Fortune wants to do everything, she wants us to let her act, to remain quiet and not give her trouble, and to wait for the time when she will let men do something; and then it will be good for you to work harder and watch over things more closely, and for me to leave my farm and say: "Here I am." If I want to bestow equal favors on you, I cannot, therefore, tell you in this letter about anything other than about what my life is like, and if you think it should be exchanged for yours, I will be happy to change it.

I am living on my farm, and since my recent misfortunes happened, I have not spent twenty days in Florence, if you add them all together. I have up to now been snaring thrushes with my own hands. Arising before daybreak, I would prepare the birdlime and go out with a bundle of cages on my back, so that I looked like Geta when he was returning from the port with Amphitryon's books.[4] I would catch at least two, at most six thrushes. And so I passed all of September.[5] Then this pastime, although contemptible and alien to me, gave out, to my displeasure. Now I will tell you how my life is. I get up in the morning with the sun and go to a grove I am having cut down, where I stay for two hours to review the work of the previous day and to pass time with the wood-cutters, who always have some argument on hand either among themselves or with the neighbors. And about this grove I could tell you a thousand wonderful things that have happened to me both in connection with Frosino da Panzano and with others who wanted some of this wood. And Frosino, in particular, sent for a certain number of loads of wood without telling me anything, and at payment he wanted to hold back ten lire from me, which he says he should have had from me four years ago when he beat me at *cricca* in Antonio Guicciardini's house.[6] I began to raise hell; I wanted to accuse the carter who had come for the wood of being a thief, but finally Giovanni Machiavelli got in between us and made us make peace. Battista Guicciardini, Filippo Ginori, Tommaso del Bene, and certain other citizens each took a load of it from me when that north wind was blowing.[7] I made promises to all of them, and I sent a load to Tommaso, which turned up in Florence half its size because he, his wife, his servants, and his children piled it up so that they looked like Gabbura when he cudgels an ox with his boys on Thursdays.[8] As a result, seeing who was profiting here, I told the others that I had no more wood, and all of them got really angry about it, and especially Battista, who counts this along with his other misfortunes in Prato.[9]

Leaving the grove, I go off to a fountain, and from there to my bird snares. I have a book with me, either Dante or Petrarch or one of those minor poets, such as Tibullus, Ovid, and the like: I read of their amorous passions and loves, remember my own, and enjoy myself a bit with these thoughts. Then I move on along the road to the inn, speak with those who pass, ask for news about their towns, learn various things, and note the varied tastes and the diverse fancies of men. In the meanwhile, the hour for dinner arrives, when I feed myself with my gang on that food which this poor farm and my tiny patrimony allow.[10] Once I have eaten, I return to the inn: there, ordinarily, there are the innkeeper, a butcher, a miller, and two kiln-tenders. With these I lower myself to the knave's level the entire day, playing at *cricca* and backgammon, and then there arise a thousand squabbles and countless insults and injurious words, and most of the time we are fighting over a penny, but nevertheless, we are heard shouting in San Casciano. Caught thus with these lice, I wipe away the mold from my brain, and I get my feelings about this malicious fate of mine off my chest: I am content that she should trample on me in this way just to see if she will be ashamed of it.

When evening arrives, I return home and go into my study, and at the threshold, I take off my everyday clothes, full of mud and filth, and put on regal and courtly garments; and decorously dressed anew, I enter the ancient courts of ancient men, where, lovingly received by them, I feed myself on the food that is mine alone and for which I was born, where I am not ashamed to speak with them and to ask them about the reasons for their actions, and they, in their humanity, respond to me. And for four hours at a time, I do not feel any boredom, I forget every difficulty, I do not fear poverty, I am not terrified at death: I transfer myself into them completely. And because Dante says that there is no knowledge unless one retains what one has understood,[11] I have noted down what I have taken away as profit from their conversations, and have composed a little work *On Principalities*, where I delve as deeply as I can into thoughts on this subject, discussing what a principality is, what species there are of them, how they are acquired, how they are maintained, why they are lost. And if ever any of my whimsies has pleased you, this one should not displease you; and to a prince, and especially to a new prince, it should be welcome. Therefore, I have directed it to his Magnificence, Giuliano.[12] Filippo Casavecchia has seen it; he will be able to give you some account of it, both of the thing itself and of the conversations I have had with him about it, although I am still fattening it up and polishing it.

You would like it, Magnificent Ambassador, if I left this life behind and came to enjoy yours with you. I shall do it in any case, but what detains me today are certain affairs of mine that I shall have to take care of in the next six weeks. What gives me pause is that the Soderini are there, so that I would be forced, if I came there, to visit them and talk with them.[13] I would worry that on my return I could not count on dismounting at home, but would dismount at the Bargello, for although this regime has very substantial foundations and great security, nevertheless, it is new and for this reason suspicious, nor does it lack rogues who, to appear like Pagolo Bertini, would put others on the bill to dine, but leave the reckoning to me. I beg you to relieve me of this fear, and then, no matter what, I will come to visit you within the timeframe mentioned.

I have spoken with Filippo of this little work of mine about whether it would be a good idea to give it or not give it [to Giuliano de' Medici], and if it is a good idea to give it, whether it would be better for me to bring it or to send it to you. Not to give it would make me worry that it would not be read, to say the least, by Giuliano, and that this Ardinghelli would take the credit for this latest work of mine.[14] To give it I am being driven by need, which compels me to do so, for I am wasting away and cannot stay in this condition for long before I will become contemptible because of my poverty. Besides, there is the desire I have that these Medici lords should start making use of me, even if they would begin by having me roll a stone about.[15] For then, if I did not win them over, I would have only myself to blame. And by means of this thing, if it were read, they would see that for the fifteen years that I have put into studying statecraft, I have not been either sleeping or playing around, and anyone ought to be happy to be served by one who is full of experience at the expense of others. Nor should they worry about my loyalty, for, having always kept my word, I would not now learn how to break it, and whoever has been loyal and honest for forty-three years, as I have, cannot change his nature, and to my loyalty and honesty my poverty bears witness.[16]

I should like you, therefore, to write me what you think about this subject, and I commend myself to you. May you be happy.[17]

On the tenth day of December, 1513.

                                        Niccolò Machiavelli in Florence

Notes to the *Letter*

1. Machiavelli's close friend Francesco Vettori (1474–1539) came from an old Florentine family and was a writer and a diplomat. He served on a diplomatic mission to Germany with Machiavelli in 1507 and was the Florentine ambassador to Rome from 1513 to 1515.

2. Machiavelli is citing, inexactly, line 13 from Petrarch's *Trionfo dell' eternità* (*Triumph of Eternity*), which means, essentially, that God's grace can never come too late. The Italian *grazia* can mean both "grace," which makes sense here, and "favor," which I have used for the word in the next sentence.

3. Machiavelli is referring to two of his close friends, Filippo Casavecchia and Paolo Vettori, Francesco's brother.

4. This is an allusion to an incident in *Geta and Birria*, a popular tale of the fifteenth century, based on Plautus's comedy *Amphitryon*, in which the title character has returned from a sea voyage and, in order to let his wife know he has arrived in the port, has his servant, Geta, carry a load of books to her.

5. This may be a mistake for "November."

6. *Cricca* is a card game in which the object is to get three of a kind.

7. Although Machiavelli's reference to the north wind here may be literal, some editors have interpreted it as a veiled allusion to the difficulties he experienced after the fall of Florence, including his incarceration and torture because of his supposed connection with the Boscoli conspiracy against the Medici.

8. Gabbura seems to have been a butcher, although his exact identity is unknown. Machiavelli is comparing the way that Gabbura and his assistants pounded meat to make it thinner with the way that Tommaso del Bene and his family stacked the wood so tightly that it seemed only half a load.

9. Battista Guicciardini was the Podestà of Prato, which is just north of Florence, when it was taken by Spanish troops in 1512; its fall was brutal and led directly to the return of the Medici to Florence.

10. By "gang" (*brigata*) Machiavelli is referring in a jocular manner to his family, conceived broadly to include servants as well as wife, children, and relations.

11. See Dante, *Paradiso*, 5.41–42.

12. Machiavelli originally dedicated *The Prince* (which he calls here *On Principalities*, or, as he puts it in Latin, *De Principatibus*) to Giuliano de' Medici, but after his death on March 17, 1516, Machiavelli dedicated it to Lorenzo de' Medici, duke of Urbino. His description of his work here, which seems to refer just to its first ten chapters, has suggested to some scholars that he had only completed those chapters when he wrote the letter. However, there is no consensus as to when he finished the entire work, some scholars arguing that it was complete at this time, others that it was finished later in 1513 or in early 1514, and still others holding out for dates as late as 1516 or even 1518.

13. The Soderini in question were Piero, formerly the head of the Florentine Republic, under whom Machiavelli had served in the Second Chancery, and Piero's brother Francesco, who was a cardinal. Both had been given permission by Pope Leo X, a member of the Medici family, to reside in Rome. Machiavelli's concern is that if he came to Rome to visit Vettori, he would feel obligated to visit the Soderini brothers, too, and that might expose him to new reprisals from the Medici in Florence. In the following sentence, he worries that after such an encounter, he might return home to be thrown into prison (the Bargello). His allusion to Pagolo Bertini

is unclear, but he may be referring to one of the conspirators against the Medici, since Machiavelli's name was found on an incriminating list ("the bill"), for which he was arrested and tortured (paid "the reckoning").

14. Piero Ardinghelli was one of Leo X's secretaries and had advised Giuliano to have nothing to do with Machiavelli. The latter obviously fears that Ardinghelli might steal his ideas and offer them as his own to the Medici.

15. The idea that poverty is contemptible was a classical commonplace. When Machiavelli says that he would be willing to "roll a stone about" to serve the Medici, he underscores the desperation of his desire to return to Florence and to reenter political life there; his phrase may be an allusion to the punishment inflicted in Hell on sinners such as Sisyphus (see Dante, *Inferno*, 7.16–66, and Virgil, *Aeneid*, 6.616).

16. Machiavelli was born in 1469, so he was actually forty-four when he wrote this letter.

17. Machiavelli's final words in Latin, *Sis felix*, can mean either "May you be happy" or "May you be prosperous."

EXCERPTS FROM THE
*DISCOURSES ON THE FIRST TEN
BOOKS OF TITUS LIVY*

Book 1

Preface

BECAUSE OF THE ENVIOUS nature of men, it has always been no less dangerous to find new methods and institutions than to look for unknown seas and lands, since men are readier to blame than to praise the actions of others. Nevertheless, driven by the natural desire I have always felt to do without hesitation the things that I believe will be for the common good, I have decided to enter on a path as yet untrodden by anyone; although it may be irksome and difficult, it can also bring me a reward from those who are kind enough to keep in mind the goal of these labors of mine. And if my poor intellect, my slight experience of current affairs, and my feeble knowledge of ancient ones make this attempt of mine imperfect and of little use, it will at least show the way to someone with more ability [*virtù*] and a greater capacity for analysis and judgment, who can carry out this intention of mine, which, although it may not bring me praise, should not earn me blame.

When I consider, then, how much honor is accorded antiquity and how many times (leaving aside countless other examples) a fragment of an ancient statue has been bought at a great price so that the buyer may have it near him, to adorn his house with it, and to have it imitated by those who take pleasure in that art and who will, with great industriousness, make every effort to imitate it in all their works, and when I see, on the other hand, that the most virtuous [*virtuosissime*] actions which history shows us have been done in ancient kingdoms and republics by kings, captains, citizens, lawgivers, and others who have labored for their countries, and that they have been more often admired than imitated— on the contrary, they have been so much avoided by everyone in every little thing they do that no trace of the virtue [*virtù*] of the ancients remains among us—I cannot help but both marvel and grieve over it at the same time. And all the more so when I see that in the civil disputes that arise among citizens, or in the diseases that men catch, they always have recourse to the judgments or to the remedies that have been made or prescribed by the ancients. For the civil laws are nothing other than judgments made by ancient jurists, which, put in order, teach our present jurists how to judge things, and medicine is nothing other than the experiments made by ancient physicians, on which contemporary physicians base their diagnoses. Nevertheless, in setting up republics, in maintaining states, in ruling kingdoms, in organizing the military and conducting war, in pronouncing judgments on subjects, and in expanding an empire, one cannot find a prince or a republic that has recourse to the examples of the ancients.

I believe that this arises not so much from the weakness into which the present religion has brought the world, or from the harm which ambition, joined to idleness, has done to many Christian states and cities, as from not having a true understanding of histories, because in reading them, we do not extract the sense or taste the flavor that is in them. Thus it happens that countless individuals read them, deriving pleasure from hearing about the variety of events they contain, but without otherwise thinking to imitate them, for those readers have concluded that imitation is not only difficult, but impossible—as if the heavens, the sun, the elements, and men should have changed in their motion, ordering, and power from what they were in antiquity. Wishing, therefore, to lead men away from this error, I felt it necessary to write about all those books of Titus Livy which have not been taken away from us by the malignity of time, and to say what I, thanks to my knowledge of ancient and modern affairs, feel is necessary for a better understanding of them, so that those who read these discourses of mine might more easily extract from them the profit which one should seek in the study of history.[1] And although this enterprise is difficult, nevertheless, aided by those who have encouraged me to take up the burden, I believe I can carry it in such a way that only a short road will remain for some other person to bring it to its destined goal.

Note to Book 1, Preface

1. Of the 142 books that conmprise Livy's *History of Rome* (usually called in Latin *Ab urbe condita*—that is, "From the Founding of the City"), only some thirty-five survive. The first lacuna occurs after the tenth book.

Chapter 2

On How Many Kinds of Republics There Are, and of What Sort the Roman Republic Was

... SINCE I WISH TO discuss what the institutions of the city of Rome were and what circumstances led to its perfection, I say that some who have written about republics declare that there are three kinds of governments in them called principality, aristocracy, and democracy, and that those who organize a city must turn to one of these, depending on what seems most appropriate to them.[1] Others, who are wiser in the opinion of many men, think that there are six types of government, of which three are very bad, and the other three are good in themselves, although they are so easily corrupted that they, too, can become pernicious. Those that are good are the three mentioned above; those that are bad are three others that derive from the first three, each of which is similar to the one closest to it, so that they can easily slip from one form to the other: a principality thus easily becomes a tyranny; an aristocracy becomes an oligarchy with ease; and a democracy is turned into anarchy with no difficulty. Thus, if the founder of a republic establishes one of these three types of government in a city, he will establish it there for only a short time, because no remedy is capable of preventing it from slipping into its contrary because of the similarity that exists, in this case, between the virtue and the vice.

These varied forms of government arose among men by chance, for at the beginning of the world, there were few inhabitants, and they lived for a while scattered in the manner of the beasts; then, when their numbers multiplied, they came together, and in order to be able to defend themselves better, they looked among themselves for one who was stronger and more courageous, and they made him their leader and obeyed him. From this they acquired an understanding of things that are honorable and good, as distinct from those that are pernicious and evil, for if someone harmed his

160

benefactor, this produced hatred and compassion among men, who blamed the one who was ungrateful and honored the one who was grateful, and thinking. Moreover, since they saw that the same injuries could be done to them, they decided, in order to avoid such evils, to make laws and to institute punishments for those who broke them. Thus arose the understanding of justice. The result of this was that afterwards, when they had to select a prince, they did not go after the strongest, but the one who was most prudent and most just. But later, when princes began to be chosen by hereditary succession and not by election, the heirs quickly degenerated from the level of their ancestors, and forsaking virtuous [*virtuose*] deeds, they thought that princes needed only to surpass others in sumptuous display and lasciviousness and every other kind of licentiousness. Thus, the prince began to be hated and to feel fear because of this hatred, and as he quickly went from fear to offensive action, straightway tyranny was born.

From tyranny there came deaths and conspiracies and plots against the prince, plots which were not made by those who were timid or weak, but by those who surpassed others in magnanimity, greatness of spirit, wealth, and nobility, and who could not endure the dishonorable life of their ruler. The masses, then, following the authority of these powerful men, took up arms against the prince, and when he was eliminated, obeyed those men as their liberators. And since the latter hated the name of "single leader," they constituted a government made up of themselves, and at the start, still remembering the tyranny behind them, they conducted themselves according to the laws they established, subordinating what was beneficial for themselves to the common good, and they managed and preserved things, both private and public, with the greatest diligence. Then the administration passed to their children, who had not known the changeability of Fortune, had never experienced bad times, and could not be content with political equality, and they gave themselves to avarice, ambition, and rape, and made an aristocratic government into an oligarchy with no respect for civil rights. Thus, in a short time, what happened to the tyrant happened to them, for the masses, sick of their conduct, made themselves the instruments of anyone who aimed to harm their rulers in any way, so that one man soon arose who, with the aid of the masses, destroyed the oligarchy. And since the memory of the prince and of the injuries received from him was still fresh, and since they had destroyed the government of the few and did not want to restore that of the prince, they turned to democracy and set it up in such a way that neither the powerful few nor a prince would have any authority in it. And because all governments are respected at the beginning, this democratic government was maintained for a while, but not for too long, especially once the generation that had set it up had died out, for it quickly turned to anarchy in which neither private men nor public officials were feared. The result was that with each person living as he pleased, a thousand injuries were committed every day, so that, forced by necessity, or at the suggestion of some good man, or in order to escape all the licentiousness, they returned once again to princely rule; and from that they then went back, step by step, toward anarchy, in the manner and for the reasons just given.[2]

This is the cycle through which the governments of all states, past or present, go. However, only rarely do they return to the same forms of rule they started from, since there is practically no state so long lived that it can pass through these changes many times and still remain standing. Rather, it may well happen that when it is struggling, such a state, which always lacks counsel and strength, will become subject to a neighboring state that is better organized than it is. If, however, this did not happen, then a state might be capable of cycling endlessly through all these forms of government.

I say, then, that all of the forms mentioned are disastrous because of the short-lived nature of the three good ones and the malignant character of the three bad ones. Thus, since those who have been prudent in establishing laws have recognized these defects, they have avoided each of these forms in itself and have chosen one that partakes of them all, judging it to be steadier and more stable, for when one and the same city-state is a principality, an aristocracy, and a democracy, then each one of these keeps watch over the other.

Among those who have deserved great praise for such a constitution is Lycurgus, who established his laws in Sparta and, assigning the kings, the nobles, and the people their parts, created a state that lasted more than eight hundred years, which resulted in the greatest praise for him, and peace and quiet for his city.[3] The contrary happened to Solon, who established the laws of Athens, for by making it a pure democracy, he made it so short-lived that before he died, he saw the birth of the tyranny of Pisistratus. And although forty years later the latter's heirs were driven out and Athens returned to liberty, it did not last more than a hundred years, because they re-established their democracy according to Solon's laws. Even though they made many constitutional changes in order to preserve it, by means of which they restrained the insolence of the great and the license of the masses, things which Solon had not considered, nevertheless, Athens lived a very short time in comparison with Sparta, because it did not combine popular government with princely rule and the rule of the nobility.

But let us come to Rome. Although it did not have a Lycurgus to give it a constitution at the beginning so that it would be able to live free for a long time, nevertheless, because of the friction between the plebeians and the senate, so many unexpected things happened in it that what a founder did not do for it, chance did instead. Thus, if Rome did not get a first gift from Fortune, it got a second, for its first institutions, although defective, were on the right way to achieve perfection.

Romulus and all the other kings made many good laws that were also compatible with freedom, but because their goal was to found a kingdom and not a republic, when that city became free, it lacked many things that had not been instituted by those kings and that it needed in order to ensure its freedom. And when those kings lost their power for the reasons and in the ways described earlier, nevertheless, those who drove them out immediately created two consuls who took the place of the king, so that they wound up expelling from Rome the name, but not the power, of the king. Thus, since there were consuls and a senate in that republic, it came to be a mixture of only two of the three elements mentioned above, that is, princely and aristocratic rule. The only thing remaining was to find a place in it for democratic government. When the Roman nobility became arrogant for the reasons that will be discussed below, the people rose up against it, so that, in order not to lose everything, the nobility was forced to grant the people a role in the government, while, on the other hand, the senate and the consuls still retained enough authority to preserve their position in the republic. And thus came about the creation of the tribunes of the plebeians, after which the government of that republic became more stable, since all three forms of rule had a part in it. And Fortune was so favorable to Rome that although it went from government by kings and aristocrats to that of the people, passing through the same stages for the same reasons discussed above, nevertheless, they never took away all authority from the kings in order to give it to the nobility, nor did they eliminate the authority of the nobility to give it to the people; but since its government remained mixed, it produced the perfect republic.

Notes to Book 1, Chapter 2

1. Machiavelli's source for this political model is Polybius, *The Histories*, 6. Polybius's classification is, in turn, derived from book 3 of Aristotle's *Politics*.
2. Machiavelli's vision of the cyclical movement from one form of government to another is taken from Polybius, *The Histories*, 6.9–10.
3. Lycurgus was a partly legendary Spartan lawgiver who lived in the ninth century B.C.E.; after traveling extensively, he settled in Sparta and undertook the reformation of its constitution. Machiavelli's source here is Polybius, *The Histories*, 6.10. Solon (640–558 B.C.E.), who is mentioned in the next sentence, was an Athenian lawgiver who gave the city its most democratic constitution. Pisistratus (d. 527 B.C.E.) was a successful general and head of a political faction in Athens. He defeated the rival factions in battle around the year 546 and established a tyranny in the city that lasted thirty-six years. Machiavelli's source for information about Solon and Pisistratus is not Polybius, but Plutarch's *Life of Solon*, 18.

Chapter 9

How It Is Necessary for a Man to Act Alone in Order to Organize a Republic Anew, or to Reform It with Complete Disregard for Its Ancient Institutions

IT MAY PERHAPS SEEM to some that I have gone too far along in Roman history without having yet made mention of the founders of the state or of its laws concerning religion and the military. Therefore, not wishing to keep in suspense the minds of those who would like to know something about this subject, I say that many may perchance judge it to be a bad example that the founder of a civil society, such as Romulus, should have first killed his brother and then acquiesced in the death of Titus Tatius, the Sabine, who had been elected his co-ruler in the kingdom.[1] From this example, they might conclude that a prince's subjects would feel free to take him as their model, and, because of their ambition and desire to rule, harm those who opposed their authority. This opinion would be true, but only if the reason for which Romulus committed such a murder were not considered.

This should be taken as a general rule: never or rarely does it happen that a republic or a kingdom is organized well at the start, or reformed totally with complete disregard for its old institutions, unless this is done by one man; in fact, it must be a single man who alone, by himself, provides the method and on whose mind any organization of this sort depends. Thus, the prudent founder of a state, who has the intention of aiding not himself, but the public good, and not his own heirs, but his native land, which is common to all, must do his utmost to have authority all to himself. Nor will a wise man ever blame anyone for any deed he does that transcends the laws, if he is acting in order to organize a kingdom or found a republic. It is certainly appropriate to say that although the deed accuses him, its outcome excuses him, and when what is done is good, as was the case with Romulus, it will always excuse him, for he who is violent in order to destroy, not he who is violent in order to mend things, ought to be blamed.

Such a man must certainly be sufficiently prudent and virtuous [*virtuoso*] so as not to bequeath the authority he has seized to another, for, men being more prone to evil than to good, his successor might use in the pursuit of ambition what he had used virtuously [*virtuosamente*]. Besides this, although one man alone is fit for organizing a government, the government which has been organized will not last long if it rests on the shoulders of one man. However, it will do so if it is left to the care of many, provided that preserving it is something dear to their hearts. For just as the many are not fit to organize a government, since they do not understand what is good in it because of all the different opinions they hold, so, once they have understood that they have such a good government, they will never agree to give it up. And that Romulus was among those who might merit an excuse for the deaths of his brother and his co-ruler, and that he did what he did for the common good and not out of personal ambition—this is demonstrated by the fact that he immediately organized a senate with which he took counsel and whose opinions he deliberated on. Moreover, anyone who considers carefully the authority that Romulus reserved for himself will see that he only reserved for himself the authority to command the army when war had been decided and to convene the senate. This was confirmed later when Rome freed itself by driving out the Tarquins and they did not change any aspect of their ancient institutions, except that instead of a permanent king, they had two consuls chosen annually.[2] This bears witness to the fact that all the original institutions of the city were more consistent with a free form of self-government than with an absolute or a tyrannical form of rule.

Countless examples could be supplied in support of the things mentioned above, such as those of Moses, Lycurgus, Solon, and other founders of kingdoms and republics, men who were able to fashion laws appropriate for the common good because they had seized the authority to do so. However, I wish to omit this since it is common knowledge. I will adduce only one example that is not so famous but that ought to be considered by those who desire to frame new laws, and that example is this. Agis, the king of Sparta, wanted to return the Spartans to limits within which the laws of

Lycurgus had enclosed them, for he thought that ever since his city had departed from those laws, it had lost a great deal of its ancient virtue [*virtù*], and, as a consequence, of its power and its empire. However, he was killed at the very start of his efforts by the Spartan ephors as a man who wanted to rule as a tyrant.[3] Cleomenes succeeded him as king, and when the same desire arose in him, thanks to the memoirs and writings of Agis which he had found and which revealed Agis's thoughts and intentions to him, he realized that he could not do this good for his country unless he was the sole authority there, for he felt that, because of men's ambitions, he could not do something useful for the many against the will of the few.[4] And so, he found a suitable opportunity and had all the ephors killed as well as anyone else who might oppose him. Then he restored in their entirety the laws of Lycurgus. This decision might have revived Sparta and given Cleomenes the same reputation as Lycurgus if it had not been for the power of the Macedonians and the weakness of the other Greek states, because just after that reorganization Cleomenes was attacked by the Macedonians, and since his forces were inferior and he could not get help from outside, he was defeated, and that design of his, however just and praiseworthy, remained incomplete.

Considering all these things, then, I conclude that in order to establish a state, one must act alone, and that Romulus deserves to be excused, not blamed, for the deaths of Remus and Titus Tatius.

Notes to Book 1, Chapter 9

1. Romulus was the legendary founder of Rome, who supposedly ruled between 753 and 715 B.C.E. According to the legend, he and his twin brother Remus were foundlings who were initially nurtured by a she-wolf. The two founded Rome, and Romulus slew Remus when the latter jumped over the walls they had built. Titus Tatius was the king of the Sabines, a neighboring people, and was made co-ruler of Rome with Romulus after the two peoples were reconciled in the wake of the "rape," or abduction, of the Sabine women. Titus was killed in mysterious circumstances while officiating at a religious ceremony.
2. The Tarquins were early kings of Rome. The last of them, who was also the last king Rome was to have, was Lucius Tarquinius Superbus, who ruled from 534 to 510 B.C.E. After his son raped the Roman matron Lu-

cretia, who committed suicide as a result, the people, led by her husband
Lucius Tarquinius Collatinus and by Lucius Iunius Brutus, rose against
him and drove him out of the city.

3. Agis (c.262–241 B.C.E.) ruled Sparta for only three or four years before he
was killed. The ephors were magistrates who were elected annually and
were intended to balance the power of the Spartan kings. Machiavelli's
source here is probably Plutarch's *Lives of Agis and Cleomenes*.

4. Cleomenes III was the king of Sparta from about 235 to 222 B.C.E. He did
indeed attempt to restore Lycurgus's laws, but his efforts at reform were
cut short when his army was beaten by the Macedonians at the battle of
Sellasia in 222. Cleomenes fled to Egypt, where he attempted to stir up a
revolution, but failed and committed suicide in the winter of 220/219.
Machiavelli's sources here are Polybius, *The Histories*, 2.45–70, and Plutarch's *Lives of Agis and Cleomenes*.

Chapter 11

On the Religion of the Romans

EVEN THOUGH ROME HAD Romulus as its first lawgiver, and like a daughter, she owed her birth and her education to him, nevertheless, the heavens decided that the institutions of the Romans would be insufficient for such a great empire, and they inspired the Roman senate to select Numa Pompilius as Romulus's successor, so that the things left out by Romulus were put in by Numa.[1] The latter, finding a very savage people and wanting to lead them to civil obedience by the arts of peace, turned to religion as something absolutely necessary to maintain a city-state, and he established it in such a way that for many centuries there was never such fear of God as in that republic.

And anyone who examines the many deeds of the Roman people as a whole, or of many of the Romans individually, will see that those citizens were much more afraid of breaking an oath than of breaking the laws, since they respected the power of God more than that of men. This is clearly manifest in the examples of Scipio and Manlius Torquatus.[2] For after Hannibal routed the Romans at Cannae, many citizens came together and, despairing of their country, agreed to abandon Italy and go away to Sicily; and when Scipio heard of this, he went to find them and with his naked sword in his hand, he forced them to swear not to abandon their country. Lucius Manlius, the father of Titus Manlius, later called Torquatus, had been accused of a crime by Marcus Pomponius, Tribune of the People, and before the day of the trial arrived, Titus went to find Marcus, and threatening to kill him if he did not withdraw the accusation against his father, forced him to swear it, and Marcus, having sworn out of fear, withdrew his accusation. Thus those citizens, whom neither the love of their country nor its laws could keep in Italy, were kept there by an oath they were forced to take, and that tribune set aside the anger he had at the father, the injury he received from the son, and his own honor, in order to obey the oath he had taken—and this arose from nothing other than the religion which Numa had introduced into that city.

And for anyone who considers Roman history carefully, it is clear how much religion helped in commanding armies, in inspiring the plebeians, in keeping men good, and in making the wicked feel shame. Thus, if one were to debate about the prince to whom Rome owed the most, Romulus or Numa, I think that Numa would sooner obtain the first place, for where there is religion, one can easily introduce arms, but where there are arms, but no religion, the former can only be introduced with difficulty. And it is clear that it was not necessary for Romulus to have the authority of God in order to set up the senate and establish other civil and military institutions, but that authority was necessary for Numa, who feigned being on familiar terms with a nymph who counseled him about the advice he had to give to the people, because he wanted to introduce new and unfamiliar institutions into that city and feared that his own authority would not suffice.[3]

And truly, there was never any legislator who gave the people extraordinary laws who did not have recourse to God, because otherwise they would not have been accepted, for there are many benefits which a prudent man recognizes, but which in themselves are not so clear and reasonable that others can be persuaded to accept them. Therefore, wise men who want to remove this difficulty have recourse to God. This is what Lycurgus did, and Solon, and many others who had the same goal as they did. Thus the Roman people marveled at Numa's goodness and prudence, and yielded to every decision he made. It is certainly true that those times were very religious and the men with whom he had to work so simple that they made it very easy for him to carry out his designs and to imprint on them with ease any new form whatever. And without a doubt, anyone who might want to create a republic in the present would find it easier to do so among men in the mountains, where there is no culture, than among those who are used to living in cities, where the culture is corrupt—just as a sculptor will get a beautiful statue out of a rough piece of marble more easily than out of one that has been badly blocked out by someone else.

Considering everything, then, I conclude that the religion introduced by Numa was among the primary causes for the success of
that city, for it produced good institutions, good institutions made
its good fortune, and from its good fortune came the happy results
of its undertakings. And as the observance of religious teaching is
the cause of the greatness of republics, similarly, disdain for it is the
cause of their ruin. For where the fear of God is lacking, the state
must necessarily either come to ruin or be held together by the fear
of a prince that will compensate for the lack of religion. But because
princes are short-lived, that state will probably fail quickly, declining
in the same measure that the ability [virtù] of the prince does. Thus,
states that depend entirely on the ability [virtù] of a single man do
not last very long, because that ability [virtù] comes to an end with
his life, and rarely does it happen that it is revived by his successor,
as Dante prudently remarks:

> Rade volte discende per li rami
> l'umana probitate, e questo vuole
> quei che la dà, perché da lui si chiami.[4]

Therefore, the salvation of a republic or a kingdom does not lie
in having a prince who governs prudently during his life, but one
who organizes the state in such a way that even after he dies, it will
survive on its own. And although it is easier to persuade uncultured
men to accept a new institution or idea, it is not, for that reason,
impossible to persuade even civilized men and those who do not
consider themselves uncultured to do so. The people of Florence
do not suppose themselves either ignorant or uncultured, yet they
were persuaded by Brother Girolamo Savonarola that he talked with
God.[5] I will not judge whether it was true or not, because one ought
to speak with reverence about such a great man, but I will certainly
say that countless people believed him without having seen anything
extraordinary to make them believe him, for his life, his teaching,
and the subjects he chose from the Bible were sufficient to make
them have faith in him. Therefore, no one should fear that he will
not be able to accomplish what has been accomplished by others,
for men, as we said in our preface, are born, live, and die, always
in the same manner.

Notes to Book 1, Chapter 11

1. Numa Pompilius (traditionally 715–673 B.C.E.) was the legendary second king of Rome; he created most of the basic rites and practices of Roman religion.

2. Publius Cornelius Scipio Africanus, the Elder (236–183 B.C.E.), was the Roman general responsible for the defeat of Hannibal and the Carthaginians at the battle of Zama in 202. For the incident concerning him that Machiavelli is about to describe, see Livy, *History of Rome*, 22.53. Titus Manlius Imperiosus Torquatus was a Roman politician and general who was active in the period 360–340 B.C.E. Renowned for his sense of filial duty and his severity, he was called Torquatus because of the golden torque, the metal collar or neck chain, he took from the body of a Gaul he defeated in a duel.

3. For Numa's relationship with a nymph, see Livy, *History of Rome*, 7.4–5.

4. From Dante's *Purgatorio*, 7.121–23: "Rarely does human worth ascend through the branches, and He wills this who gives it, so that it should be asked for from Him." The "branches" refer to one's family tree. Dante's conception here is that God has arranged it so that a person cannot pass his or her virtues on to a descendant, and thus everyone will recognize that those things come from God and pray to Him for them. In the next sentence, Machiavelli refers to *la salute* of a republic or a kingdom, a noun I have translated as "salvation" in keeping with the quotation from Dante, but which can also be rendered as "health," which fits Machiavelli's frequent identification of the prince as a physician.

5. Girolamo Savonarola (1452–1498) was a religious reformer who became the spiritual leader of Florence after the Medici were driven out in 1494. For more details, see note 5 in chapter 6 of *The Prince*.

Chapter 12

How Important It Is to Take Religion Into Account, and How Italy, for Lack of It, Thanks to the Church of Rome, Has Been Ruined

THOSE PRINCES AND REPUBLICS that want to keep themselves uncorrupted have to keep, above everything, the ceremonies of their religion uncorrupted, and hold them always as something to be venerated, for there is no greater indication of the ruin of a country than to see divine worship despised. This is easy to understand once one knows on what basis the religion of a man's birthplace is established, for every religion has, as the foundation of its life, one of its principal institutions. The religious life of the pagans was based on the responses of the oracles and on the caste of diviners and augurs. All their other ceremonies, sacrifices, and rites depended on these things, for they readily believed that the god who could predict your future for you, whether good or ill, could also grant it to you. From this came their temples, from this their sacrifices, from this their supplications and every other ceremony they used in venerating the gods, and from this they had the oracle of Delos, the temple of Jupiter Ammon, and other famous oracles which filled the world with wonder and devotion.[1] When the oracles later began to say what was pleasing to the powerful, and this falsehood was discovered by the people, men became unbelievers and were ready to subvert all their good institutions.

Therefore, the rulers of a republic or a kingdom should preserve the foundations of the religion that they profess, and once they have done this, it will be easy to keep their state religious and, in consequence, good and united. And they must support and augment everything that favors their religion, even if they think it is false, and they will do this the more, as they are more prudent and more knowledgeable about natural phenomena. And because this method has been followed by wise men, belief in miracles arose, miracles that are celebrated even in false religions, for the prudent magnify them, no matter what sort of origin they have, and their authority then makes everyone believe in them. Of these miracles there were a great many at Rome, among which there was this one: when Roman soldiers were sacking the city of Veii, some of them entered the temple of Juno, and when they approached her image and said to her, "Do you want to come to Rome?" some thought they saw her nod in assent, and others thought she said yes.[2] For those men were very religious (which Titus Livy shows us, because in entering the temple they went in without disorder, wholly devout and full of reverence), and so they thought they heard the response to their question that they perhaps anticipated. This opinion and this belief were fully supported and magnified by Camillus and by the other leaders of the city.[3]

If such religiosity had been maintained by the princes of Christendom just as its founder ordained it, Christian states and republics would be much more united and prosperous than they are. Nor can one make a better conjecture about its decline than to note how those peoples who live closest to the Church of Rome, the head of our religion, are the least religious. And anyone who considers its foundations and sees how different its present practices are from what they were, would conclude, without a doubt, that its ruin or its scourging are close at hand.

And because many are of the opinion that the well-being of the cities of Italy derives from the Church of Rome, in opposition, I want to present the necessary arguments, among which I will offer two very powerful ones, which, in my opinion, cannot be refuted. The first is that through the bad examples of that court this country has lost all piety and religion, and this has brought in its train countless improprieties and disorders, because just as where there is religion, one takes it for granted that everything is good, so, where it is lacking, one takes the contrary for granted. We Italians, therefore, owe this first debt to the Church and the priests: that we have become irreligious and wicked. But we also have a greater one, which is the second cause of our ruin: this is that the Church has kept, and still keeps, this country divided. And truly, no country was ever united and prosperous if the whole of it were not under the sway of one republic or one prince, as has happened to France and Spain.

And the reason why Italy is not in the same situation and why she, too, does not have a republic or a prince who governs her, is the Church alone. For although it has been established and held temporal power here, it has not had enough power or ability [*virtù*] to be able to create a tyranny in Italy and make itself the ruler, nor has it been so weak, on the other hand, that, for fear of losing its dominion over temporal affairs, it could not call in a foreign power to defend it against any state in Italy that had become too powerful. There are many examples of this in earlier times, as when, with the help of Charlemagne, the Church drove out the Lombards, who were practically the kings of all of Italy; and there are many in our times, as when it took away the power of the Venetians with the help of France and then drove out the French with the aid of the Swiss.[4] The fact that the Church has not been strong enough to take possession of Italy and has not permitted another to take possession of her has been the reason why Italy has not been united under one head, but has been under many princes and lords. From them there has come so much discord and weakness that she has been brought to the point of being the prey not only of powerful barbarians, but of anyone who attacks her. For this we Italians owe a debt to the Church and not to anyone else. And should someone wish to see the truth of this more directly through an actual experiment, he would have to be so powerful that he could send the Roman court, with the same authority it has in Italy, to reside in the towns of the Swiss, who are the only people who live like the ancients with regard to both religion and military institutions. And he would see that in a short time the wicked customs of that court would create more disorder in that country than any other event which might have occurred there at any time.

Notes to Book 1, Chapter 12

1. The oracle of Delos was located in a temple dedicated to Apollo on the island of Delos, which was itself sacred to the gods Apollo, Artemis, and Leto; the pronouncements of the oracle were famous throughout the Greco-Roman world. Ammon, or Amun, was an Egyptian deity who was the king of their pantheon and was thus later identified with the Greek Zeus and the Roman Jupiter.
2. On this episode, see Livy, *History of Rome*, 5.22.

3. Marcus Furius Camillus (d.365? B.C.E.) was a Roman politician and general whom Livy usually depicts as something like the second founder of Rome.

4. The Lombards, a Germanic tribe, invaded Italy between 568 and 572, eventually creating a kingdom that occupied most of the northern part of the peninsula. Pope Stephen II asked for aid against them from the Franks in 754, and in 774 the Frankish king Charlemagne succeeded in dislodging the Lombards from their kingdom. When speaking of what occurred in his own times, Machiavelli is referring to the exploits of Pope Julius II, who formed the League of Cambrai (1508–1510) with France, Spain, the Holy Roman Empire, and several Italian city-states against the Venetians, whom they defeated decisively at the battle of Agnadello in 1509. Julius was then reconciled with his enemies and formed the Holy League with them and with Spain, the Holy Roman Empire, and the Swiss against the French. Although the French defeated the troops of Julius II at Ravenna on April 11, 1512, they lost many men there, including their leader Gaston de Foix, and the next month 20,000 Swiss troops came to the aid of the pope and defeated them. The French were then expelled from Italy after the battle of Novara the next year.

Chapter 14

The Romans Interpreted Auspices According to Their Needs, and Prudently Made a Show of Observing Religion, Even When They Were Compelled Not to Do So; and They Punished Anyone Who Was So Foolhardy As to Disparage It

NOT ONLY WERE AUGURIES in large part the basis of the ancient religion of the pagans, as we said above, but they were also the cause of the well-being of the Roman republic. Consequently, the Romans took more care of them than of any other religious institution, and they made use of them at the meetings of their consuls, at the beginning of campaigns, in sending forth their armies, when engaging in battles, and in every one of their important actions, whether civil or military; nor would they have ever gone on an expedition unless they had persuaded their soldiers that the gods promised them victory. And among the other augurs in their armies they had a certain order of diviners whom they called poultrymen, and whenever they were preparing to engage the enemy in battle, they asked the poultrymen to take the auspices, for if the chickens pecked their food, they considered it a good sign and would fight, but if the chickens did not peck, they would abstain from battle. Nevertheless, when reason showed them that something had to be done, notwithstanding the fact that the auspices were adverse, they would do it in any case, but they were so clever at turning things around with their words and actions that it did not seem as though they were doing anything to disparage their religion.

This cleverness was used by the consul Papirius in a very important battle he was fighting with the Samnites, after which the latter were left completely weak and broken.[1] For when Papirius was encamped opposite the Samnites, feeling sure he would be victorious in the battle and wanting to choose the day, he ordered the poultrymen to take the auspices. But the chickens did not peck. And seeing that the army was ready and willing to fight and that the captain and all the soldiers felt that they would win, the chief of the poultrymen, in order not to deprive the army of the opportunity to do their best, reported to the consul that the auspices had gone well. So, Papirius ordered up the troops. But some of the poultrymen told certain soldiers that the chickens had not pecked; the soldiers told it to Spurius Papirius, the consul's nephew; and he reported it to the consul. The latter replied immediately that his nephew should pay attention to doing his duty and doing it well, and that, as for himself and the army, the auspices were good, and if the poultryman had told lies, it would turn out to his disadvantage. And to make the outcome correspond to his prognostication, he ordered the legates to put the poultrymen in the first lines of the battle. Whence it came about that when they were moving against the enemy, a Roman soldier shot an arrow and by chance killed the head of the poultrymen. When the consul heard of this, he said that all was going well and with the favor of the gods, for with the death of that liar the army had purged itself of any blame and of any anger that the gods might have felt against it. And so, by knowing how to adjust his plans to the auspices, he made the decision to go into battle without his army's ever realizing that he had neglected the laws of their religion in any way.

Appius Pulcher did the opposite in Sicily in the First Punic War.[2] Wishing to engage the Carthaginian army, he had the auspices taken by the poultrymen, and when they reported that the chickens would not peck, he said: "Let's see if they want to drink!" and he had them thrown into the sea. He then began the attack and lost the battle. For this he was condemned in Rome, whereas Papirius was honored, not so much because the one conquered and the other lost, as because the one had acted against the auspices with prudence and the other with rashness. Nor did this means of taking the auspices aim at any goal other than that of making the soldiers go into battle with confidence, for that confidence almost always produced victory.

Notes to Book 1, Chapter 14

1. Lucius Papirius Cursor was a Roman general who won victories over many of the Romans' enemies, including one over the Samnites in 293 B.C.E. at

the battle of Aquilonia. This is the battle Machiavelli is referring to. See Livy, *History of Rome*, 10.38–42.

2. Publius Claudius Pulcher (note: not Appius Claudius) was consul in 249 B.C.E. and defied the auspices by attacking the Carthaginian fleet at Drepana, where he lost 93 of 123 ships. He was put on trial and publicly disgraced in Rome and died some time before 246. Machiavelli's source here is either Polybius, *The Histories*, 1.49–52, or Cicero, *On the Nature of the Gods*, 2.3.7.

Chapter 58

The Masses Are Wiser and More Constant
Than a Prince

NOTHING IS MORE FICKLE and inconstant than the masses, as our Titus Livy, like all the other historians, affirms. For in the narratives of men's actions, we often see how the masses condemn someone to death, and then the very same people weep for him and ardently wish he were alive, as the Roman people can be seen to have done with Manlius Capitolinus, for they condemned him to death and then ardently wished he were alive. These are the author's words: "The people were immediately filled with desire for him as soon as he no longer were a danger to them."[1] And elsewhere, when Livy discusses the events that occurred in Sicily after the death of Hieronymus, the grandson of Hieron, he says: "This is the nature of the masses: either they obey with servility, or they rule with arrogance."[2]

I do not know if I should undertake a task that is hard and full of so many difficulties that I shall either have to abandon it with shame or pursue it with great effort; for I want to defend an argument which is attacked by all the writers. But however that may be, I do not think, nor shall I ever think, that it is wrong to defend an opinion by using rational arguments and without invoking authority or employing force. I say, then, that all men, and especially princes, can be blamed individually for having this fault for which writers criticize the masses, since everyone whose conduct is not regulated by the laws will make the same mistakes that the unregulated masses make. And this can be easily seen, for there are, and have been, a great many princes, but of good and wise ones, there have been few. I am speaking of the princes who have been able to break the bridles that might have held them in check, among whom are not the kings who were born in Egypt, when in the most ancient time of antiquity that country was governed by laws; nor the kings who were born in Sparta; nor those of our times who have been born in France, a kingdom which is regulated more by the laws than any other contemporary kingdom we know about. The kings who were born under such constitutions as these should not be put in the same group as those whose natures we have to consider individually in order to see if they are similar to the masses. For those other kings should be compared to the masses who are controlled by the laws just as much as they are; and in those masses we will find the same goodness that we find in those kings, and we will see that they neither rule with arrogance, nor obey with servility. The Roman populace was like this, for as long as the republic remained uncorrupted, it never obeyed with servility or ruled with arrogance; on the contrary, with its laws and its magistrates, it honorably preserved its place in society. When it was necessary to rise up together against some powerful man, it would do so, as it did against Manlius, the Decemvirate, and others who sought to oppress it, and when it was necessary to obey the dictators and the consuls, for reasons of public safety, it would do so.[3] And if the Roman people longed for Manlius Capitolinus after his death, that is no wonder, for they longed for his abilities [virtù], which were such that the memory of them aroused compassion in everyone, and they would have had the power to produce the same effect in a prince, since, in the opinion of all the writers, ability [virtù] is praised and admired even in one's enemies. But if Manlius had been brought back to life in response to this longing, the people of Rome would have pronounced the same judgment on him as they did when they took him from prison and condemned him to death. Still, we see that some princes are considered wise who have had someone killed and then deeply longed for him, as Alexander did for Cleitus and other friends of his, and Herod did for Mariamne.[4] But what our historian says about the nature of the masses, he is not saying about them when they are regulated by the laws, as the Romans were, but about the unrestrained ones, like the Syracusans, who made the errors which men commit when they are infuriated and unrestrained, just as Alexander and Herod did in the examples mentioned. Therefore, the nature of the masses is not more to be blamed than is that of princes, for all do wrong in the same way when there is nothing to make them refrain from doing wrong. Of this, beyond what I have said, there are a great many examples both among the Roman emperors and among other tyrants and princes, in whom one sees as much inconstancy and changeability in behavior as would never be found in any multitude.

I conclude, therefore, against the common opinion which says that the people, when they are in power, are variable, fickle, and ungrateful, and I affirm that they commit these sins in the same way that individual princes do. And anyone who blames both the people and princes alike might be speaking the truth, but by excepting princes, he deceives himself, for a people that rules and is well regulated will be stable, prudent, and grateful just like a prince, or better than a prince, even though he is considered wise; and on the other hand, a prince unrestrained by the laws will be ungrateful, fickle, and imprudent more than the people will. Nor does the difference in their behavior derive from a difference in nature, for that is the same in everyone—and if there is a positive advantage here, it lies with the people—but rather, the difference between them derives from their having more or less respect for the laws under which both of them live.

Anyone who considers the Roman people will see that for four hundred years they hated the title of king and loved the glory and the common good of their country, and he will see many examples in them that bear witness to both attributes. And if anyone should allege the ingratitude they displayed toward Scipio, I will reply with what was said at length above about this subject, where I showed that the people were less ungrateful than princes.[5] But as for prudence and stability, I say that the people are more prudent, more stable, and better judges than a prince. And not without reason is the voice of the people compared to that of God, for popular opinion has been seen to predict things in such a marvelous way that it is as if some occult power [*virtù*] enables it to foresee the evil and the good that may befall it.[6] As for judging things, when the people listen to two speakers who argue different views with equal ability [*virtù*], very rarely do we see them fail to choose the better opinion and show themselves incapable of understanding the truth they hear. And if they do err in matters of courage or utility, as was said above, a prince often errs, too, because of his own passions, which are more numerous than those of the people. It is also evident that in choosing magistrates they make by far better choices than a prince does, nor will the people ever be persuaded that it is good to put in public office a man of bad repute and corrupt habits, something which a prince is persuaded to do in a thousand different ways. When the people begin to have a horror of something, one sees that they keep to this opinion for many centuries—something not found in a prince. And for both of these things I will let the Roman people suffice as evidence, for in so many hundreds of years and so many elections of consuls and tribunes, they did not make four choices of which they had to repent. And they had, as I have said, so much hatred of the name of king that no sense of obligation they felt toward any citizen who was trying for that title would allow him to escape the punishment he deserved for doing so. Furthermore, we see that cities where the people rule expand enormously in a very short time, and much more than those cities which have always been under a prince, as Rome did after the expulsion of the kings, and Athens after it freed itself from Pisistratus.[7] This cannot arise from anything other than the fact that governments of the people are better than those of princes. Nor do I wish anyone to cite in opposition to this opinion of mine that which our historian says in the text cited earlier, or in any other one, for if we consider all the faults of the people and all the faults of princes, all the glories of the people and all those of princes, it will be seen that the people are far superior in goodness and in glory. And so, if princes are superior to the people in instituting laws, forming civil societies, and establishing statues and new institutions, the people are so superior in preserving the things that have been established that they, without a doubt, attain the same glory as those who established them.

In short, to conclude this subject, I say that just as princely states have lasted a very long time, so, too, have republics, and both needed to be regulated by the laws, for a prince who can do what he wants is mad, and a people that can do what it wants is not wise. If we are speaking, therefore, about a prince who is bound by the laws and about a people that is enchained by them, we will see more worth [*virtù*] in the people than in the prince; if we are speaking about both of them when they are unrestrained, we will see fewer errors in the people than in the prince, and they will be less serious and will have better remedies. For a good man can speak to a li-

centious and disorderly people and easily lead it back to the right
road, whereas no one can speak to a wicked prince, nor is there any
remedy for him except the sword. From this one can conjecture
about the seriousness of the maladies of both: if words suffice to
cure the malady of the people, and if the sword is necessary for that
of the prince, no one would fail to conclude that where the cure
was greater, there the errors are greater. When a people is truly
unrestrained, one need not fear its foolish actions; one does not
have to be afraid of present evils, but of that which could arise, since
a tyrant might appear in the midst of so much confusion. But the
contrary is the case with wicked princes: one fears present evils while
feeling hope for the future, since men persuade themselves that the
ruler's wicked life may lead to a resurgence of freedom. Thus you
see the difference between the two, which is between the things that
are and those that are to come. The cruelties of the masses are
directed against those they fear will usurp the common good; those
of a prince are against people he fears will usurp his own property.
But the prejudice against the people arises because everyone can
speak evil of the people without fear and in freedom, even while
they are ruling, but of princes one always speaks with a thousand
fears and hesitations.

Notes to Book 1, Chapter 58

1. Livy, *History of Rome*, 6.20. In 390 B.C.E., the half-legendary Marcus Manlius Capitolinus supposedly repulsed the Gauls from the Capitol (hence
   his nickname Capitolinus) after being awakened to the danger by Juno's
   geese. He was put to death in 384 because of his tyrannical ambitions.

2. Livy, *History of Rome*, 24.25. For Hieron, see *The Prince*, chapter 6, note
   6. Hieronymus succeeded Hieron II to the throne of Syracuse in 216 B.C.E.
   He was persuaded to break the traditional alliance his city had with the
   Romans in order to support the Carthaginians and was about to lead an
   army into the field to assist them when he was assassinated in 215.

3. On Manlius, see book 1, chapter 11, note 2. According to Roman tradition,
   all regular magistracies were suspended in 450 B.C.E. and replaced by a
   board composed of ten men, the Decemvirate (from *decem*, "ten," and
   viri, "men"). This board was largely made up of former consuls and was
   charged with rewriting the Roman law code. It was appointed for one year
   and was succeeded by a second board in 451. That second board attempted

to extend its powers and to exceed its term in office, and it is that board which the Roman plebeians resisted.

4. As an absolute monarch, Alexander the Great (356–323 B.C.E.) did not tolerate criticism at court. When his friend Cleitus (d. 328 B.C.E.) criticized him at a banquet, Alexander killed him in a drunken fury, though he later regretted it. Herod the Great (c. 73–4 B.C.E.) ruled over Judea and other areas of Palestine under the Romans. Toward the end of his life he became increasingly savage toward members of his own family, and in the year 7 B.C.E. intrigues led him to have his favorite wife Mariamne and her two sons executed.

5. Machiavelli discusses this subject in chapters 29 and 30 of book 1. He argues there that both princes and peoples are ungrateful either out of avarice or out of suspicion and fear, so that when a general leads their army to victory, they both have two motives for ingratitude: they may be ungrateful to him either because they are greedy and do not wish to reward him, or because they fear he may become too powerful. Machiavelli argues that the people, unlike princes, are not moved by greed and also that they are much less likely to be fearful and suspicious of those who fight on their behalf. He then goes on to praise the Roman people as the least ungrateful of all, despite their treatment of Scipio. Publius Cornelius Scipio Africanus, the Elder (236–183 B.C.E.), was the Roman general responsible for the defeat of Hannibal and the Carthaginians at the battle of Zama in 202. His success brought him great glory and esteem, but also made him suspect to many at Rome, who opposed him repeatedly in the political arena. Finally, in 184, he was accused of embezzling state funds and taking bribes, but avoided trial by going into voluntary exile, where he died the next year.

6. Machiavelli translates here the Latin saying *Vox populi, vox dei*: "the voice of the people is the voice of God."

7. See book 1, chapter 2, note 3.

Book 2

Preface

MEN ALWAYS PRAISE ANTIQUITY and fault the present, although not always reasonably, and they are partisans of things past such that not only do they celebrate those ages that they know from what historians have preserved of them, but also those that as old men they recall having seen in their youth. And if this opinion of theirs is false, as it is most of the time, I am persuaded that there are various causes that lead them into this deception. The first, I believe, is that we do not fully understand the truth about antiquity and that most of the time the things that are hidden about it would bring it into disgrace, while those that could bestow glory on it are presented magnificently and in the greatest detail. For most writers are so obsequious in response to the fortune of those who win that, in order to render their victories glorious, they not only enhance that which those men accomplished by means of their prowess [*virtuosamente*], but also embellish the actions of their enemies, so that anyone born afterward in the two countries, whether that of the winner or that of the defeated, has reason to marvel at those men and those times and is forced to praise them and love them in the highest degree. Moreover, since men hate things out of fear or envy, two very powerful reasons for the hatred of things in the past are eliminated, since they cannot harm you and give you no reason to envy them. But the contrary is the case with things where we are actors or spectators, for, nothing about them being hidden, you can have a full understanding of them, and since you see that, in addition to what is good, there are other things in them that you dislike, you are forced to judge them inferior to things in the past, even though present ones might be much worthier of glory and renown. I am not speaking about matters related to the arts, which are so lustrous in themselves that time can hardly take away or give

186

them more glory than they merit in and of themselves, but I am talking about things pertaining to the lives and customs of men about which we do not see such clear evidence.

I reply, therefore, that it is true that the habit of praising the past and blaming the present exists. However, it is not always true that they are in error who do so, for sometimes their judgment is necessarily correct, since human affairs, being always in motion, are either rising or falling. And so, one city or country is seen to have been given a well-organized government by some excellent man, and for a time, thanks to the ability [*virtù*] of its founder, it just gets better and better. A person who is born in such a state and praises ancient times more than modern ones deceives himself, and his deception is caused by the things said above. But those who are born later in that city or province, when the time has arrived for it to descend to a worse condition, do not then deceive themselves. And when I think about how these things go on, I conclude that the world has always been in the same condition and that there has been as much good as bad in it, but the bad and the good vary from country to country, as is seen in what we know about ancient kingdoms, which differed from one another in their customs, although the world always stayed the same. There was only this difference, that whereas the world had first placed its talents [*virtù*] in Assyria, it then put them in Media, then in Persia, so that they finally came to Italy and Rome; and if the Roman empire was not succeeded by an empire that lasted, nor was there any place in which the world kept together all of its talents [*virtù*], nevertheless, we see that they have been scattered among many nations where people live ably [*virtuosamente*], as formerly in the kingdom of the French, the kingdom of the Turks, and that of the Sultan, and today among the people of Germany, and earlier with that Saracen tribe which accomplished so many great things and occupied so much territory after it destroyed the Eastern Roman Empire.[1] In all of these countries, then, after the Romans came to ruin, and in all of these peoples, there have been, and still are in some part of them, the talents [*virtù*] that people long for and that are praised with true praise. He who is born in those countries and praises times past more than the present could be deceiving himself, but he who is born in Italy and Greece—not someone who has come into Italy from beyond the mountains, nor a Turk in Greece—has reason to find fault with his own times and to praise others. For in those other countries there are a great many things they do that are marvels; in these two there is nothing that redeems them from every sort of extreme misery, infamy, and vituperation; in them no care is given to religion, none to laws, none to military matters; and everything is stained with filth of every sort. And these vices are all the more detestable as they are more to be found in those who preside at tribunals, rule over others, and wish to be adored.

But returning to our discussion, I say that if men's judgment is defective in deciding whether the present century or antiquity is better with regard to those things which, because of their antiquity, we cannot have as perfect a knowledge of as we do of our own times, then that ability to judge should not be defective in old men when judging the times of their youth and their age, since they have known and seen both equally. This would be true if men always judged the same way and had the same appetites at all times in their lives, but since these change, even though the times do not, things will not seem the same to men who have other appetites, other pleasures, and other concerns in their age than in their youth. For as men age, they lose vigor, while gaining in judgment and prudence, so that those things which seemed tolerable and good in their youth must necessarily become intolerable and bad as they grow older, and where they ought to blame their judgment for this, they blame the times. Besides, since the appetites of humans are insatiable—for they have from nature the power and the will to desire everything, and from Fortune the ability to obtain very little—the result of this is a continual discontent in human minds and a weariness with the things they possess, which makes them fault the present, praise the past, and long for the future, even though they are not moved by any reasonable cause to do so. I do not know if I deserve to be numbered among those who deceive themselves if in these discourses of mine I praise the times of the ancient Romans too much while finding fault with our own. And truly, if the virtue [*virtù*] that ruled then and the vice that rules now were not clearer than the sun, I would be more restrained in speaking, fearful of falling into the same deception for which I blame others. But since the matter is so manifest that everyone sees it, I will be bold and will say clearly what I understand of ancient and of modern times, so that the minds of the young men who read my writings might turn away from the latter and prepare to imitate the former whenever Fortune should give them the opportunity to do so. For it is the duty of a good man to teach others about the good which you yourself have not been able to achieve because of the malignity of the times and of Fortune, so that since many have the capability, someone who is more loved by Heaven will be able to put it into effect.

Note to Book 2, Preface

1. The "Sultan" is the Sultan of Egypt; Machiavelli is referring here to the Mamelukes, a dynasty of warrior-princes who ruled Egypt as sultans from the thirteenth century until they were displaced by the Turks in 1517. The "Saracen tribe" is the Turks, who completed their conquest of the Byzantine Empire by taking Constantinople in 1453 and then continued to spread into the Balkan peninsula and central Europe during the next three centuries.

Chapter 13

Men Go from a Low Station to Great Fortune More Often by Means of Fraud Than of Force

I BELIEVE IT IS very true that rarely, if ever, it happens that men of small fortune arrive at elevated positions without force and fraud, although others may acquire that position as a gift or an inheritance. Nor do I believe that force alone has ever been found to have sufficed, although it will be found that fraud alone is often enough, as anyone will see clearly who reads the life of Philip of Macedonia, that of Agathocles of Sicily, and those of many other similar men who from the lowest, or at least a low, station have acquired either kingdoms or very large empires.[1] Xenophon shows in his *Life of Cyrus* the necessity of deception: considering that the first expedition Cyrus made against the king of Armenia is full of fraud and that he used deception and not force in order to take possession of his kingdom, one cannot conclude from such actions anything other than that a prince who wants to accomplish great things must necessarily use deception.[2] Xenophon says, moreover, that Cyrus deceived his maternal uncle Cyaxeres, the king of the Medes, in many ways, and he demonstrates that without that fraud Cyrus could never have attained the greatness that he did. Nor do I believe that anyone who was placed in a low station ever achieved a great empire by means of open force alone and without guile, but one can indeed do so by fraud alone, as did Giovan Galeazzo Visconti who took the state and the government of Lombardy from Messer Bernabò, his uncle.[3]

What princes are obliged to do when beginning the expansion of their realms, republics are also obliged to do until they have become powerful and force alone is sufficient. And because Rome, whether by chance or by choice, in every instance used all the means necessary to attain greatness, she did not fail to use this one, too. She could not have adopted a greater deception at the start than to have used the method described by us above of obtaining allies for herself, for under this name she made them her slaves, as were the Latins and the other peoples around her.[4] First, she availed herself of their armies in order to subdue neighboring peoples and to acquire a reputation as a state; then, once they were subdued, she became so great that she could beat everyone. And the Latins never realized they were totally enslaved until they saw her defeat the Samnites twice and force them to make peace.[5] As this victory increased greatly the reputation the Romans had among distant princes, who heard about the name of Rome through it, but had no experience of her armies, so it generated envy and suspicion in those who both heard about and saw her armies, among whom were the Latins. And this envy and this fear were so great that not only the Latins, but the colonies they had in Latium, together with the Campanians, who had been defended just before then by the Romans, conspired against the Roman nation. And the Latins brought about this war in the manner in which, as we described above, most wars are brought about, not by attacking the Romans, but by defending the Sidicini against the Samnites, who were waging war against them with the permission of the Romans. And that it is true that the Latins brought about this war because they recognized the Romans' deception, Titus Livy shows us, speaking through the mouth of the Latin praetor Annius Setinus, who spoke these words to them in their council: "For if even now we can endure slavery under the cover of a treaty of equals, etc."[6] Thus it is clear that in their initial expansion the Romans also did not fail to use fraud, which those who want to rise from humble beginnings to the loftiest heights must always use, and which is less to be criticized the more it is concealed, as was this of the Romans.

Notes to Book 2, Chapter 13

1. Philip II of Macedonia (382–336 B.C.E.) had a fairly obscure youth in Thebes, but eventually claimed the throne of Macedonia and was the architect of its expansion into an empire. Agathocles of Syracuse (361–289 B.C.E.) came to power in 316, thanks to a military coup; in chapter 8 of *The Prince* Machiavelli says he was the son of a potter, although his father was actually the wealthy owner of a pottery factory.

2. On Cyrus and the king of Armenia, see Xenophon, *Cyropaedia*, 2.4.31

through 3.1.6. On Cyrus and Cyaxeres in the next sentence, see *Cyropaedia*, 4.5.8–34. Machiavelli is, perhaps deliberately, misremembering Xenophon, who presents Cyrus as engaging in deception only when he was involved in military campaigns.

3. Giovan (or Gian) Galeazzo Visconti (1351?–1402) inherited Pavia from his father in 1378, assassinated his uncle in 1385 (he had been the joint-ruler of Milan with him), and was made duke of Milan in 1395 by the Holy Roman Emperor.

4. In the fourth chapter of this book, Machiavelli praises Rome for the way that it contracted alliances with various peoples in the Italian peninsula, using them in its wars of expansion, but always making sure that it controlled the alliances it had made.

5. The Samnites were defeated twice in 343 B.C.E.; see Livy, *History of Rome*, 7.33, 36–37.

6. See Livy, *History of Rome*, 8.4.2. Machiavelli discussed briefly the way that the Latins brought about this war in the ninth chapter of this book of the *Discourses*.

Chapter 29

Fortune Blinds Men's Minds When She Does Not Want Them to Oppose Her Designs

IF ONE CONSIDERS CAREFULLY how human affairs proceed, one will often see things arise and accidents happen against which the heavens did not wish us to make any provision at all. And if what I am describing happened at Rome, where there was so much ability [*virtù*], religion, and order, it is no wonder that it occurs much more often in a city or a country which is lacking those things. And because this topic is very noteworthy for demonstrating the power of heaven in human affairs, Titus Livy unfolds it at length and with the most moving words.[1] He says that since heaven wanted the Romans, for whatever reason, to know its power, first it caused the Fabii to err when they went as ambassadors to the Gauls, and through their actions it excited the Gauls to wage war on Rome; then it ordered that nothing worthy of the Roman people should be done in Rome in order to put a stop to that war, since they had earlier ordered that Camillus, who might have been the sole remedy for such a great evil, should be sent into exile in Ardea; and then, when the Gauls were approaching Rome, the Romans, who had often created dictators as a remedy to deal with the assaults of the Volscians and of other neighboring peoples who were their enemies, did not create one when they saw the Gauls coming. Moreover, in choosing soldiers, they did it feebly and without much care, and they were so slow in taking up arms that they almost failed to arrive in time to meet the Gauls at the river Allia, ten miles outside of Rome. There the tribunes set up their camp without any of their usual diligence, not inspecting the site first, not surrounding it with a ditch and a stockade, and not availing themselves of any remedy, human or divine, for the situation; and in setting things up for the battle, they made their formation thin and weak, so that neither the soldiers nor their captains were doing anything worthy of Roman discipline. Then they fought without bloodshed because they fled before they were attacked, and the greater part of them went away to Veii, while the others retreated to Rome, where they entered the Capitol without first going to their houses; the senate, without a thought for defending Rome, did not close the gates, or anything else, and part of them fled and part of them entered the Capitol with the others. However, in defending the Capitol, they used methods that were not disorderly, for they did not burden it with useless people and stored all the grain there they could in order to survive a siege; and as for the useless crowd of old people, women, and children, the majority fled to neighboring towns, while the remainder stayed in Rome at the mercy of the Gauls. Thus, anyone who would have read about what that people had done many years before and then read about them in this period would not have believed in any way that they were the same people. And Titus Livy, having described all the disorders just mentioned, concludes by saying: "Fortune blinds men's minds to such an extent when she does not want them to check her growing power."[2] This conclusion could not be truer: men who ordinarily experience either great adversity or great prosperity deserve less praise or less blame, for one usually sees that they have been urged on to ruin or to greatness by some great advantage that the heavens have held out to them, thereby either giving them the opportunity to act effectively [*virtuosamente*], or taking it away from them.

Fortune certainly does this: when she wants to accomplish great things, she selects a man who has so much courage and so much ability [*virtù*] that he will recognize the opportunities she places before him. Similarly, when she wishes to bring about great disasters, she puts forward men who will contribute to them. And if there is anyone who opposes her, either she kills him, or she deprives him of any means to bring about anything good.

We certainly see from this passage how, in order to make Rome greater and lead it to the grandeur it achieved, Fortune judged that it was necessary to beat it down (as we will discuss at length at the start of the next book), although she did not wish to ruin it entirely. And for this purpose we see that she had Camillus exiled and not killed; had Rome captured and not the Capitol; commanded that the Romans, in order to protect Rome, should not think of anything good, but then, in order to defend the Capitol, should not overlook any good preparation. Once Rome was taken, she caused the majority of the soldiers who were defeated at Allia to go to Veii, thus eliminating any way to defend the city of Rome. But in commanding all this, she prepared everything for Rome's recovery, since she had led an entire Roman army to Veii, and Camillus to Ardea, so that they could put a great force in the field under a captain who, not spotted with ignominy because of defeat, had his reputation intact, so that they might recapture their native city.

In confirmation of what has been said, some modern examples might be adduced, but we will omit them as unnecessary since we feel the one we have given should satisfy everyone. I certainly affirm once again that this is most true, according to what we see in all the histories: men can assist Fortune, but not oppose her; they can weave the warp of her designs, but not break it. They should certainly never abandon the struggle, for, since they do not know her purpose, and since she goes by crooked and unknown roads, they always have hope, and having hope, they should never give up, no matter what fortune and what difficulty they find themselves in.

Notes to Book 2, Chapter 29

1. See Livy, *History of Rome*, 5.35–37, 48–55. Livy recounts how the Gauls had been invited into Italy and were in the town of Clusium in the northeastern part of the peninsula when Quintus Fabius Ambustus and two of his brothers were sent to negotiate their withdrawal in 391 B.C.E. Instead, the brothers violated protocol by fighting the Gauls. Upon returning to Rome, they were elected to lead Rome's army, but at the river Allia they were defeated by the Gauls, who then proceeded to sack the city. Marcus Furius Camillus (d. 365? B.C.E.) was a Roman politician and general who was elected consular tribune six times and dictator five times during his life. Despite his victories over various neighboring peoples, the plebeians grew discontented with him and sent him into exile in 391. He was, however, recalled the next year after the Gauls invaded, was appointed dictator, and defeated the Gauls, driving them out of Italy. He then expanded the empire by leading successful campaigns against several other Italian states. Livy generally depicts him as something like a second founder of Rome.
2. *History of Rome*, 5.37.1.

Book 3

Chapter 3

How It Is Necessary to Kill the Sons of Brutus in Order to Preserve a Newly Acquired Freedom

THE SEVERITY OF BRUTUS was no less necessary than useful to preserve in Rome the liberty that he had acquired for her. It is a rare example in all of history to see a father sit in judgment and not only condemn his sons to death, but to be present at their execution.[1] And those who read ancient history will always recognize this: after a change of government, whether from a republic to a tyranny or from a tyranny to a republic, there must be a memorable punishment of those who are the enemies of the present state of affairs. And so, he who creates a tyranny and does not kill Brutus, and he who establishes a free state and does not kill the sons of Brutus, will not last long. Since I discussed this at length above, I refer to what was said there.[2] Here I will adduce just one example from our times and our city that is worthy of being remembered. And this is Piero Soderini, who believed that with his patience and his goodness he could overcome the desire in the sons of Brutus to put themselves back under another form of government—and in this he deceived himself.[3] Although he, being prudent, recognized what was necessary, and although chance and the ambition of those who fought against him gave him the opportunity to wipe them out, nevertheless, he could never make up his mind to do so. For, in addition to believing that with patience and goodness he could eliminate those bad humors[4] and that with rewards he could extinguish some men's hostility, he thought (and many times assured his friends) that in order to take vigorous action against the opposition and beat his adversaries, he would have to assume extraordinary authority and break the laws of civic equality, and he felt that such authority, even if he did not use it tyrannically, would so dismay the general public that after his death they would never again agree to appoint a *gonfaloniere* for life, something he thought it a good idea to strengthen and preserve.

This hesitation was wise and good. Nevertheless, one should never let an evil continue out of respect for a good when that good can easily be overwhelmed by that evil. And Soderini should have believed that since his deeds and his intentions were going to be judged by their outcome (if his fortune and his life lasted that long), he would have been able to convince everyone then that what he had done had been done for the safety of the state and not because of his ambition, and that he would have been able to arrange things so that his successor could not use for an evil end what he had used for a good one. But he was deceived in his first opinion, not recognizing that malevolence is not mastered by time or placated by any sort of gift. Thus, because he did not know how to imitate Brutus, he lost, together with his country, his position in the government and his reputation.

Notes to Book 3, Chapter 3

1. See Livy, *History of Rome*, 2.5. In Livy's account, Lucius Iunius Brutus was the republican hero who was responsible for the expulsion of Tarquinus Superbus and the ending of the Roman monarchy in 509 B.C.E. Admired for his rigor, he supposedly had two of his sons killed for plotting to bring back the kings. The more famous Brutus, Marcus Iunius Brutus, who participated in the assassination of Julius Caesar, stressed his connection to this figure who was his ancestor.
2. Machiavelli may be referring to chapter 16 of book 1 of the *Discourses*, but he covers some of the same material in *The Prince*, chapters 5–8.
3. Piero di Tommaso Soderini (1452–1522) was a Florentine statesman who was elected *gonfaloniere* for life in 1502 in an attempt by the Florentines to provide some sort of stability for their republican government. He was responsible for creating a citizen militia and was recognized for the mildness of his rule. However, he was forced to flee Florence in 1512 when papal troops restored the Medici to power, and although he was later reconciled with the Medici Pope Leo X and served him in Rome, he was never allowed to return to Florence. Note: a *gonfaloniere* was a "standard-bearer," someone who held the banner or flag (*gonfalo*) when leading troops into battle. In 1289 the Florentines created the *gonfaloniere del popolo* ("standard-bearer of the people"), also called the *gonfaloniere della*

repubblica ("standard-bearer of the republic") and the *gonfaloniere di giu-stizia* ("standard-bearer of justice"), who headed a force of a thousand armed men that protected the civil magistrates of the city. By the fifteenth century, the term had lost its military meaning and identified instead the person who was elected as the executive head of the civil government. This was the position that Soderini held.

4. Machiavelli refers here to "humors," by which he means the different classes or political factions that exist in the state; he is thinking of the state as being like the body—as a body politic—in which an imbalance of bodily fluids, or humors, was an indication of disease or ill health. For a more detailed discussion of the humors, see *The Prince*, chapter 9, note 1.

Chapter 9

How One Must Change with the Times If One Wants Always to Have Good Fortune

I HAVE OFTEN NOTED that the cause of the bad and of the good fortune of men is the fit between their mode of proceeding and the times, for it is clear that some men proceed impetuously in their affairs, and some, diffidently and cautiously, and because in both of these modes men go beyond the proper limits and are not able to keep to the true path, they make errors in both. However, that man turns out to err less and to enjoy a more prosperous fortune when the times fit his mode of action, as I said, and when you always proceed in the way nature forces you to go. Everyone knows how Fabius Maximus proceeded in a diffident and cautious manner with his army, far removed from all the impetuousness and audacity typical of the Romans, and his good fortune made his method sort well with the times. For since Hannibal, a young man with a fresh fortune, had come into Italy and had already beaten the Roman people twice, and since that republic was almost deprived of its best troops and was terrified, it could have had no better fortune than to have had a captain who with his hesitation and caution kept the enemy at bay.[1] Nor could Fabius have ever found times more suited to his methods, all of which redounded to his glory. And that Fabius did this because of his nature and not by choice is evident in the fact that when Scipio wanted to cross over into Africa with their armies in order to terminate the war, Fabius, as a man who could not detach himself from his methods and his habits, vigorously opposed Scipio's plan, so that if it had been up to him, Hannibal would still be in Italy, for Fabius did not perceive that the times had changed and that it was necessary to change the methods of waging war.[2] And if Fabius had been the king of Rome, he could have easily lost that war, for he would not have known how to vary his ways in keeping with changing circumstances. But he was born in a republic where there were different kinds of citizens and different kinds of humors,[3] and just as Rome had Fabius, who was the best leader when the times required that the war be drawn out, so it later had Scipio when the time was ripe to win it.

This is why it happens that a republic has a longer life and enjoys good fortune longer than a principality does, for it can adapt itself to changes in circumstances, thanks to the different kinds of citizens in it, better than a prince is able to do. For a man who is used to acting in one way will never change, as has been said, and when the times change and no longer harmonize with his methods, he will come to ruin.

Piero Soderini, cited on other occasions, acted in all his affairs with humanity and patience.[4] Both he and his country prospered when circumstances conformed to his mode of proceeding, but when the time came later for him to put aside his patience and humility, he did not know how to do so, so that he, together with his country, was ruined. Throughout the entire duration of his pontificate, Pope Julius II acted impetuously and passionately, and because the times suited him well, all of his undertakings succeeded.[5] But if other times had come that would have required a different method, he would necessarily have come to ruin, for he would not have changed either his methods or his way of behaving. And there are two reasons why we cannot change ourselves: first, we cannot oppose the way in which nature is leading us; second, if a man has prospered greatly using one mode of proceeding, it is not possible to persuade him that he can do well by proceeding differently. The result is that Fortune will change for that man, since she makes the circumstances change, but he does not vary his methods. From this the ruin of cities also comes about, since republics do not change their institutions with the times, as we discussed at length above; rather, they move quite slowly, and it is more difficult for them to change, since that requires circumstances that will unsettle the entire state, and then it will not be enough to have just one man who adapts his methods to the times.[6]

Notes to Book 3, Chapter 9

1. Quintus Fabius Maximus Cunctator (d. 203 B.C.E.) was the great opponent of Hannibal in the first, defensive phases of the Second Punic War (218–201 B.C.E.); his policy of cautiously refusing to engage in battles he knew he would lose earned him the sobriquet of Cunctator, "the hesitator."

2. Publius Cornelius Scipio Africanus (236–183 B.C.E.) was a Roman general and statesman who defeated the Carthaginians in Spain and then carried the war to Africa, where he decisively defeated Hannibal at the battle of Zama in 202.

3. Machiavelli refers here to "humors," by which he means the different classes or political factions that exist in the state; he is thinking of the state as being like the body—as a body politic—in which an imbalance of bodily fluids, or humors, was an indication of disease or ill health. For a more detailed discussion of the humors, see *The Prince*, chapter 9, note 1.

4. Machiavelli mentions him, for example, in chapter 3 of book 3 of the *Discourses*, which is included here. See note 3 to that chapter.

5. Machiavelli discusses Julius II at length in chapter 25 of *The Prince*.

6. Machiavelli discusses the inability of republics to adapt swiftly to new circumstances in the first chapter of book 3 of the *Discourses*.

Chapter 19

Whether Indulgence or Punishment Is More Necessary in Ruling the Masses

THE ROMAN REPUBLIC WAS stirred up by hostility between the nobles and the plebeians, yet when war was upon them, they sent out Quintius and Appius Claudius with the armies.[1] Because he was cruel and harsh as a commander, Appius was scarcely obeyed by his men, so that, on the brink of defeat, he fled from the province, whereas Quintius, because he was kind and of a humane disposition, had obedient soldiers and carried away the victory. From this it seems that to govern the masses it would be better to be humane than haughty, merciful than cruel. Nevertheless, Cornelius Tacitus, with whom many other writers agree, reaches the opposite conclusion in one of his maxims, when he says: "In ruling the masses punishment is worth more than indulgence."[2] In considering how these two opinions can be reconciled, I would say that you will be ruling either men who are normally your equals, or men who will always be your subjects. If they are your equals, you cannot simply use punishments or that severity of which Cornelius speaks. And because the Roman plebeians had equal authority with the nobility in Rome, a man who became their ruler there for a time could not treat them with cruelty and harshness. Moreover, it is clear that Roman captains who got their armies to love them and treated them with indulgence often got better results than did those who made themselves extraordinarily feared, unless they were endowed with exceptional ability [*virtù*], as Manlius Torquatus was.[3] But the man who commands subjects, of whom Cornelius was speaking, must incline toward punishment rather than indulgence so that they do not become insolent and trample all over you because of your easy-going nature. But this should also be done in a moderate way so as to avoid hatred, for making himself hated never turns out to be for the good of a prince. The way to avoid it is to leave your subjects' property alone, for, except when the act disguises greed, no prince desires to shed blood, unless he is forced to do so, and this necessity seldom appears. But when greed is involved in the act, the necessity appears all the time, for there is never a lack of reasons, or of desire, to spill blood, as I explain in detail in another treatise on this subject.[4] Thus, Quintius merits more praise than Appius, and the maxim of Cornelius, within its limits, also deserves to be approved, although not in the way Appius applied it.

Notes to Book 3, Chapter 19

1. Titus Quintius Barbatus Capitolinus and Appius Claudius Sabinus were elected consul in 471 B.C.E. and put in charge of the Roman army during a period of internal disorder. Titus Quintius (b. 501? B.C.E.) was elected consul six times between 471 and 439, and was known for his moderation and mildness and his desire for concord between the patricians and the plebeians. Appius Claudius, by contrast, was known for his violent opposition to the plebeians. He imposed harsh discipline on the army, and when it fled from a battle, he had it punished brutally. In 470, according to Livy, accusations were brought against him by the tribunes, but he died before going to trial. In other accounts, he is said to have killed himself. There is, however, evidence of an Appius Claudius who was made consul in 451 and who was also bitterly hostile to the plebeians; this may have been the same person or perhaps his son. Machiavelli's point in this sentence is that the army, which was composed of plebeians, was being led by patricians. On this episode, see Livy, *History of Rome*, 2.55–60.

2. Tacitus, *Annals*, 3.55.4. Publius (?) Cornelius Tacitus (c.56–120) was a Roman historian of republican sympathies who produced a variety of works, including minor ones on Germany and oratory, and two major histories, the *Annals* and the *Histories*, which deal with the reigns of the emperors of the first century.

3. Titus Manlius Imperiosus Torquatus was a Roman politician and general who was active in the period 360–340 B.C.E. He was renowned for his sense of filial duty and his severity. One story has him executing his son for having fought a duel against orders. See *Discourses*, book 1, chapter 11, note 2.

4. Machiavelli is referring to *The Prince*, chapter 17.

Chapter 49

If a Republic Is to Preserve Its Freedom, New Acts of Foresight Are Needed Every Day; and for What Good Qualities Quintus Fabius Was Called Maximus

As I HAVE SAID at other times, in a great city emergencies occur every day that require a physician, and the more serious they are, the wiser the physician needs to be. And if such emergencies ever occurred in any city, they occurred in Rome, both strange and unexpected ones, as, for example, the one in which all the Roman women seemed to have plotted together to murder their husbands, for quite a few were found who had poisoned them, and quite a few who had prepared the poison to do so.[1] There was also the plot of the Bacchanals that was discovered during the Macedonian war, in which many thousands of men and women were actually involved, and if it had not been discovered, and if the Romans had not been accustomed to punishing large numbers of wrong-doers, it would have been dangerous for that city.[2] If the greatness of that republic and the power of its actions were not apparent from countless other signs, they can be seen in the nature of the punishments she inflicted on wrong-doers. She did not hesitate to sentence an entire legion and a city to be put to death at once, or to banish eight or ten thousand men, imposing extraordinary conditions on them which had to be met not just by one man, but by so very many. This happened, for example, to those soldiers who had fought unsuccessfully at Cannae:[3] she banished them to Sicily and required that they should not find lodging in town and that they had to eat standing up.

Of all her actions, however, the most terrible was the decimation of her armies, in which one of every ten in an army was put to death by lot. Nor could they find a more terrifying punishment than this to chastise a multitude, for when a multitude does wrong and the author of the misdeed is uncertain, all of them cannot be chastised, since they are too numerous, and to punish some of them and to let some go unpunished would wrong those who were punished and would encourage those unpunished to do wrong a second time. But if one kills a tenth of them by lot, when all deserve it, then the one who is punished complains about fate, and the one who is not punished is afraid that it will be his turn the next time and takes care to avoid wrong-doing.

Thus, the poisoners and the Bacchanals were punished as their crimes deserved. And although these diseases in a republic produce bad effects, they are not fatal, because there is almost always time to cure them. But one does not have time with those that affect the state, for if they are not cured by a prudent man, they will bring the city to ruin. Thanks to the liberality with which the Romans used to grant citizenship to foreigners, there were born in Rome so many new citizens who came to control such a large percentage of the vote that the government began to change and to depart from the ways and the men it was accustomed to follow. Quintus Fabius perceived this when he was censor, and put all of these newcomers, who were the source of this disorder, into four tribes, so that, limited to a very small arena for action, they could not corrupt all of Rome.[4] This problem was well diagnosed by Fabius and an appropriate remedy was applied to it without causing any civil disorder, and it was so well received by that city-state that he deserved to be called "Great."

Notes to Book 3, Chapter 49

1. This episode appears in Livy, *History of Rome*, 8.18, and refers to events that took place in 331 B.C.E.
2. Livy describes the discovery of orgiastic cults in Rome around the year 186 B.C.E.; see *History of Rome*, 39.8–9, 41.
3. See Livy, *History of Rome*, 23.25, 25.5–7. Cannae was a town in southern Italy where the Roman army was badly defeated by Hannibal in 216 B.C.E. Although it outnumbered his forces by perhaps as many as two to one, it was out-maneuvered by him and its ranks were decimated.
4. Quintus Fabius Maximus Rullianus was consul five times between 322

and 295 B.C.E. and censor in 304. The "Maximus" in his name means "Great." For this episode, see Livy, *History of Rome*, 9.46. Note that the *Discourses* ends not just with this last reflection on Fabius's political acumen, but with the title "Great," which he earned because of it.

Comments & Questions

In this section, we aim to provide the reader with an array of perspectives on the text, as well as questions that challenge those perspectives. The commentary has been culled from sources as diverse as reviews contemporaneous with the work, letters written by the author, literary criticism of later generations, and appreciations written throughout history. Following the commentary, a series of questions seeks to filter Niccoló Machiavelli's The Prince and Other Writings *through a variety of points of view and bring about a richer understanding of this enduring work.*

Comments

THOMAS BROWNE
Every Country hath its Machiavel.

—from *Religio Medici* (1643)

LORD THOMAS BABINGTON MACAULAY
Out of his surname they have coined an epithet for a knave, and out of his Christian name a synonym for the Devil.

—from *On Machiavelli* (1827)

THE SPECTATOR
[Machiavelli] recognised the higher morality as the true standard; but he saw it everywhere set at naught. On the other hand, he saw his beloved Italy turn into factions and reduced to misery by the oppressive rule of the stranger; and he yearned and laboured for a United Italy. Republican though he was, he saw that Italy could only be made free by the strong arm of a single ruler; and *The Prince* is a manual of political statecraft, to help such a ruler to defeat the foes of a unified Italy with their own weapons. Machiavelli does not attempt to justify the doctrines of *The Prince* on moral grounds; but he thought them justifiable as instruments of political strategy.

—July 21, 1883

P. F. WILLERT

The very circumstances and qualities which had been so favourable to the progress of Italy in the arts and humanities of life had been hostile to moral growth. Over-great subtlety of intellect, and a tendency to analyze motives and conduct, are always fatal to delicacy of moral fibre. Whatever the origin of conscience may be, it does not bear arguing with; the devil still proves the better logician. The numerous little courts of the despots were centres of culture, they vied in encouraging artists and men of letters, but they were also centres of a corruption brought close to the door of every citizen. All the demoralising effects of despotism were intensified tenfold by the narrowness of the dominions, and also by the skill and vigour of many of these petty tyrants. The only public life open in most cases to an Italian was to enter the service of some despot, the only object of his ambition to win his master's favour, or perhaps to supplant him; and it is obvious what the means were by which alone these ends could be attained.

Machiavelli's writings were, perhaps, more influenced by the evil atmosphere in which he lived than his actions; yet if it be allowed that Machiavelli's political career was straightforward and comprehensible, neither do I believe that an unprejudiced reader will find in his books that strange confusion of good and evil which Macaulay so characteristically describes when he tells us that "the whole man seems to be an enigma, a grotesque assemblage of incongruous qualities, selfishness and generosity, cruelty and benevolence, craft and simplicity, abject villainy and romantic heroism. One sentence is such as a veteran diplomatist would scarce write in cipher for the direction of his most confidential spy; the next seems to be extracted from a theme composed by an ardent schoolboy on the death of Leonidas." To be understood, Machiavelli's works must be read as a whole, and we must not isolate sentences from their context and discuss them as maxims of universal applicability; and especially we must not separate the *Discourses on Livy* and *The Prince*, but remember that they were written at the same time, and that they do not represent different phases in the development of their author's political opinions, but supplement and explain each other.

—from *Fortnightly Review* (February 1884)

T. S. ELIOT

Machiavelli has been the torment of Jesuits and Calvinists, the idol of Napoleons and Nietzsches, a stock figure for Elizabethan drama, and the exemplar of a Mussolini or a Lenin.

—from *For Lancelot Andrewes: Essays on Style and Order* (1928)

ERNST CASSIRER

The Prince is neither a moral nor an immoral book: it is simply a technical book. In a technical book we do not seek for rules of ethical conduct, of good and evil. It is enough if we are told what is useful or useless.

—from *The Myth of the State* (1946)

FELIX GILBERT

Although [Machiavelli] indicated that amoral action might frequently be the most effective measure which can be taken in any situation, he never showed a preference for amoral actions over moral actions. He was not a conscious advocate of evil; he did not want to upset all moral value. But it is equally misleading to maintain the opposite: that Machiavelli wanted to replace Christian morality by another morality and that he encouraged politicians to disregard customary morality because their motives for acting ought to be the good of the political society which represented the highest ethical value.

—from *Machiavelli and Guicciardini: Politics and History in Sixteenth-Century Florence* (1965)

Questions

1. Is it possible to formulate Machiavelli's highest value? What is it that he places above such values as honesty, a ban on murder, peace, family, charity, a concern for the well-being of one's countrymen and women?

2. Is there a system of values from which Machiavelli can be judged? If you wanted to convince him that he was wrong in some important ways, what would you say?

3. Has any prominent recent American political leader—president, vice president, cabinet member, senator, labor leader—been what could reasonably be described as a Machiavel? If so, who and why?

4. Take any important public issue, national or international, and try to figure out how Machiavelli would advise us to handle it. Would his way be the best?

For Further Reading

Biographies

De Grazia, Sebastian. *Machiavelli in Hell.* Princeton, NJ: Princeton University Press, 1989. A Pulitzer-Prize-winning intellectual biography of the author; in a class by itself.

Ridolfi, Roberto. *The Life of Niccolò Machiavelli.* Translated by Cecil Grayson. Chicago: University of Chicago Press, 1963. For years the "standard" biography, and still very reliable.

Viroli, Maurizio. *Niccolò's Smile: A Biography of Machiavelli.* Translated by Antony Shugaar. New York: Farrar, Straus and Giroux, 2000. A recent work with much to offer.

Recommended Studies

Ascoli, Albert R., and Victoria Kahn, eds. *Machiavelli and the Discourse of Literature.* Ithaca, NY: Cornell University Press, 1993. A useful collection of essays, including translations of material by leading Italian scholars that is otherwise unavailable in English.

Chabod, Federico. *Machiavelli and the Renaissance.* Translated by David Moore. New York: Harper and Row, 1958. A seminal study by one of Italy's best historians.

Fleisher, Martin. *Machiavelli and the Nature of Political Thought.* New York: Atheneum, 1972. An indispensable study of Machiavelli's political thought in its context.

Garver, Eugene. *Machiavelli and the History of Prudence.* Madison: University of Wisconsin Press, 1987. A stimulating study of an important aspect of Machiavelli's thought.

Gilbert, Felix. *Machiavelli and Guicciardini: Politics and History in Sixteenth-Century Florence.* Princeton, NJ: Princeton University Press, 1965. A classic study that sets Machiavelli and his great contemporary in their historical context.

Hale, J. R. *Machiavelli and Renaissance Italy.* New York: Collier, 1963. A good general overview of Machiavelli and his times.

Hulliung, Mark. *Citizen Machiavelli.* Princeton, NJ: Princeton University Press, 1983. A brilliant interpretation of Machiavelli's works by a political scientist who disputes the claim that Machiavelli should be read as a "scientific" thinker.

Kahn, Victoria Ann. *Machiavellian Rhetoric: From the Counter-Reformation to Milton.* Princeton, NJ: Princeton University Press, 1994. A splendid, though demanding, reading of Machiavelli's work, the political theorists who came after him in the Renaissance, and the political thought of Milton.

Mansfield, Harvey C. *Machiavelli's Virtue.* Chicago: University of Chicago Press, 1996. A stimulating study of Machiavellian ethics.

Najemy, John M. *Between Friends: Discourses of Power and Desire in the Machiavelli-Vettori Letters of 1513–1515.* Princeton, NJ: Princeton University Press, 1993. A historian's splendid re-creation of the intellectual milieu in which Machiavelli produced *The Prince.*

Parel, Anthony J. *The Machiavellian Cosmos.* New Haven, CT: Yale University Press, 1992. A subtle, thoughtful reading of Machiavelli's intellectual world.

Pitkin, Hanna F. *Fortune Is a Woman: Gender and Politics in the Thought of Niccolò Machiavelli.* Berkeley: University of California Press, 1984. An absolutely brilliant, feminist reading of Machiavelli's works.

Pocock, J. G. A. *The Machiavellian Moment: Florentine Political Thought and the Atlantic Republican Tradition.* Princeton, NJ: Princeton University Press, 1975. "The" classic study of Machiavelli's role in creating the modern conception of republicanism.

Rebhorn, Wayne A. *Foxes and Lions: Machiavelli's Confidence Men.* Ithaca, NY: Cornell University Press, 1988. A prize-winning account of the "literary" dimensions of Machiavelli's princes.

Skinner, Quentin. *Machiavelli.* New York: Hill and Wang, 1981. A masterly overview of Machiavelli's works by one of the leading historians of political thought.

Index

Look for the following titles, available now from
BARNES & NOBLE CLASSICS

Visit your local bookstore for these and more fine titles.
Or to order online go to: WWW.BN.COM/CLASSICS

Adventures of Huckleberry Finn	Mark Twain	1-59308-112-X	$5.95
The Adventures of Tom Sawyer	Mark Twain	1-59308-139-1	$5.95
The Aeneid	Vergil	1-59308-237-1	$8.95
Aesop's Fables		1-59308-062-X	$5.95
The Age of Innocence	Edith Wharton	1-59308-143-X	$5.95
Alice's Adventures in Wonderland and Through the Looking-Glass	Lewis Carroll	1-59308-015-8	$7.95
Anna Karenina	Leo Tolstoy	1-59308-027-1	$8.95
The Arabian Nights	Anonymous	1-59308-281-9	$9.95
The Art of War	Sun Tzu	1-59308-017-4	$7.95
The Autobiography of an Ex-Colored Man and Other Writings	James Weldon Johnson	1-59308-289-4	$5.95
The Awakening and Selected Short Fiction	Kate Chopin	1-59308-113-8	$6.95
Billy Budd and The Piazza Tales	Herman Melville	1-59308-253-3	$7.95
The Brothers Karamazov	Fyodor Dostoevsky	1-59308-045-X	$9.95
The Call of the Wild and White Fang	Jack London	1-59308-200-2	$5.95
Candide	Voltaire	1-59308-028-X	$6.95
The Canterbury Tales	Geoffrey Chaucer	1-59308-080-8	$9.95
A Christmas Carol, The Chimes and The Cricket on the Hearth	Charles Dickens	1-59308-033-6	$6.95
The Collected Oscar Wilde		1-59308-310-6	$9.95
The Collected Poems of Emily Dickinson		1-59308-050-6	$5.95
The Complete Sherlock Holmes, Vol. I	Sir Arthur Conan Doyle	1-59308-034-4	$7.95
The Complete Sherlock Holmes, Vol. II	Sir Arthur Conan Doyle	1-59308-040-9	$9.95
Confessions	Saint Augustine	1-59308-259-2	$6.95
The Count of Monte Cristo	Alexandre Dumas	1-59308-151-0	$9.95
Don Quixote	Miguel de Cervantes	1-59308-046-8	$9.95
Dracula	Bram Stoker	1-59308-114-6	$6.95
Emma	Jane Austen	1-59308-152-9	$6.95
Essays and Poems by Ralph Waldo Emerson		1-59308-076-X	$6.95
The Essential Tales and Poems of Edgar Allan Poe		1-59308-064-6	$7.95
Ethan Frome and Selected Stories	Edith Wharton	1-59308-090-5	$5.95
Fairy Tales	Hans Christian Andersen	1-59308-260-6	$9.95
Founding America: Documents from the Revolution to the Bill of Rights	Jefferson, et al.	1-59308-230-4	$9.95
Frankenstein	Mary Shelley	1-59308-115-4	$5.95
Great American Short Stories: From Hawthorne to Hemingway	Various	1-59308-086-7	$9.95
The Great Escapes: Four Slave Narratives	Various	1-59308-294-0	$6.95
Great Expectations	Charles Dickens	1-59308-116-2	$6.95
Grimm's Fairy Tales	Jacob and Wilhelm Grimm	1-59308-056-5	$9.95
Gulliver's Travels	Jonathan Swift	1-59308-132-4	$5.95
Heart of Darkness and Selected Short Fiction	Joseph Conrad	1-59308-123-5	$5.95
The Idiot	Fyodor Dostoevsky	1-59308-058-1	$7.95
The Importance of Being Earnest and Four Other Plays	Oscar Wilde	1-59308-059-X	$7.95
The Inferno	Dante Alighieri	1-59308-051-4	$6.95
Jane Eyre	Charlotte Brontë	1-59308-117-0	$7.95

(continued)

Jude the Obscure	Thomas Hardy	1-59308-035-2	$6.95
The Jungle	Upton Sinclair	1-59308-118-9	$7.95
The Last of the Mohicans	James Fenimore Cooper	1-59308-137-5	$7.95
Les Liaisons Dangereuses	Pierre Choderlos de Laclos	1-59308-240-1	$8.95
Little Women	Louisa May Alcott	1-59308-108-1	$6.95
Lost Illusions	Honoré de Balzac	1-59308-315-7	$9.95
Main Street	Sinclair Lewis	1-59308-386-6	$9.95
Mansfield Park	Jane Austen	1-59308-154-5	$5.95
The Metamorphosis and Other Stories	Franz Kafka	1-59308-029-8	$6.95
Moby-Dick	Herman Melville	1-59308-018-2	$9.95
My Ántonia	Willa Cather	1-59308-202-9	$5.95
Narrative of Sojourner Truth		1-59308-293-2	$6.95
The Odyssey	Homer	1-59308-009-3	$5.95
Oliver Twist	Charles Dickens	1-59308-206-1	$6.95
The Origin of Species	Charles Darwin	1-59308-077-8	$7.95
Paradise Lost	John Milton	1-59308-095-6	$8.95
Persuasion	Jane Austen	1-59308-130-8	$5.95
The Picture of Dorian Gray	Oscar Wilde	1-59308-025-5	$5.95
A Portrait of the Artist as a Young Man and Dubliners	James Joyce	1-59308-031-X	$7.95
Pride and Prejudice	Jane Austen	1-59308-201-0	$6.95
The Prince and Other Writings	Niccolò Machiavelli	1-59308-060-3	$5.95
The Red Badge of Courage and Selected Short Fiction	Stephen Crane	1-59308-119-7	$4.95
Republic	Plato	1-59308-097-2	$7.95
Robinson Crusoe	Daniel Defoe	1-59308-360-2	$5.95
The Scarlet Letter	Nathaniel Hawthorne	1-59308-207-X	$5.95
The Secret Agent	Joseph Conrad	1-59308-305-X	$8.95
Selected Stories of O. Henry		1-59308-042-5	$5.95
Sense and Sensibility	Jane Austen	1-59308-125-1	$5.95
Siddhartha	Hermann Hesse	1-59308-379-3	$6.95
The Souls of Black Folk	W. E. B. Du Bois	1-59308-014-X	$5.95
The Strange Case of Dr. Jekyll and Mr. Hyde and Other Stories	Robert Louis Stevenson	1-59308-131-6	$5.95
A Tale of Two Cities	Charles Dickens	1-59308-138-3	$5.95
Three Theban Plays	Sophocles	1-59308-235-5	$7.95
Thus Spoke Zarathustra	Friedrich Nietzsche	1-59308-278-9	$7.95
The Time Machine and The Invisible Man	H. G. Wells	1-59308-388-2	$6.95
Treasure Island	Robert Louis Stevenson	1-59308-247-9	$4.95
The Turn of the Screw, The Aspern Papers and Two Stories	Henry James	1-59308-043-3	$5.95
Uncle Tom's Cabin	Harriet Beecher Stowe	1-59308-121-9	$7.95
Vanity Fair	William Makepeace Thackeray	1-59308-071-9	$7.95
Walden and Civil Disobedience	Henry David Thoreau	1-59308-208-8	$6.95
The War of the Worlds	H. G. Wells	1-59308-362-9	$5.95
Ward No. 6 and Other Stories	Anton Chekhov	1-59308-003-4	$7.95
Wuthering Heights	Emily Brontë	1-59308-128-6	$5.95